W9-AMZ-638

The Future of the Mass Audience focuses on how the changing technology and economics of the mass media in postindustrial society will influence public communication. It summarizes the results of a five-year study conducted in cooperation with the senior corporate planners at ABC, CBS, NBC, Time Warner, the *New York Times*, and the *Washington Post*. The central question is whether the new electronic media and the use of personal computers in the communication process will lead to a fragmentation or "demassification" of the mass audience. Some analysts, for example, have suggested that with the growth of increasingly specialized cable television channels and on-demand electronic publishing, citizens will filter and preselect news concerning only their own special interests and prejudices, with the result that cultural and political life will be increasingly polarized, and the common culture and national media will atrophy.

This study indicates, however, that the movement toward fragmentation and specialization will be modest and that the national media and common political culture will remain robust. The analysis draws on a detailed review of the economics of advertiser- and subscriber-supported "narrowcast" media and the psychology of media use. The author concludes that the production and promotion costs and economies of scale for electronic media put natural constraints on special-interest, small-audience programming. The conclusion sets forth a policy agenda for making the most of the participatory and democratic potential of evolving electronic communications systems.

The future of the mass audience

Terrors of the telephone (From *Daily Graphic*, New York, March 15, 1877).

The future of the mass audience

W. RUSSELL NEUMAN

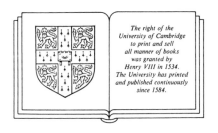

The right of the
University of Cambridge
to print and sell
all manner of books
was granted by
Henry VIII in 1534.
The University has printed
and published continuously
since 1584.

CAMBRIDGE UNIVERSITY PRESS

Cambridge
New York   Port Chester   Melbourne   Sydney

Published by the Press Syndicate of the University of Cambridge
The Pitt Building, Trumpington Street, Cambridge CB2 1RP
40 West 20th Street, New York, NY 10011, USA
10 Stamford Road, Oakleigh, Melbourne 3166, Australia

First published 1991

Printed in the United States of America

Library of Congress Cataloging-in-Publication Data
Neuman, W. Russell.
The future of the mass audience / W. Russell Neuman.
p.   cm.
Includes bibliographical references and index.
ISBN 0-521-41347-8. – ISBN 0-521-42404-6 (pbk.)
1. Mass media – Audiences.   2. Mass media – Technological
innovations.   3. Mass media – Psychological aspects.   I. Title.
P96.A83N4   1991
302.23 – dc20   91-15353
                                                        CIP

A catalog record for this book is available from the British Library.

ISBN 0-521-41347-8 hardback
ISBN 0-521-42404-6 paperback

Cover art adapted from materials provided courtesy of Apple Computer, Inc.

For
Susan

Contents

Preface

There is a story, apocryphal perhaps, that when the town fathers of a village in Poland gathered after World War II to assess their ravaged community, they realized that almost nothing could be salvaged. They would have to build the town anew from scratch. They had the opportunity to be creative, to design something fresh and new. They could move beyond the awkward hodgepodge of the old village, with its narrow, winding streets that had evolved through the Middle Ages. But, of course, they did not. Weary of all that the war had imposed on them, they wanted desperately to re-create what they had lost, and with art and precision they reproduced the narrow, winding streets and medieval architecture of the old village.

Major technological developments present opportunities of a similar sort. Like the town fathers of the Polish village, we see the new in the light of the old. Our language reveals our mind-set – the terms "horseless carriage," "wireless telephone," and "talkies" distinguished new technical wonders from what was already known and taken for granted.

As this study is being completed in the early 1990s, we stand on the threshold of what appears to be a new generation of communications technologies. We have the opportunity to design a new electronic and optical network that will blur the distinction between mass and interpersonal communications and between one-way and two-way communications. We invent terms like "micropublishing" and "two-way television" because in our experience it has been the nature of publishing to be large-scale and of television to be one-way, just as it had been in the nature of carriages to be fastened to horses.

These new technological developments are most often characterized as an explosion or proliferation of new media. The term "media" is plural, and indeed most reviews of the field have proceeded listwise through the growing array of electronic devices, identifying the special properties of each: direct-broadcast satellites, personal computers, digital, high-definition, and inter-active television, videotex and teletext, electronic mail and high-speed-computer networks, as well as a variety of enhanced services for an expanding digital telephone network (Williams 1982; Aumente 1987; Dizard 1989). A special irony is that, in the end, the new media will be one – a single, high-capacity, digital network of networks that will bridge what we now know as the separate domains of computing, telephony, broadcasting, motion pictures, and publishing (Huber 1987; Gilder 1989; Garcia 1990; Egan 1991; Elton 1991).

As a result, from the point of view of communications economics, we find ourselves living in most interesting times. Each of these industrial sectors currently enjoys a highly profitable tradition of business practice. The market boundaries between these sectors are based on a series of evolved social conventions for the repertoire of media appropriate for each category of human communication. A single integrated electronic system for high-quality video, audio, and printed output will make such artificial barriers less meaningful. As a result, each corporation in these fields will soon face three or four times the previous number of determined and well-financed competitors for its business, a prospect about as welcome as an invasion of Vandals and Visigoths.

In the tradition of the American free-enterprise system, the new media network will be designed and promoted by the currently active corporate players. But these players are ambivalent and conflicted. On the one hand, they prefer the existing system and the limited market definitions that won them, in most instances, more than adequate profit margins. If they can prevent or even just delay the entry or interconnection of some new media, they are likely to try. On the other hand, the prospect of investing in new technology to take over someone else's market, while keeping one's own, warms the hearts of all self-respecting capitalists. Industry strategists wonder if a good offense will result in a successful defense. It might be necessary only to threaten to invade a neighboring market sector to give the dominant players there second thoughts about trying to invade one's own. Strikes and counterstrikes, barbarians at the gates – military analogies abound.

The American political tradition in such matters is laissez-faire. The concept of a comprehensive industrial policy or even a broadly focused reformulation of communications policy for the information age is political anathema in the centers of power. The Federal Communications Commission (FCC), the National Telecommunications and Information Administration, and Congress's Office of Technology Assessment occasionally sponsor a study, but elected officials are not inclined to challenge the media giants on whom they depend for the means to communicate with their constituents.

We face a fascinating set of strategic issues. The corporate players have the first move. The federal establishment and the marketplace can respond. Some corporate players have succumbed to delusions of grandeur about public demand for their latest electronic gizmos. If from the aggregated business plans, one adds up all the time that the average citizen is predicted to spend each day on new video games, electronic newspapers, on-demand movies, and the like, it exceeds a 24-hour day, leaving no time for sleep or work. Clearly, not all of these visions of the future will be realized. The early and rather dramatic market failures of the videophone, videodisc, and videotex systems for home electronic information retrieval and entertainment have put the industry on notice. Although some battles may have been lost, the war is still on.

I have spent much of the past 10 years as a sort of war correspondent among the corporate strategists of the communications industries. As an academic research specialist on new media technology from the Massachusetts Institute of Technology, I was asked how the existing research literature on media use and economics might inform their strategizing. The key questions, reasonably enough, were which of the new technologies would succeed in the marketplace and how soon they would arrive. Our research team analyzed past attempts to predict the adoption of new media (Lazarus and McKnight 1983) and designed computer models, dubbed MEDIACALC and TELE-CALC, that allowed us to vary the assumptions about the costs and demands for new media and estimate the impact on the existing media (Feldman 1985; Frechter 1987; Elkington 1988). Later, in cooperation with the MIT Media Laboratory, we designed and tested prototype systems for interactive television (Neuman and Cader 1985), advanced imaging systems (Neuman et al. 1987), and home shopping (Gagnon, Neuman, and Kosloff 1988). The research program was supported by Capital Cities/ABC, CBS, and NBC, by the New York Times Company and the Washington Post Company, and by Time Inc. and Warner Communications, which at the time were separate companies. Support for supplemental research was provided by Polaroid, GTE, the Markle Foundation, and the Center for Advanced Television Study.

The program was a success; we learned a great deal, and the sponsors seemed pleased and occasionally found our models and research reports of some practical use. We formulated a generic game plan for corporate warriors that was dubbed the "Upstream Strategy." The idea is straightforward: We argue that current profits are relatively high in the media industries because competition is artificially constrained by federal regulations as a result of a perceived spectrum scarcity and a related set of economic factors tied to the production and marketing of informational and cultural goods. Entrepreneurs who wish to produce and sell new informational goods generally find it advantageous to work with the existing oligopolists who dominate the downstream marketplace, the final connection to the paying customer, such as the major motion-picture studios, large publishers, the television networks, and the local telephone company. A review of these factors is developed in Chapter

5. The changing technologies of communications (Chapter 2), however, will increasingly erode the bottleneck situation and the corresponding profitability the firms currently enjoy. "Upstream migration" will mean vertical integration and heavy investment in the creative community, because value will increasingly reside in creation rather than in delivery of media content. Thus, a newspaper needs to promote its identity not as ink-on-paper delivered in the morning but as a unique and reliable information package and a contractually exclusive source for well-known journalists, commentators, cartoonists, and reviewers. If new means of electronic communications start to compete with the existing newspapers as alternative forms of delivery, and they will, the upstream creative resources will have all the bargaining power and will increasingly derive the profits from the value they create. The same dynamics will bring increasing pressures to bear on radio and television stations, cable systems, movie theaters, and ultimately even telephone systems. We are now seeing the beginning signs of this process in global media mergers, joint ventures, and a massive six-year battle over program ownership rights between Hollywood and the television networks.

Ironically, in all our industry meetings and reports, a broader question kept getting lost in the market predictions and the military metaphors. This was the question of how the evolution of this rather perverse chess game might affect the quality of human communications and the scope of public information and popular culture. The longer-term social impacts of the new media are, as the economists might say, simply externalities, artifacts of how the marketplace works. Artifacts or otherwise, such issues provide the substance and focus of this book. I find myself strongly drawn, at this point, toward trying to answer the questions I was not asked.

Just underneath the surface of the conflicts among broadcasters, cablecasters, and telephone companies lies a decision about how to design the conduits of human communications for perhaps the next century. We face in the realm of public communications what Piore and Sabel (1984) have identified in the realm of manufacturing as a great industrial divide: a new opportunity to reconceptualize the scale and character of public communications, but only if that opportunity is recognized.

So my purpose here, in part, is to try to draw the spectators into the fray. The academic community, the regulatory establishment, and the general public generally watch with some interest as the media titans do battle. If the issue of the new media is narrowly defined in terms of who invented what technology or who will dominate which market, then spectators can watch from the sidelines or, if so inclined, bet on winners and losers in the stock market. If the issue of the new media is how to design an entirely new national infrastructure for both personal and public communications, we move from the domain of private business strategy to public policy.

As a result, I have written a book with four audiences in mind: communications professionals, who are primarily interested in the fate of their industries; social scientists, who by nature focus more on the longer-term impacts of media institutions on political and cultural life; the communications policy community, which is still debating whether or not there is any role at all for government policy in shaping the new media environment; and interested general readers. The dominating perspective, reflecting my training and the history of this particular research project, is that of the social sciences. I argue, following Rice and Williams (1984) and McQuail (1986), that the challenge of the new media productively draws our attention back to a set of fundamental questions about the social order in industrial society that go to the roots of sociology and political science as disciplines. Perhaps many researchers in this field share such views, but it is rare in this growing literature that one finds an explicit connection between the new media and traditional theoretical concerns.

The Introduction and Chapter 1 develop this thesis further. Chapter 2 focuses primarily on the technology, the emphasis being not on specific media or market trials but on the fundamental properties of the integrated electronic network. Chapters 3 and 4 assess how new forms of communications interact with both the ingrained habits and the unmet needs of the mass audience. Chapter 5 draws a series of economic and institutional issues into the analysis. Chapter 6 draws the accumulated evidence together with a special eye to how such findings might contribute to the communications policy debate.

I suspect that some specialists may be drawn only to those chapters that reflect their specific backgrounds and experiences. Such an approach is not recommended. The literature in this field is dominated by subdisciplinary studies that adhere closely to their home domains of classic cases and predictable conclusions. The whole, I contend, provides quite a different picture than would a simple sum of the parts.

In addition to the research sponsors listed earlier, many of my colleagues and numerous specialists in academe, government, and industry were most generous with their time and counsel as this project progressed. Without trying to thank them all, I would like to acknowledge the help and advice of Wally Baer, Dan Bell, Jim Beniger, Don Blackmer, Nolan Bowie, Terri Cader, John Carey, Ben Compaine, Barry Cook, Ann Crigler, Peter Cukor, Henry Elkington, Rich Feldman, Allen Frechter, Diana Gagnon, Bill Gamson, Manny Gerard, Ross Hamachek, Phil Harding, Terry Hershey, Harvey Jassem, Charles Jonscher, Gail Kosloff, Bill Lazarus, Peter Lemieux, Andy Lippman, Sean McCarthy, Scott McDonald, Lee McKnight, Bob Maxwell, Michael Maynard, Ron Milavsky, Richard Montesano, Marvin Mord, Nicholas Negroponte, Suzanne Neil, Eli Noam, Shawn O'Donnell, Tony Oettinger, Bill Page, Pepper, David Poltrack, Lucian Pye, Michael Robinson, Dan Roos, Bill Rubens, Steve Schneider, Bill Schreiber, Dorothy Shannon, Al Silk, Marvin Sirbu, Richard Solomon, Jim Sorce, Alan Spoon, Jules Tewlow, John Thompson, and Joann Wleklinski. The frontispiece graphic is a favorite of Erik Barnouw and was used in several volumes of his history of American broadcasting. It strikes me as particularly apt given the themes of this book and seems worth reprinting here in a new context. I would like particularly to express appreciation for the guidance and encouragement at the early stages of the work provided by the late Ithiel de Sola Pool. With a list so long, it may seem odd not to note all the friends and colleagues who have contributed to this project over the years, but my debts are numerous.

Introduction

Perhaps the mass media and the mass audience will prove to be historical anomalies. What we have come to take for granted in the nature of newspapers, television, books, magazines, and their audiences may, in retrospect, come to be seen as curious artifacts of the primitive communications technologies that arose in the early stages of industrialization. The modern nation-state encompasses a socially and culturally diverse citizenry numbering in the tens or hundreds of millions and a productive industrial base whose yearly output, in billions of dollars, is difficult for the human mind to grasp. These are truly mass societies. Their unprecedented scale is spanned and coordinated by high-speed printing presses and television and telephone networks. We stand at what would appear to be the pinnacle of the industrial age.

But is it possible that the engine of technology will spin out social and political effects anew? Perhaps we shall walk back down the other side of the industrial peak and return to a scale of human organization and communication more natural to participatory democracy. Sometimes the social effects of technological developments are cyclical rather than one-directional in character. That would be something new indeed, a postindustrial society that would self-consciously use technology to return to smaller-scale institutions and a renewed commitment to the traditional norms of civic participation. Declining audience shares for television networks and growing economic pressures on mass magazines may set the stage for the growth of more individualized desktop publishing, two-way video telephony, and electronic mail. Perhaps just as the cotton gin and the assembly line symbolized the onset of industrialization and mass society, the personal computer may come to symbolize the onset of deindustrialization and the decentralization of information processing.[1]

The term "postindustrial society" and its associated theories of social change are closely linked with the studies that Daniel Bell published through the 1960s, culminating in *The Coming of Post-Industrial Society* in 1973. "Postindustrialism" is a curious term. It posits a grand sweep of history from

1

the agricultural to the industrial and then the postindustrial age. The term tells us only that the new era is significantly different from the preceding ones. It lacks a central concept such as agriculture or industry to define its character.

If there is a single concept that captures the thrust of postindustrial society, it is, no doubt, the explosion of information. Indeed, the terms "information age" and "communications age" frequently are used interchangeably with "postindustrialism."

Whither postindustrial society?

According to the evolving theory, the key elements of postindustrialism are as follows:

- the expansion and increasing importance of the service sector of the economy relative to manufacturing and agriculture,
- the growth in the numbers of managerial, professional, and technical occupations within all sectors,
- the increasingly central position in the society and economy of education, theoretical knowledge, research, and the manipulation and communication of information,
- continuing economic affluence and material productivity through automation, especially new forms of automation based on computer-aided information processing and artificial intelligence,
- new flexibility, and possibly smaller scale, in computer-controlled manufacturing, allowing for more customization and responsiveness to individualized consumer needs, and
- new postmaterialist values that increasingly emphasize individual self-actualization, rather than the accumulation of material goods, as a measure of status and achievement.[2]

Most analyses of postindustrialism have focused on broad trends in employment, manufacturing technologies and structures, and economics. Relatively few have attempted to extrapolate from those trends to understand their impact on political and cultural life. Huntington (1974, 164), for example, in reviewing one prominent list of fifteen characteristics of postindustrial society, found only one that was even vaguely linked to the political sphere.

Among those who have speculated on such matters, most of their predictions have been quite sanguine. Masuda (1980), for example, stresses individualism and the increasing ability of citizens to control their own environments and to find information and education on issues of specialized interest conveniently and inexpensively. As the strictures of the industrial mass-production–mass-consumption cycle are lifted, a new individualism will flourish, and a natural diversity of life-styles will emerge. He emphasizes three central themes: (1) computerization and computerized industrial automation, freeing individuals from manual and clerical tasks, (2) new "voluntary communities" of individuals, not necessarily living near each other, but emerging out of shared special interests and increased interconnectedness through the new electronic media, and (3) self-actualization, with achievement increasingly measured against personally determined goals and special interests, rather than occupational accomplishments. It is an intriguing utopian vision, for it would allow the individual to return to the self-reliance and individualism of the small towns and villages of the eighteenth century, but with all the technical trappings and material wealth of the twentieth century.

Martin Ernst (1981) takes the historical scenario a step further by linking such social and economic changes to a fundamental evolution in human psychology. Basing his thesis on Maslow's well-known hierarchy of human needs, Ernst contrasts the prominent role of basic industrial production in recent history with the increasing emphasis on higher-order needs in postindustrial society. Thus, barring a significant recession or political upheaval, he predicts continued growth and expansion in the information, cultural, and leisure sectors of the marketplace. Ernst's theory is, in effect, a theory of affluence. There is evidence that households with more discretionary income spend a much larger proportion of that income in the leisure sector in pursuit of self-esteem and self-actualization. Ernst projects that finding onto the course of history.

Huntington is less sanguine. He is concerned that the politics of postindustrial society may strain the capacities of the political institutions that evolved in earlier times. He worries, for example, that "the mass media make it possible for 'magnetic and attractive personalities' to command the attention and mobilize the support of 'millions of unorganized citizens.' On the one hand, the citizen is drawn into politics; on the other, his feeling of impotence and the futility of politics escalate." As in the case of the transition from agricultural life to industrial society, he posits that the changes may occur too fast and in too disconnected a manner for political institutions to adjust. When that happens, just as in the earlier age, each group acts in its own interest with its own weapons: "the wealthy bribe, the students riot, workers strike, mobs demonstrate and the military coup." Furthermore, social strata that are in decline and are not integral to the new information economy may, as did the middle class of shopkeepers and small businessmen during the preceding transition, support extremist movements in a desperate attempt to reverse the economic changes. Or new cleavages, such as a standoff between the executive bureaucracy and the media, may lead to political paralysis.

Social cohesiveness will be threatened by the enthusiasms of the newly empowered as they come into conflict with the bitter and increasingly intense
neotraditionalism of those strata they supplant (Huntington 1974).

Rethinking postindustrialism

Postindustrialism is a broad historical concept that draws its strength and
emotional resonance from its intellectual breadth. The original clarity and
forcefulness of the concept, however, have mellowed with use and receded
a bit in the face of criticism. Many of the trends identified by Bell and others
continue in the trajectories originally identified, but overall the processes of
change have turned out to be more gradual, more complex, and more problematic in the resulting balance of social gains and losses. One way to characterize the more mature and still-evolving theory of postindustrialism is that
it has focused more on the problem of keeping social forces in balance in
times of sweeping changes than on just trying to grasp the enormous scale
of the forces involved.

Some of the changes may turn out to be more accurately characterized as
long-term cycles, or long waves, rather than radical shifts (Miles 1985).
Numerous critics warn that although the service sector has expanded, one
must remember that "manufacturing matters" (Cohen and Zysman 1987).
Advanced industrialism cannot be seen as a development independent of an
increasingly global economy, in a world the great majority of whose citizens
still live outside of the industrialized arc of Europe, North America, and
Japan. Some forms of technological advance lead to a deskilled work force
and a dual economy, factors that could increasingly polarize political and
economic disputes (Berger and Piore 1980). The data on changing socioeco-
nomic values reveal multidirectional patterns that are much more complex
than can be captured by a term such as "postmaterialism" (Inglehart 1977).
Although there has been a most intriguing move toward the adoption of
Western market and electoral norms within the Second World nations, the
notion of an end of ideology appears, in retrospect, to have been quaintly
hopeful (Lipset 1985). Even the fundamental presumption that advanced
information technology would lead to productivity gains equivalent to those
that came with automation in manufacturing has met with highly qualified
empirical support (Jonscher 1983, 1986). Further, the postmodern movement
would have us turn to a deeper set of issues about maintaining individual
and cultural identity and a sense of purpose in an increasingly homogenized
global culture (Kariel 1989; Giddens 1990).

Thus, although the term "postindustrialism" may have receded somewhat
behind the expansion of such similar summative terms as the "knowledge
economy" and the "information society," its central concerns remain very

much with us. Perhaps in the Kuhnian sense, the paradigm has been set, and work proceeds apace on the elements of the puzzle and the relationships of forces we still do not understand.

This book focuses on one element of the puzzle: a set of institutions and social spheres caught up in the turbulence of change but not fully addressed in the original formulations. We focus on the changes in the nature of the technologies, practices, and institutions of mass communications and their effects on political culture. The central question is how significant changes in the mass media may affect the day-to-day functioning of the democratic process.

This study is a continuation of earlier efforts to try to understand the complex dynamics of communications between political elites and the mass citizenry (Neuman 1986). That earlier work relied heavily on survey research data; in this study, both the methodologies and the historical focus have been broadened. The purpose of this introductory section is to set the stage, to put a few props in place and block out the positions and movement of the primary heroes and villains. The hero of the piece is communications technology, or at least its increasing capacity to enhance communications and empower the individual to control the communications process. There is no villain per se. There are, however, social, economic, and political forces that threaten to constrain, to limit, and perhaps to pervert the new technology's potential for intellectual diversity and openness. But if there are to be heroes, powerful oppositions are required for a true test of their mettle.

The following sections will identify key themes, the strategy of analysis, and underlying theories of social life and politics in which this study is grounded. Further sections will attempt to clarify what this book is not, as well as to set some distance between the present study and those that portend to predict the future or to argue that if technology is to determine our future, it will do so independently of the human values and institutions of the present.

The social effects of the new media

The hypothesized social effects of the new media have come to compose a long list.[3] Popular authors such as Toffler (1980) and Naisbitt (1982) have drawn on the understandable concern of individuals caught in the process of change and have developed best-selling lists of key changes and hints for keeping a step ahead of the competition. Also, numerous scholarly studies have attempted to assess the impacts of individual trends. But the collection of prophecies and assessments is inchoate, unwieldy, and full of contradictions. It has been argued in various quarters that the new media have

- begun to overwhelm the individual with a paralyzing overload of information

- diminished the importance of political parties in the American political system
- increasingly displaced general-interest, mass-audience media with more specialized narrow-interest media
- enhanced the effectiveness of education and instruction through the use of computer-aided, graphically enriched instruction that is individualized to meet the needs and learning style of each learner
- given governments and security agencies the ability to closely monitor the behavior of citizens, including what they read and see in the media, what they say through electronic media, and every economic transaction they conduct involving a bank or credit card
- freed the individual from having to rely on news and information provided by big media conglomerates
- changed the fundamental economics of commercial communications from an indirect, advertiser-supported, mass-audience orientation to a new audience-oriented system in which special-interest audience segments pay the producers directly for what they want to see and hear
- shrunk long-distance communications costs and time delays, to recreate a "global village"
- shifted the balance of power toward the executive and away from the legislative branch of the American political system, as a result of the president's singular visibility and many more resources for subtly manipulating the media agenda
- increased the international influence of American economic interests by reinforcing American cultural imperialism and American dominance of commercial entertainment around the globe through the dramatic expansion of satellite- and videocassette-delivered television
- pushed the cultural expectations for information and interpersonal correspondence to a frenzied pace of instantaneous facsimile and next-day delivery
- pushed the cultural expectations for economic transactions to a frantic clamor for instant cash and telephonic purchases
- created a new "information underclass" that cannot afford the high costs of information: the computer-based equipment needed to access it and the training necessary to operate the complex equipment
- created a new, powerful class of executives and technicians who control and have expertise in the utilization of the information technologies and the evolving network
- opened up the possibility of a direct, plebiscitary democracy not practiced since the days of tribal councils and small town meetings, in which even minor decisions of governance and public welfare can be determined by the electronically tabulated views of the mass populace.[4]

Although it is widely recognized that something important is afoot, the social meanings of these changes in the technologies of human intercourse are matters of diverse and contradictory speculation. What is missing, I would propose, is a historically grounded linkage between the broadly based analysis of postindustrialism and this loose collection of propositions about the role of the media. The frustration of a list such as this is that although each proposition has some promise of significance, they focus on quite different aspects of media institutions and technologies and would require very different approaches for meaningful empirical analysis. How might we bring together the diverse results from different research methods and levels of analysis for an integrated assessment? Is there a hidden, underlying theme that could guide such a task?

Pool's thesis and time's arrow

What I refer to as Pool's thesis was never a fully articulated theory, but rather a body of speculation and observation that arose during the course of other work (Pool 1978, 1983 b,c). Ithiel de Sola Pool died before he was able to return to the issues involved and develop a coherent theory. His ideas might be paraphrased as follows: Within the time frame of human life on earth, such creations as large-scale social institutions, vast cities, and mass media must be recognized as quite recent developments. Imagine a 24-hour-long stage play starting at midnight and continuing to the next midnight, scaled to represent the million years of human existence. The invention of speech (which occurred about 100,000 years B.C.) does not take place until 9:30 in the evening, and writing is not invented until eight minutes before midnight. The ability to store and transmit speech and writing electronically, by means of the telegraph, telephone, phonograph, radio, and television, comes only at the denouement, for the inventors of those devices do not begin to appear on stage until 11 seconds before midnight. The developers of digital electronics and the computer make their grand entrance only 2 seconds before midnight.

The first truly mass medium did not arise with Gutenberg's printing press, but rather with the steam-driven cylindrical press of the 1830s, and for the next 90 years it provided inexpensive printed material, primarily newspapers and magazines, to the increasingly literate mass populace in industrializing societies. Beginning in the 1920s, print was joined by film, radio, and television as competing mass media, spanning the cities and nation-states with a common culture and similar sets of interpretations of the day's events. Never before, from the earliest civilizations of Mesopotamia and the Far East, to Greece and Rome, through the Renaissance, to the edge of the industrial age, had there been anything similar to this new capacity for immediate, unfiltered, direct communication from the centers of power to the entire population.

For those of us who grew up surrounded by books, newspapers, radio, and television, taken for granted as part of the environment, it may be difficult to grasp the concept that mass communication, as such, is a historical anomaly, the exception to the rule. Now, because of the proliferation of digital networks and user-controlled, horizontal, person-to-person communications, we may find ourselves returning to an earlier dynamic of communication: public and private discussion and interpretation of ideas in a manner more akin to that of the preindustrial age than to that of the age of mass communications. This is an attractive and romantic notion – a return to a communal society, or at least a community-centered society, while still retaining the affluence, pluralism, and cosmopolitan culture of the industrial city. When humans had only the primitive technologies of early writing and unmediated human speech, the reach of an idea was limited by the energy of the scribe, the cost of papyrus, and the maximum volume of the speaker's voice before the milling crowd (Innis 1951). In the exciting but brief age of mass communications, artificial barriers of advertising economics and a limited electromagnetic spectrum have kept the number of public voices to a minimum. By their nature, these media have discouraged two-way communication, interpretation, marginal notation, and group discussion. They have been strictly one-way, vertical conduits of information and interpretation from the elite among politicians, journalists, and ordained experts to the rest of us.

The new developments in horizontal, user-controlled media that allow the user to amend, reformat, store, copy, forward to others, and comment on the flow of ideas do not rule out mass communications. Quite the contrary, they complement the traditional mass media, a factor of central importance. Today, centralized vertical communications and decentralized horizontal communications and interpretations can find their own balance as they reflect the human energies and cultural inclinations of the populace across the range of public issues of the day.

Pool's thesis is that the new media will permit us to return to the political dynamic of an earlier time. One thinks of the Committees of Correspondence in the 1770s that disseminated ideas and kept the spirit of the American revolution alive. One thinks of the tradition of the town meeting and the vibrant diversity and engagement of nineteenth-century American culture based on the overlapping identities of church, school, workplace, and neighborhood, as captured in de Tocqueville's notebooks (1856).

The unique promise of the new communications media has been captured graphically by Tetsuro Tomita of Japan's Ministry of Posts and Telecommunication (1980). He plotted out the currently dominant mass media (and more limited person-to-person media) in terms of audience size and the immediacy of communications. An adaptation of his model is reproduced here as Figure I.1. The horizontal axis organizes media by the size of the typical audience, and the vertical dimension shows the delay between the time the information is composed and the time it is received. The payoff from his effort was the discovery of a special zone, a curious gap in the structure of the personal and mass media at the critical intermediate level of the small interest group or the community organization. No doubt most citizens have not been acutely aware of this gap,[5] but it draws attention to the possibility that subtle patterns in communications flows can, over time, have significant effects on the nature of our habits and expectations of public and political life. The "media gap" identifies an area in which small-group and special-interest-group communications are precisely suited to the strengths of the new media – to mention but a few examples, broadcast telephony,[6] computer discussion groups, electronically filtered news, and community-produced cable television.

Figure I.2 reformulates the Tomita model slightly by emphasizing the dynamics of human communications rather than the media of communications. In this iteration, the special properties of the new media come into sharper focus. Clearly, both the number of people involved and the delay in communication will affect how reactive each participant can be to what others have said and thus how meaningful and viable the deliberative process can be. A central historical symbol of community participation in the United States has always been the town meeting, but there are times when citizens may not wish to participate on all issues under consideration, may not be able to participate at the scheduled time, or may wish to participate actively on other than local issues. The evolving electronic network offers rich promise of new forms of quasi group activity that can easily respond to each of those concerns. If the subtle chemistries of technological change and social norms can be harnessed, we may develop a new format for bridging the gap between public and private life (Habermas 1989).

It is important to add a caveat so that Pool's thesis will not be misconstrued as some sort of romantic conservatism or a call for a return to nineteenth-century politics, a danger he understood well (Pool 1977). I rely on the notion of "time's arrow" to make my meaning clear (Hartz 1955; Huntington 1968): There is no prospect of resurrecting the technologies, life-styles, and values of the small town and rural society to have a reborn industrial political culture; time's arrow does not suddenly reverse course. The nature of the small-scale media, if they continue to thrive in the years ahead, will bear the stamp of a century and a half of mass-media-based politics and culture. This book is an exploration of precisely that process.

Our future will not necessarily be determined by the new technologies;

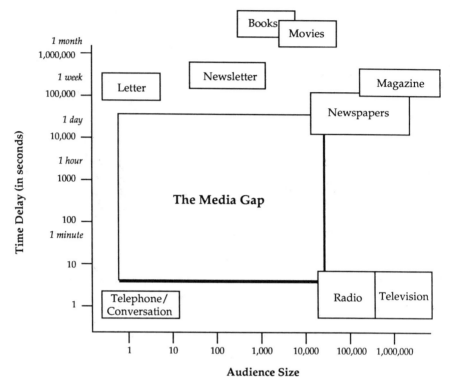

Figure I.1. Tomita's discovery of the media gap. (Adapted from Tomita 1980.)

they will not force a change. They offer an opportunity, but only if we are able to grasp its meaning. Pool's thesis helps to center this discussion and clarify its relevance to the postindustrialism debate. The central question for the future of the mass audience is one of balance, a balance between the forces of cohesive central authorities and shared values, as opposed to the diversity and pluralism of the changing mass population.

The exhaustion of mass society theory

The enterprise I propose would be much more straightforward if somehow amid the hubbub of the social sciences a theory of how communications institutions affect social and political life had evolved that could serve as our foundation. Does such a theory already exist?

This is a particular irony: The answer is yes, such a theory exists, but it has all but been abandoned as a quaint artifact of the 1950s and 1960s. I refer to the theory of mass society and its close kin – systems models of

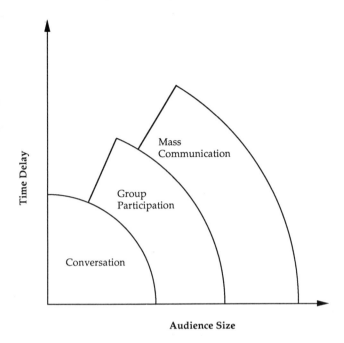

Figure I.2. Reformulating the Tomita model.

political communications, pluralist theory, and political development theory. The demise of mass society theory would seem to offer a new model for Thomas Kuhn to consider in his characterization of the dynamics of paradigmatic change and scientific progress. Kuhn's model of scientific revolutions would posit that if one theory declines and falls into disuse and inattention, some new theory with a new generation of adherents has arisen to push it aside and take its place. However, no new theory of media and democratic politics has emerged and demonstrated itself to be more parsimonious, realistic, or historically appropriate.

Mass society theory and pluralist theory have been criticized for being incomplete and less than fully developed, but such criticisms could as easily be addressed to any social science theory of equivalent breadth. This tradition has also been criticized for being inherently conservative in its nature, but such criticism mistakes a part for the whole. Although these perspectives may have been embraced by some conservative thinkers, I am skeptical that there is anything inherent about that. Many elements of mass society theory have also been embraced by the left as explanations for public acquiescence, false consciousness, and the weakness of protest movements. In any case, neither of these criticisms has contributed significantly to the demise of the mass society perspective.

Apparently, through the complex process of scholarly fads and fashions, attention has simply turned to other issues – Gunnell (1983) refers to a theoretical diaspora, and Bell mentions that such notions have the aroma of being out of date and obsolete as analysts search for fresh insights (Bell 1973). Perhaps the best characterization is simply theoretical exhaustion. Such exhaustion reflects the fact that the problems of mass media and mass democracy have not been resolved, and the models and hypotheses derived from the 1940s to the 1960s have not lost their relevance, only their youthful exuberance. The theoretical movement simply ran out of steam (Beniger 1987; Neuman 1991).

That exhaustion is certainly understandable. The imagery of Hitler and European fascism had faded, along with the worry that through some perversion, such as McCarthyism or neofascism or some sort of mass media, demagoguery would again subvert the political process. The end-of-ideology component of the theory became a particular embarrassment of overreaching and wishful thinking (Lipset 1985). It is particularly ironic that three decades later, some elements of the predicted weakening of ideological polarizations have come to pass as Japan and Europe have developed elaborate state bureaucracies for long-term industrial planning and coordination, whereas the Soviet Union and Eastern Europe have embraced market incentives and more open borders. It may simply be that the theory will find better success at explaining longer-term social trends than immediate events from the day's news.

The next chapter will develop the argument that the tension between centralized authority and the pluralism of public interests continues to be a relevant and revealing analytic dimension for understanding the impact of the new technologies on social and political institutions. Perhaps Kuhn's model needs to be expanded to incorporate cycles of fashion and rediscovery, in addition to the invention of new paradigms.

The central themes of this book

The impact of electronic integration

The quintessential characteristic of the new electronic media is that they all connect with one another. We are witnessing the evolution of a universal, interconnected network of audio, video, and electronic text communications that will blur the distinction between interpersonal and mass communications and between public and private communications.

On first consideration, one is likely to imagine such a development as an imminent political and social disaster. The imagery is of "Big Brother" electronically monitoring everything, from what the citizen watches on television and says on the digital phone to when the microwave oven is turned on. Indeed, it is technically possible for centralized authorities to determine what information and entertainment will be made available to the public, but that has been true since the first days of royal control over the printing industry in Europe.

The special character of the new media is that they can as easily be extended horizontally (among individuals and groups) as vertically (in the more traditional connection between the centralized authorities and the mass populace.) Thus, although in some political cultures attempts no doubt will be made to try to disable and constrain horizontal connectivity, the explosive growth in the volume of communications and the ease of personalized encryption will make such restrictions increasingly difficult to enforce. Such efforts would be like trying to design a telephone network that would allow the citizen to call only the government bureaucracies, never another citizen. Such a network is technically possible, but neither economically nor politically viable anywhere but in the most extremely authoritarian political culture.

Furthermore, because of the proliferation of channels, the lowering of costs, and the increasing computer-based intelligence of the digital network, the individual is increasingly empowered to retrieve information from diverse sources and to confirm its veracity from multiple sources. The ultimate result of electronic integration into a single integrated system, paradoxically, will be intellectual pluralism and personalized control over communications.

The counterforces of mass society

A second theme is that although the thrust of the changing communications technologies is important in its character and significant in its scope, its net effects will be relatively modest. We can identify three forces in tension. The first is the push of the new technologies and the network that connects them toward individualization and pluralism. This "technology push" will be met head-on by two countervailing forces that will constrain and shape its effects. One countervailing force is the political economy of the American communications system. It turns out that the economies of scale in print and broadcast production generate strong counterpressures toward mass-produced, common-denominator, mass-audience media. These economies of scale in production and promotion will not be changed by the new technologies. The other force is the psychology of the mass audience, the semiattentive, entertainment-oriented mind-set of day-to-day media behavior. When, for example, individuals are offered sophisticated interactive media for electronic information retrieval in the home, they are not always enthusiastic.

Thus, I argue that although the technology of mass communications will change dramatically, the mass psychology and commercial economics of public communications will not. At the moment, most of what is found in newspapers, on television, and in bookstores focuses on general-interest and entertainment content. Politics, in the grand sense of the word, and matters of specialized or community interest make up a very small part of the overall flow of public communications. This is not likely to change suddenly with the advent of new media; personal computers and optical fibers will not reshape social life and political culture overnight. The gradual changes that will evolve from the interactions of new communications technologies and new social institutions, however, will be significant, even if less sudden and dramatic than some early prophets had predicted.

A strategy of analysis

The best-known works analyzing social changes are those that identify a single determining mechanism, usually a phenomenon that the author sees as having previously been misunderstood or ignored. I use the term "monist" in characterizing this intellectual tradition to emphasize the characteristic singularity of the causal focus.[7] This study stands in pronounced counterpoint to the monistic tradition, and because monistic work dominates this field of inquiry, I would be remiss not to try to make my strategy clear.

The lure of monism

In the competition for the most influential monistic theory of the past century, we have strong contenders, but there is a clear winner: Karl Marx's analysis of the evolution (and predicted decline) of the capitalist political economy. Marx's key explanatory mechanism is the ownership of the means of production, and both the analysis of history and the prediction of future trends are singular and deterministic. Such distracting and complicating factors as the possibility that the Communist party apparatus might come to exercise the same kind of centralized, self-serving political power previously exercised by capitalist robber barons lie outside of the theory's monistic focus. Generalizations and modifications, such as Dahrendorf's thoughtful expansion and qualification of Marxist theory (1959), rarely receive the attention or exercise the influence of the original. Over time, monistic theories tend to lose their punch, with their focus being broadened and their causal structure elaborated to include multiple explanatory variables.

Not to pick on Marx. Adam Smith, the intellectual godfather to neoclassical economics, and certainly the bête noire of the Marxist tradition, shows a similar flair for monism in his singular emphasis on the "market mechanism" as the solution to all problems of social scarcity. Likewise, Freud's concentration on infantile sexuality and its influence on adult psychodynamics earned him a central position in psychological theory.

These were tremendously influential, creative, and thoughtful analysts. They stand out because each developed a new idea and pushed it to an extreme to test its limits. To win attention for new and potentially threatening ideas, the spokesperson must make a powerful case. Among the many students and teachers who follow in the footsteps of the great masters, attention tends to be focused on the seminal works themselves and the vitriolic critiques they provoked, not on evenhanded and qualified reformulations. It is more exciting to follow the original debate between monists of different callings than to plod through a careful weighing of the evidence for each constituent point in a theory. In Kuhn's view, this is the natural sociological process of scientific evolution.

Balance theories

There is a contrasting style of social theorizing, one that emphasizes multiple variables and the interactions of multiple social domains and levels of analysis. Neither unicausal nor deterministic, such theories assess the balance of opposing and overlapping forces and pursue a more complex teleology of multiple means and ends. I use the term "balance theory" to characterize this tradition of analysis.[8]

Pluralist democratic theory is a characteristic example of a balance-theory orientation. The works of Dahl, Huntington, Lipset, Coser, and Moore, among others, emphasize the importance of counterbalancing forces and an open and dynamic equilibrium of competing elites and interest groups. The Federalist papers provide the classic statement of this balance-of-powers approach in American political history. In historical analysis, one thinks of the cyclical theorizing of Spengler, Toynbee, and, more recently, Paul Kennedy in this tradition. In their analyses, forces that are out of balance are continually altering the military and economic dominance of successive political centers and coalitions. In sociology, functionalist analysis plays a similar role in modeling the forces of balance and disruption in the dynamics of pressure for the status quo versus social change (Alexander 1985).

This contrast between the monist and balance traditions helps put my strategy of analysis in perspective. The provocative monist arguments about how one or another critical factor will determine the future of the media and public life, although misleading in their singularity, become valuable grist for the mill as we pursue a multivariate theory of the future of the mass audience. The starting point for this study is the push of new technologies. By focusing on such matters, I run the risk of appearing to take a monistic approach, in this case, obsession with technology as a causal factor. Is it possible to take technology seriously without falling into technological determinism?

Putting technological determinism in perspective

Calling someone a technological determinist is a little like calling someone a communist.[9] It conjures up wonderful imagery of an individual smitten by an obsessive commitment to a dream and an ideology, blind to the real-world constraints of personal motives, institutional self-interests, and unintended consequences. Marx himself might qualify as a technological determinist on the basis of the historically determined causal equation that the transition from water power to steam power "caused" capitalism (Gilpin 1979). But such equations are implicit in much of the early work in sociology and political economy, as such theorists as Durkheim, Weber, Tönnies, and others attempted to build a theory of social evolution parallel to physical evolution in which the industrial revolution was defined as stimulating entirely new and "advanced" forms of social organization based on a complex division of labor. Somewhat later, Ogburn would develop a theory of "cultural lag" that posited a delay as social institutions responded belatedly to technical change.

There is no lack of examples of single-minded determinism. Czitrom (1982), for example, documents the firmly held conviction that the invention of the telegraph would end war for all time, based on an obvious behavioral fact: If men could communicate their differences instantaneously, why would they need to fight? Moyer reports that the telephone "caused" the city (Pool 1977), and Slack (1984, 56) sadly notes that the telephone destroyed the American family. The list is long. Ithiel de Sola Pool compiled a most interesting review of the literature of predictions and causal equations based on the evolution of the telephone, for the period 1876 to 1940. He accumulated 186 distinct causal propositions, including the beliefs that the telephone would abolish loneliness, rebuild rural life, make skyscrapers possible, and democratize hierarchical relations (Pool 1983a).

To put such monistic theorizing in perspective, however, it is helpful to assess the theoretical competition. Although there are many who would attribute to technology all of the causal energy that brings social change, there are those who are equally convinced that the causal roots are cultural or economic.

Cultural determinism. Why has democracy thrived as a political system in the United States for the past 200 years while experiencing such turmoil and instability elsewhere in the industrialized and developing worlds? Have religious values such as self-reliance had more to do with the evolution of capitalist institutions than steam power? Why do extensive pockets of poverty and unemployment persist in the United States, despite enormous economic expansion, universal free education, and significant commitments to job training and affirmative action? Such questions provoke cultural rather than technological or economic answers. Although the term is not widely used, one can as fairly characterize many social theorists as "cultural determinists" who insist that the values and beliefs of individuals have causal primacy.

The accumulated research on the historical uniqueness of the American political system is subsumed under the term "American exceptionalism." One finds no arguments in this tradition that the technologies of the industrial age operate differently in the Western Hemisphere. The arguments are cultural, focusing on the values and unique cultural history of colonial times and the self-selective migrations that followed (Hartz 1955; Huntington 1981).

The theme of the connection between religious values and capitalism is, of course, due to Weber, who has been characterized as spending his intellectual life in a debate with the ghost of Marx, though Weber appropriately takes the corresponding contrary view that values and culture are primary. Industrial technologies are invented by industrious workers. Hard work and the accumulation of capital are not caused by steam power.

The culture-of-poverty argument approaches the same issue of economic inequalities from the other direction. If Calvinist values enhance the growth of industrial capitalism, which beliefs and cultural traditions appear to impede its growth? Scholars such as Lewis and Liebow, writing about the developed world, and Pye, Pool, Lerner, Huntington, and Almond, writing about the developing world, all emphasize cultural and institutional primacy.

Economic determinism. Finally, there are those analysts who would characterize issues of technology or culture as mere artifacts, resultant conditions derived from economic interest. Barrington Moore, for example, criticizes rather forcefully the notion that values make a difference independently of economic interest:

To explain behavior in terms of cultural values is to engage in circular reasoning. If we notice that a landed aristocracy resists commercial enterprise, we do not explain this fact by stating that the aristocracy has done so in the past or even that it is the carrier of certain traditions that make it hostile to such activities: the problem is to determine out of what past and present experiences such an outlook arises and maintains itself. [Moore 1966, 486]

Marx, of course, is associated with the concept of material determinism, which can be loosely defined as positing that economic interests are prior and determining in political history.

Such perspectives do not surrender easily to counterargument; they are holistic and paradigmatic in character. It is, however, on the turbulent boundaries between these paradigms that new ideas and perspectives are most likely to emerge.

The search for interaction effects

Although we must appreciate the need of the intellectual pioneer to emphasize and perhaps exaggerate a position for effect, in the longer run we must adopt a more balanced and multivariate model for understanding social change. Simply put, we must give each variable its due. The evolution and uses of some new technologies (and the failures of others) are not exclusively due to the nature of the technology or the nature of the economic or cultural system into which it is introduced, but rather reflect the interactions of these factors. Such analyses are perhaps less dramatic and normatively urgent, but ultimately more satisfying. It is important to trace the interpenetration of different levels of analysis as psychological, institutional, cultural, and economic factors intertwine.

Pool uses the term "soft determinism" to try to characterize such an approach to understanding the social effects of technology. He notes that technologies do indeed have generic properties that make a difference in how they are used, but that historically the causal arrows point in both directions: "Institutions that evolve in response to one technological environment persist and to some degree are later imposed on what may be a changed technology" (1983b, 5). Pool's insight is important, because it alerts us to the importance of timing and historical sequence in these subtle interactive processes.

The interaction approach can be characterized as focusing on the issue of technology-in-use rather than as an abstracted or theoretical approach to social change and technology. The key data are derived from a broad-ranging set of present-day and historical case studies of technical–social interactions. One of the most fascinating examples of this interactive process is the approach of the Soviet bureaucracy to telecommunications. A universal system of voice communication is by its nature egalitarian; access is universal. Communications are horizontal (citizen to citizen), for the most part, rather than vertical (citizen to authority). Universal switching is not hierarchical, in that anyone can call anyone else; there is no inherent system of going "through channels" or through a chain of command. The idea that anyone could call anyone was abhorrent to the authoritarian sensibilities of traditional Soviet political culture. As a result, telephone books simply were not made available. The authorities, of course, had all the telephone books they needed, and it is doubtful that they had any reluctance to tap the lines of potential dissidents. So, with modest adjustments, the system has worked quite well. It will be interesting to see how these norms of technical communication will be affected by *perestroika*.

A parallel example is the use of wired radio in the People's Republic of China. In getting messages to the mass of the population, broadcast radio would be as efficient economically as is the system of wires, amplifiers, and loudspeakers; however, it was the latter system that was installed in the early days of the republic. The particular advantage of radio is that one can broadcast multiple messages on different portions of the broadcast spectrum. But when there is only one message to be broadcast, why bother with multiple channels? Besides, the wired system is even more amenable to centralized control. It could have been otherwise, of course. The authorities could simply have designed and manufactured radios without tuners.

The interaction approach acknowledges that technologies do indeed have properties. The properties of the technology and the environment interact to produce an outcome: the social use of the technology. Thus, the outcome can be seen as a variable, rather than as being predetermined. At a different time or in a different context, the introduction of a new technology could have widely divergent effects.

In this approach, one is drawn to Daniel Bell's critique of the cultural lag theory of technological impact first put forward by Ogburn. There are indeed leads and lags in this interactive process, but the term "cultural lag" implies a one-way causal path (Bell 1973). One must recognize that to a degree, the development of a new technology, such as the invention of telegraphy, broadcasting, or semiconductors, follows its own scientific logic. But the direction of research funding, the control of design and implementation, and the pace of development of any new technology are highly constrained by the values and priorities of the host culture.

The related debate concerning when and where technologies are and are not value-free may have done more to retard the study of technology and social change than to move it forward; it has become a bit of a bugaboo, akin to the epithet "technological determinist." It is a natural enough human impulse to assign qualities of good and evil to machines, but this should be treated more as a matter of poetic license than as analytic insight. It is the tar baby of monist determinism again. To identify technology as evil is to ignore the variability of its design and use. The impulse to do so is strong, however, because the idea of forbidding or destroying a technology and therefore its associated social evil has strong allure. But from the days of the

Luddites to their modern-day counterparts who wish to regulate all media that might serve as conduits for morally offensive content, it has been and is an unpromising strategy for guiding social change.

The interaction approach may also serve to counterbalance the impulse to focus only on what is new and different. Imagine a banner newspaper headline asserting that nothing much new happened today. Such a headline likely would be an accurate summary of the state of the world; much more has remained the same than has undergone fundamental change. In fact, both journalists and scholars probably would do much better to move toward a better balance when explaining the forces for continuity versus change (Moore 1966, 486). But journalists are trained to seek out the latest trend, not to bore the reader with unnecessary background information, and historians will continue to specialize in times of disruptive change, such as the American Revolution and the Civil War.

The view of the future that results from this impulse, however, is unbalanced. The powerful prose of those who would unveil a new era dawning attracts attention; there is the sense that by being in the know early, one might be in a position of advantage. But we would be better advised to seek a deeper understanding of the present, for that is likely to provide a better road map to the future.

A note on method

It is a well-known trait of social scientific research that the choice of method and research design has both subtle and conspicuous effects on the types of conclusions reached. Were we to confine ourselves to an examination of only experimental studies of reactions to new media, we likely would be drawn to exaggerated estimates of both the demand for new media and the resultant changes in communications behavior. Subjects in experiments are reluctant to disappoint the researchers, who obviously have gone to a great deal of trouble to set up the experiment and recruit their participation. Furthermore, given the focus on the individual subjects taken one at a time, we are unable to assess the effects of social structural and organizational variables. The artificial environment of the laboratory focuses their attention on the experimental stimulus, without distraction or counterstimulus, in a fashion very unlike the introduction of new ideas or technologies in the real world. The result is that laboratory experiments permit an analytic focus rarely reproducible in field studies, but having ripped a phenomenon from the complexities of its social context, we are able to study only a simplified and artificial reproduction of the phenomenon at hand. On the other hand, were we to rely exclusively on field studies and historical metaphors, we would be likely to misunderstand those properties of a new phenomenon in which we are most interested, those properties that are new and unique.

Accordingly, the strategy undertaken here is what I would characterize as a meta-analytic approach.[10] The attempt is to assess and integrate evidence across historical periods, across methods, and across levels of analysis. There are weaknesses in such a strategy. Given the diversity of materials the analyst can draw on, it is difficult to convince the reader that the selection of evidence is systematic and fair-minded. It is extraordinarily difficult to weigh and integrate evidence from different levels of analysis. The focus and analytic rigor that single-method studies permit is beyond reach. Nevertheless, the diversity and breadth of some phenomena require a meta-analytic approach. The nature of the social scientific enterprise, such as it is, requires a movement back and forth between the rigor and focus of the individual study and the integrative and evaluative efforts of others who would put these accumulated findings in perspective and hope to tease out insight to guide further research.

One recent meta-analytic study of political theory offers an additional insight into the evolution of scientific consensus (and, more typically, the elusiveness of such ambitions). Alford and Friedland (1985) point out that most theoretical perspectives have what they call a "home domain," a set of findings and exemplary historical cases that demonstrate the theory's relevance and veracity. The Marxist, for example, is drawn to study economic inequities or the interlocking directorates of corporate boards to demonstrate the character of capitalist institutions and their inevitable social consequences. Those of a more pluralist persuasion are drawn to a case study of community decision making to illustrate the crosscutting pressures and interests that are likely to contribute to political decisions about the allocation of public resources. In each home domain, the analyst is most likely to find reinforcing evidence, and few analysts are rewarded or motivated to venture outside of it other than to denigrate whatever evidence lies outside the received paradigm and its exemplars of proper research practice. The enterprise of the meta-analytic study, however, attempts to span the work of multiple home domains in more broadly conceived comparative analysis.

1

Two theories of the communications revolution

At the end of World War II, just as the process of rebuilding was about to begin, there was a chance to pause and reflect. It was an opportunity to think carefully about what had happened, what might have happened if the Axis powers had won and spread their totalitarian utopia around the globe, and what would happen next as the Soviet Union and the United States, with their contrasting political traditions, were thrust to the front of the world's stage. That era produced two new perspectives among social scientists who were trying to understand the roles of communications media in holding large, diverse, and potentially contentious societies together as nation-states.

Those were heady times: The war effort had led to some spectacular technological breakthroughs in rocketry, atomic energy, high-frequency radio, and electronic computing. Those technologies would play important roles in defining the character of the decades to follow: The world tried to adjust to living with the bomb; television sets quickly found their way into virtually every home in the industrialized world; rockets lifted communications satellites to connect the world with instantaneous electronic communications; and the computer moved from a room-size, multi-million-dollar prototype to a desktop model for the home, priced in the same range as a color television set.

This book is about the impacts of that revolution in communications technology on public life and political culture. We begin with two contrasting views of the technological future that were put forward at the close of World War II. Those views anchored the ends of a continuum: At one end, the new electronic technologies were seen as unprecedentedly powerful new tools for political control and oppression, irresistibly tempting to political and economic elites; at the other end, those technologies were seen as new, inexpensive information tools for use by the mass citizenry that by their nature would tend to promote an open flow of information and to strengthen democratic institutions.[1]

The purpose of this chapter is to examine the connection between such

22

analyses of the new media and several enduring themes in social theory concerning continuity and change in social institutions. All too many studies in this field have approached the new electronic network as if it were a unique event: the first case on record of social change stimulated by technical developments. The approach undertaken here, in contrast, will strongly emphasize the development of new communications media as a case study in the ongoing traditions of communications research and the sociology of technological change.

Mass society theory and the perils of propaganda

The most famous prophecy in this area is George Orwell's ominous *1984*. Orwell's technology of the future is symbolized by the omnipresent telescreen. He describes it as a large metal plaque, with a surface like a dulled mirror, covering almost an entire wall in each home and workplace. It is wired directly into the Ministry of Truth and drones on about the production of pig iron, war and peace, and the need for total obedience. At appropriate times, the screen is filled with the strong features and deep voice of Big Brother himself. The telescreen can be dimmed, but there is no way of turning it off. Most important, it is a two-way technology. Every movement one makes, except in darkness, and every word above a whisper can be scrutinized in the central offices of the Thought Police. Orwell's imagery is so powerful and his writing so widely circulated that the theme and ideas of his novel have now become part of our common culture and language.

The central theme of Orwell's book is the power of a government-controlled social system to force a singular pattern of thought on every citizen. No wonder it is still so frequently read today. The omen of propaganda is a powerful political symbol, and its connection to technologies makes it more so (Ellul 1964; Wicklein 1981; Ganley and Ganley 1982; Mosco 1982; Pool 1983b; Noelle-Neumann 1984; Dizard 1989).[2]

Orwell's *1984* is modeled on the totalitarian political systems of Nazi Germany and Soviet Russia. Studies of real-world totalitarian propaganda and political mobilization campaigns have revealed that attempts at total thought control over mass populations have fallen far short of Orwell's haunting scenario, although all too many regimes continue to persist in the tradition of Goebbels and Lenin (Hiniker 1966; Mueller 1973; Pool 1973; Mickiewicz 1981).[3]

Our focus here, however, is on political communications and the new electronic mass media of modern industrial democracies, particularly the United States. It may seem odd to assert that Orwell's exaggerated fantasy should be taken seriously and bears important lessons for American politics of the 1990s, but that is precisely my point. If there is an irony in the way

Orwell is read today, it is certainly the confidence with which modern readers seem to reject the scenario as quaint and improbable. Orwell's imagery seems more rooted in World War II than in the 1990s, as, of course, was the case. But, writing in 1949, Orwell argued that the political issues of propaganda and domination had not been settled simply because fascism in Europe had been defeated militarily. Orwell's *1984* was forward-looking. The delicate balance between too much and too little government influence on public communications continues to be a fundamental and critical public issue (Schiller 1982; Le Duc 1987; Pool 1990).

In order to better understand the potential impact of new media technologies, it is important to build from the base of what is already known about the relationship between communications structure and social structure. Much of the work on these issues was conducted in the decade following the war and was motivated by the same set of concerns that moved Orwell to write his novel. What is the nature of propaganda and mass persuasion? What are the unique powers of these new electronic mass media? How can the delicate balance be maintained between the need for central authority and the need to protect social and political pluralism?

Although these issues had their roots in the evolving disciplines of psychology, sociology, and political science, the interdisciplinary effort to understand these dynamics took on new urgency during and after the war, yielding what came to be known as the theory of mass society. It represents a substantial corpus of theoretical and empirical work. Ironically, the shifting fads and fashions of the social sciences and the urban and student unrest of the 1960s drew attention to what were perceived to be new issues of media, ideology, and mass politics. The underlying issues, however, were hardly new. Concepts such as pluralism, propaganda, and mass society gradually became passé and were overtaken by new terms with a more critical bite, such as media hegemony, media cultivation of values, and the rather ominous European theory of a spiral of silence.

Given the lack of clear-cut progress in resolving the puzzle of mass society, the impulse to start afresh on "new" and hopefully more tractable problems was understandable. But it is increasingly clear now that the adrenaline of immediate events has worn off, that Vietnam, which through television became the first "living-room war," Hitler's rousing radio addresses, and Roosevelt's discovery of the instantaneous, nationwide, fireside chat all contributed to a theoretical heritage we would be ill-advised to ignore.

The discovery of mass society

A mass society is characterized by homogeneity of the mass population and a weakness of interpersonal and group life. Riesman's phrase (1953) "the lonely crowd" captures the essence of the concept. Various essays in this literature emphasize different factors, but the loss of a sense of community and political belonging remains a central theme. The theory posits that since the turn of the century, the rapid urbanization and industrialization of Europe and the United States have resulted in the following trends: (1) The decline of family life: The nuclear family replaces the extended family; family members spend less time together; children attend large, centralized, anomic school systems; working mothers may be absent from the home; television watching replaces family conversation. (2) The alienating workplace: Mobility from job to job and isolating work conditions in large organizations make both the workplace and work associates less important to the individual. (3) The decline of local community: Dispersed suburban areas separated from central, integrating cultural institutions of the city give residents little sense of community. (4) The weakening of religious ties: Although the majority of people may identify themselves as religiously affiliated, such affiliation is nominal, and participation is irregular or nonexistent. (5) The weakening of ethnic ties: Over time, ethnic communities blur into a massified urban landscape. (6) The decline of participation in voluntary associations: The lack of group life further weakens the individual's sense of identity and connectedness (Fromm 1941; Riesman 1953; Arendt 1951; Kornhauser 1959, 1968; Bramson 1961; Bell 1962, 1973, 1979; Shils 1962; Wilensky 1964; Pinard 1968; Giner 1976; Beniger 1987; De Fleur and Ball-Rokeach 1988).

The historical argument is that just as these social forces reach a stage of crisis, the evolving mass media technologies, including radio and television, become available to provide a new nationally centered identity for the isolated and rootless individual who seeks a sense of belonging. Hannah Arendt, in exploring the origins of totalitarianism, characterizes the process as follows:

The masses grew out of fragments of a highly atomized society whose competitive structure and concomitant loneliness of the individual had been held in check only through membership in a class. The chief characteristic of the mass man is not brutality and backwardness, but his isolation and lack of normal social relationships. Coming from the class-ridden society of the nation-state, whose cracks had been cemented with nationalist sentiment, it is only natural that these masses, in the first helplessness of their new experience, have tended toward an especially violent nationalism, to which mass leaders have yielded against their own instincts and purposes for purely demagogic reasons. [1951, 310–11]

Kornhauser (1959) follows this line of argument, tracing the Nazis' mobilization of alienated and restive youth groups in Germany in the 1920s. Those young Germans had abandoned their traditional religious ties and community ties and had substituted a sense of direction and belonging derived from Hitler's charismatic leadership. An intensive propaganda campaign in 1924 helped to coordinate a number of diverse groups into a Greater German

Youth Movement. The character of those propaganda appeals focused on remote and abstract political symbols, rather than on the more specific and concrete political issues of day-to-day political life. Those media symbols represented a pseudoauthority in that they were concocted and manipulated to sway the masses, were shallow in content, impinged directly on individuals through the media, rather than being filtered through the community or educational system, and encouraged a compulsive, irrational form of loyalty and attachment (Kornhauser 1968).

A rapid breakdown of traditional norms of behavior may suddenly provide more freedom than the individual is psychologically prepared to handle (Fromm 1941; Riesman 1953), and such anomic individuals may find comfort in the pseudoauthority and pseudocommunity of the mass media (Herzog 1944; Boorstin 1961). But these cultural dynamics lead to political instability, because such individuals are easily mobilized by authoritarian and demagogic appeals. This cluster of concerns has stimulated a large corpus of social science research on persuasion, attitude change, mass psychology, and political communications (Hovland, Janis, and Kelley 1953; Berelson, Lazarsfeld, and McPhee 1954; Katz and Lazarsfeld 1955; Milgram 1965; McGuire 1969). Michael Robinson (1976) developed a theory that the increasing dependence of the mass population on television for political news fosters the growth of political malaise, and he demonstrated that connection in a series of empirical studies. Other found evidence that isolated individuals were more easily persuaded and were prone to extreme political views (Kornhauser 1959; Kerr and Siegel 1954). As with Orwell's work, the historical fact of Hitler's rise to power in Weimar Germany and a special concern about the fragility of democratic institutions serve as the intellectual backdrop. There remains the haunting question – under what conditions might it happen again (Hamilton 1972; Linz and Stepan 1978).

Although such critics as Daniel Bell have characterized the concept of mass society as a rather slippery and odd mixture of moral philosophy and systematic social analysis, he describes it, nonetheless, as one of the most influential social theories of the mid-twentieth century (Bell 1962, 21). Indeed, it traces its legacy directly to the founding studies in the field of sociology, having to do with the maintenance of social integration during times of change, conducted at the turn of the century by such luminaries as Weber, Durkheim, Tönnies, and Comte.[4]

Mass society rediscovered

By the 1960s, the term "propaganda" had returned to use primarily as an epithet, rather than as an analytic concept in the study of political communications. An important exception to that general trend is the work of the prolific French philosopher-sociologist Jacques Ellul. He argues that the concept of propaganda is no less appropriate to the study of modern industrial democracies than to the study of fascism or communism (Ellul 1965). His view is that the phenomenon of propaganda and its connection to the dominant technologies of communication need not to be the planned outcome of a nefariously scheming totalitarian elite:

A common view of propaganda is that it is the work of a few evil men, seducers of the people, cheats and authoritarian rulers who want to dominate a population; that it is the handmaiden of more or less illegitimate powers. . . . This view seems to me completely wrong. A simple fact should lead us to question it: nowadays propaganda pervades all aspects of public life. [Ellul 1965, 118–19]

Ellul goes on to discuss what he calls the necessity of propaganda. Some of his arguments may sound strange to American ears. His point is that pervasive, purposeful political mass communication is an inevitable outgrowth of modern technology. He asserts that Goebbels's theories of propaganda were based in part on the work of Freud and that Stalin's strategies drew on Pavlovian psychology. So far so good. But he proceeds to argue that American propaganda is similarly based on John Dewey's theories of education.

This is a point central to Ellul's thesis. Propaganda, he argues, is very much akin to mass education. It is used more often to reinforce existing tenets of civic culture than to persuade or change attitudes. It is a subtle and natural phenomenon of modern politics, emphasizing unquestioned half-truths more than intentional falsehoods. It draws on common myths, simplifies complex realities, and more often than not provides welcome and comforting assurance that all is well to a half-attentive mass audience. Perhaps that is why Ellul makes such good reading for American audiences today; in the American vocabulary, the concepts of education and propaganda seem such distant cousins. It is refreshing to think through the parallels.

Ellul's work, like Orwell's, takes the strategy of warning its readers of the dangers of allowing the centralized political institutions to accumulate too much control over the cultural technologies. This theory focuses on the extreme case and the end point of the process: the totalitarian regime. The allusions to the symbols, strategies, and extremes of European fascism are integral to the case each book presents. Such arguments may not always succeed in convincing readers that these issues are as relevant to the 1990s as to the 1940s, but that connection should be made.

This study focuses not on modern-day totalitarian media but rather on the potential structural weaknesses of mass democratic institutions. How do democracies break down? Will the new media upset a potentially delicate balance by overloading the flow of communications, by exacerbating social tensions and inequalities, or by providing elites or potential elites an irresistibly tempting tool for manipulation? Or, instead, will the new media, on balance, serve to bolster democratic practice by stimulating the flow of political information and deepening mass participation?

Orwell imagined how Hitler or Stalin might have used the technology of two-way wall-size telescreens. Indeed, today we have large-screen and two-way cable television. It is, however, the product of industrial capitalism, and the video cables are connected to corporate headquarters rather than to a governmental Ministry of Truth. There are many channels and as many Big Brothers, and they hawk consumer products as well as politics and religion. One might speculate on the type of book Orwell might have written had he chosen to explore the future excesses of industrial capitalism, rather than those of state socialism.

Although the term "mass society" is less often used today, and the power of its connection to seminal theory in sociology and political science has been weakened, its critical focus on manipulation of the population by centralized media has been picked up by new voices with quite different perspectives. Many are Marxists, who in their attempt to understand the false consciousness of public enthusiasm for capitalist democracies tend to attribute rather spectacular powers of persuasion to the mass media. Unlike the situation with totalitarian propaganda, which is singular in its argument and anything but subtle, this modern critical literature identifies a more sophisticated form of cultural dominance based on the ability to deflect critical views rather than outlaw them. Another strand of media criticism quite independent of Marxist views simply identifies negative values and practices of the media, such as an emphasis on commercialism, sex, and violence, and particularly the manipulation of children. This group is inclined to recommend regulations and prohibitions in the spirit of institutional media reform. Others focus on the international flow of communications or on citizens' privacy. All share a certain stridency and an innocence of the roots of these concerns in the concept of the mass society. But from diverse starting points, several currently active research traditions have come to a position quite like Ellul's. They find the media to be successful seducers, addictively pacifying and fundamentally inimical to social pluralism.

Critical media theory

Among the champions of this point of view one might include Herbert Marcuse, Jürgen Habermas, Hans Magnus Enzenberger, Armand Mattelart, Ariel Dorfman, and Herbert Schiller. They focus on what they describe as a subtle but very effective repression of contrary ideas in the name of tolerance and democratic pluralism. Marcuse (1964) argues that we have a one-dimensional society that assimilates contrary ideas into the commercial mainstream by romanticizing and personalizing them into apolitical fragments of advertiser-supported network news-drama. He refers to the modern media system in his characteristic language as providing a "comfortable, smooth, reasonable, democratic unfreedom." Can we, he asks, really distinguish between the mass media as agents of information and entertainment and as agents of manipulation and indoctrination?

Likewise, Enzenberger, the German poet, playwright, and essayist, asserts that

George Orwell's bogey of a monolithic consciousness industry derives from a view of the media which is undialectical and obsolete.... With the development of the electronic media, the industry which shapes consciousness has become the pacemaker for the social and economic development of societies in the late industrial age. It infiltrates into all other sectors of production, takes over more and more directional and control functions, and determines the standard of the prevailing technology. [1974, 95, 98]

The ultimate use of the new technologies, Enzenberger argues, has not yet been determined. The expansion of international flows of communications and user-controlled technologies could shift the momentum of control over the flow of the public debate from the established authorities to progressive movements in society, if only they can recognize that the monolithic media need not be monolithic. His optimism about the potential of new art forms and populist or, as some have put it, guerrilla video has drawn a worldwide readership.

Media criticism

There is another literature, curiously parallel in its thrust to the Marxist critique, that denounces the mass media, especially television, for their negative influence on culture and society. There is not much of Marxism in its roots, however. It simply denounces the media for their undue commercial influence, especially on children. Among the popular spokespersons here one might include Marie Winn, Jerry Mander, Neil Postman, Frank Mankiewicz, Joel Swerdlow, Rose Goldsen, Dorothy and Jerome Singer, Ben Bagdikian, and George Gerbner. The media are seen as having a variety of effects: inducing passivity; distracting individuals from other, more serious pursuits, such as education; forcing adult values and expectations on children at much too early an age; inculcating superficial, acquisitive, materialistic values; desensitizing viewers to real-world violence; and, most closely associated with the critical school, trivializing political life. This literature shares both a stridency and a sense of urgency with the Marxist writings, but in contrast, it bases many of its conclusions on experimental and survey studies of viewers and their social attitudes. Although the data and findings from most of the individual studies can be and have been disputed, it is difficult to argue with the conclusion that somehow the mix of media content in the United States could be richer, more diverse, and more humane.

The Third World critique

A third stream of criticism comes from those in the Third World who are concerned about their inability to control the seemingly inexorable onrush of Western commercial entertainment and news media. The problem here is exacerbated by the simple economic fact that once the production costs for American and European television programs and motion pictures have been covered in their country of origin, they can be sold profitably around the world at prices much lower than the costs of producing indigenous programming. Among the voices of concern here one might include Kaarle Nordenstreng, Jeremy Tunstall, Herbert Schiller, Dallas Smythe, and L. Ramiro Beltran. An issue of tension is drawn between the acknowledged value of a free flow of information across international boundaries and the need for developing countries to nurture and protect their own indigenous cultures and values. Because programming tends to flow from the more to the less developed nations of the world, the nature of the process is most often characterized in conspiratorial and neocolonial terms. Thus, in parallel to the analysis of economic flows, one hears a call for a "new world information order" that would somehow attempt to redress the imbalance (MacBride 1980).

The privacy issue

The final strand of the literature concerns the issue of personal privacy. Because so much of economic life involves computers that are increasingly interconnected by routine data communications, every economic act is likely to leave an electronic footprint. Telephone companies, of course, keep records on every long-distance call. Banks and credit companies have detailed records and profiles of purchasing behavior. The Internal Revenue Service, the Census Bureau, and the Social Security Administration know a great deal about the physical, social, and economic well-being (or lack thereof) of the great bulk of the citizenry. In homes monitored by the A. C. Nielsen Company, electronic "people meters" send data instantaneously to centralized computer banks in Florida detailing which member of the household watched which program or videotape. The "universal product codes" on each item brought to the checkout counter allow a store to keep up-to-date inventories and also, if so motivated, to keep track of exactly who bought what. Even if the data-collecting organizations have no intention of using information for anything more than internal bookkeeping, it is difficult to anticipate all the possible uses of the data after they are collected. The QUBE two-way cable system in Columbus, Ohio, for example, keeps records of who watched which movie, for billing purposes only. But in 1980, defense lawyers for the operators of a local X-rated movie house subpoenaed those computerized records, because the movie at issue in the trial, one *Captain Lust*, had recently been shown on QUBE, and the question of community standards regarding sexually explicit material was central to the legal determination of obscenity.[5]

Privacy is a delicate issue. Charles Ferris, former chairman of the Federal Communications Commission, did not mince words in summarizing his view: "The fundamental problem I see with the coming information age is that it will rob us of one of our more important rights in a free society, the right to privacy" (Burnham 1983, 246). The issue of personal privacy in the electronic age grew in significance and ultimately became the subject of a series of investigatory commissions, resulting in the landmark legislation of the 1970s and 1980s (Belair 1980). Among the principal spokespersons here one might include John Wicklein, David Burnham, Robert Ellis Smith, and Gary Marx.

These streams of research and analysis converge in their concern regarding the unconstrained and pervasive power of the established communications media. The abilities of the dominant media to frame the political debate, to subsume and repress messages contrary to the established orthodoxy, and to collect and integrate data from diverse sources allow them to exert a form of power that is especially dangerous because of its subtlety. These concerns are redoubled in the face of the new generation of communications technologies, whose powers to monitor, to engage, and to persuade are perhaps several orders of magnitude stronger than those of their predecessors.

It is fitting that Orwell chose to conclude his book with the ultimate and complete defeat of his hero's independence and self-control. The ultimate form of propaganda is brainwashing. In the final pages of the narrative, Winston Smith, the book's protagonist, was worn down by concentrated, continuing torture and thought control. No one has the strength to resist brainwashing forever. Such imagery lies at the very core of concern about the future of public and private electronic communications.

Democratic theory and the promise of political pluralism

Vannevar Bush's idea for Memex, a brilliant vision in 1945 of what was to evolve 40 years later into the personal computer, represents, on the range of technological potential, the polar opposite of Orwell's telescreen. Professor Bush's ideal was more akin to the famous library in Alexandria that substantially succeeded in accumulating the entire store of the world's knowledge in the third century B.C. But in Bush's scenario, the storehouse of accumulated wisdom would be instantaneously and conveniently available via electronic delivery to anyone in the world who might care to inquire. A more recent paper by Alan Hald fleshed out what the Memex might look like:

> Within this decade [the 1980s] a typical office or home could have an affordable computer system integrated with high-capacity information storage and recording devices such as video disc players and video cassette recorders. This equipment would be tied into a global communications network through the telephone system, cable television and other media.
>
> A small library could be quickly accessed through this equipment. For example, if you ask about zebras you are shown a zebra running and told about its habitat and characteristics. Information is automatically adjusted to your level of understanding whether you are a five-year-old child or a doctor of zoology. I can see the children of the future bouncing through this playground of knowledge, motivated by curiosity and the fun of instantly having their questions answered, assisted by either a human or a computer guide through human knowledge.
>
> Imagine what it would be like to be exposed from birth to this type of medium. A child would quickly become experienced in searching for and finding information on anything – relating ideas and weaving patterns of understanding, developing a form of thinking that would be highly conceptual. By today's standards, such a child would appear to be a genius. The impact on an entire generation would be dramatic. Our children's children may become the first genius generation. [1982, 10–11]

The basic difference between the visions of Orwell and Bush lies in who controls the cultural technology. In Orwell's future, every aspect of the communications process is monitored and controlled to protect the interests of the state and to reinforce its ideology. Vannevar Bush's future, in contrast, posits that control of communications and information will reside increasingly with the individual, a natural outgrowth of technological evolution.

Indeed, this is the normative engine that drives much of the research in this field. If we are to understand the future of the mass audience, the question to guide our inquiry is how new technologies might be structured to strike a new balance in the control of information between centralized authorities and the public at large. If such a new equilibrium were to be achieved, it no doubt would become one of the defining characteristics of the postindustrial age.

A central metaphor for this literature is the computer as an intellectual tool, a natural extension of the human mind in the second industrial revolution, just as machines extended and gave power to the human hand in the first industrial revolution (McLuhan 1964; Bell 1973; Dertouzos and Moses 1979; Masuda 1980; Nora and Minc 1980; Zuboff, 1988). Thus, mathematical problems that once taxed Newton's powers can be solved quickly and effortlessly by high-school students with calculators and computers.

A corollary is that the new technological basis of society will lead to a new politics. Fred Williams, for example, characterizes this view:

The political order of nations is being rapidly transformed from the written document and spoken word to an electronic communications network enveloping everybody. The new political order is the communications infrastructure. . . . The new communications technologies offer the opportunity for citizen information and participation undreamed of by our Founding Fathers. . . . We may have to adjust our democracy away from the constraints of the eighteenth century and toward the advantages of the twenty-first. [Williams 1982, 199]

Communications and political development theory

The belief that the communications media are central and prerequisite elements for the evolution of the modern, pluralistic democratic state has its roots in a corpus of research on comparative politics and political development. This literature underpins Vannevar Bush's arguments and forecasts, just as mass society theory supports Orwell's. Also, like mass society theory, this work had clear ties to the historical circumstances that spawned it. Gabriel Almond, in a recent retrospective analysis of this tradition of research, describes a generation of young social scientists following World War II who tried to make sense out of the reconstruction of governments and economies in Europe and the explosion of new nation-states around the globe. Their mood was optimistic, and their theories were of grand scale. As Almond describes it, these young scholars sought to apply the concepts of the Enlightenment and the social theories developed in Europe and the United States in the nineteenth and early twentieth centuries to derive a model for the world at large. They shared a faith in human progress, and they developed theories of critical "takeoff points" based on the spread of knowledge and technology, the development of new markets, higher standards of living, and lawful, humane, and liberal politics, beckoning nations newly freed from the bonds of colonial exploitation (Almond 1990).

Among all the technological developments sweeping the Third World, communications technologies were singled out as having the most pervasive effects on human societies (Millikan 1967) and as the key prerequisite to democracy (Lipset 1960).[6] Perhaps the quintessential statement of this literature is Daniel Lerner's *The Passing of Traditional Society* (1958). He describes a causal model that posits critical roles for mass literacy and the growth of media institutions in the process of political and economic development. It reflects the logic and optimism of Walt Rostow's notion of a critical takeoff point for economic development. In the original formulation, Lerner described four variables arrayed in causal sequence:

urbanization $\rightarrow$ literacy $\rightarrow$ media development $\rightarrow$ political development

That basic model provided the stimulus for a succession of comparative and time-series studies (McCrone and Cnudde 1967; Frey 1973; Duch and Lemieux 1986; Neuman in press). Those empirical studies uncovered mixed and sometimes conflicting results. Duch and Lemieux, in particular, argue that the type of political regime may affect media growth as much as the latter affects the former. Thus, although the causal ordering is subject to debate, there is little doubt that these variables constitute a highly interrelated cluster.

The emphasis in this literature is on the role of communications technology in national integration and nation building. Karl Deutsch (1963), for example, analyzes the delicate trade-offs between the vested interests of the local and traditional geographic units and the common benefits derived from national unification. Such arguments hark back to Marx's description of nineteenth-century France as a "sack of potatoes," independent homologous villages, self-sufficient clusters of peasants, not connected with each other either by communications or by economic interdependence (Marx 1852).

Ithiel de Sola Pool summarizes the view that the mass media system is the critical catalyst:

The existence of daily price quotations facilitates the establishment of a national market. Media encourage a national art and literature by holding up products against each other. The media broaden the relevant reference groups in discussions. The same kinds of processes of national organization through the media take place in social life, in cultural life, in economic life, and in party politics. [1963, 253]

Another key concept of this literature is the media's role in inculcating a psychological openness to change within the citizenry. Lerner describes the self-perpetuating psychology of the traditional peasant who in response to the question what it would be like to play the role of social leader responds emphatically that such a thing could not be imagined. Lerner uses the term "empathy" to characterize the ability to imagine change and to be alert to news and information from outside the setting of the local village. The development and nurturance of empathy thus becomes a central mechanism by which the mass media can reinforce economic and political development. In addition to fostering human empathy, the communications media are needed to develop a sense of fundamental political trust to reinforce the legitimacy of national institutions. Lucian Pye, for example, describes the delicate task of coalition building among mutually distrustful ethnic groups and the need to build a culture of acceptance of electoral defeats as well as victories (Pye and Verba 1965). Almond and Verba (1965) and, more recently, Inkeles and Smith (1974) develop the distinction between an obedient orientation and a participatory orientation, reinforced by emerging institutions of education and the mass media as critical components in the process of political growth and the development of a viable civic culture.

Of equal importance in these theories of political development is the emphasis on a need for gradual and balanced growth. Huntington (1968), for example, stresses the dangers of rapid economic growth, which can destroy traditional cultural values and institutions without adequately replacing them and can raise material expectations without providing for them. Likewise, Barrington Moore (1966), in his analysis of English economic development, stresses the importance of the fact that the process was gradual, with the economic position of the traditional ruling elite being slowly eroded, allowing political development to evolve in new directions. The central problem for this theory is the class-linked polarization of political interests. As Moore succinctly puts it, no bourgeoisie, no democracy (1966, 418). Overlapping and crosscutting religious, tribal, geographic, and economic interests are most conducive to balanced, democratic growth (Lipset and Rokkan 1967).

The critical elements of the theory of communications and political development, then, are (1) the growth of literacy and communications institutions and (2) a corresponding psychological openness to diversity and change in the context of (3) gradual economic growth and crosscutting political pluralism.

The fresh enthusiasm of Almond's generation of postwar social scientists waned somewhat as it became recognized that modernization was a slogging, brutal process, an interplay of both growth and decay. Furthermore, the paradigm of communications and development came under increasing criticism as a handmaiden of neocolonial interests and as a mode of analysis insensitive to both the realities of political economy and the richness and diversity of indigenous cultures (Rogers 1976; Almond 1990). Thus, although attention began to shift to other matters, a theoretical basis for understanding the interaction of communications technology and political growth had been established.

New research on communications and democratic pluralism

In the ensuing years, three further themes in this evolving literature came to prominence, each of which reflects the enduring faith that communications technology is an engine to drive politics in the direction of a revitalized democracy. The primary emphasis in this new work is on the new media in the First World, rather than on the existing media technologies in the Third World, and the intellectual debt to the political development literature is not always acknowledged, but the underlying logic remains unchanged. The first theme in the literature celebrates unprecedented abundance of information; the second emphasizes a new pluralism, an outgrowth of the informational diversity and open marketplace of ideas; the third identifies a growth of participatory activity stimulated by the first two factors.

Information abundance

According to one popular account, the new media have provided an "information bomb . . . exploding in our midst, showering us with a shrapnel of images and drastically changing the way each of us perceives and acts upon our private world. . . . We are transforming our own psyches" (Toffler 1980, 156).

Television is central to the communications explosion. During World War II there were only six stations in the entire United States, broadcasting one to two hours each day to a handful of sets, but within 15 years, 90% of the nation's households had television sets. For the next decade, most metropolitan areas had three network-affiliated stations, public television, and a few independent stations providing movies and reruns. But with the advent of satellite-delivered cable television, the true potential of the "tube of plenty" (Barnouw 1975) began to be realized, including extensive public-affairs, news, and religious programming, as well as programming designed expressly for little-served ethnic and linguistic minorities. One cable system in New York, for example, regularly provides programming in Korean, Italian, Greek, Hindi, Hebrew, Spanish, and Chinese (Baldwin and McVoy 1983; Neuman and Pool 1986; Heeter and Greenberg 1988). The result is that in the 1990s, most modern cable systems are broadcasting 30 to 75 channels, and the next generation of optically based cable systems will have capacities of 150 channels or more (Nicholas, Levin, and Ross 1991). Recent figures from the Nielsen Company reveal a stabilized usage pattern that results in just under 60% of American homes subscribing to cable, representing 76% of the homes passed by coaxial cable. In more remote areas, more than 2.5 million households with backyard satellite dishes can choose from over a hundred broadcast signals. In addition to this national diversity, local cable channels and the new small-scale "low-power television" broadcasters are able to provide locally produced and locally oriented video fare (Pool 1977; Arterton 1987). The video explosion, it is argued, makes possible a cultural and political pluralism that may become the hallmark of postindustrialism (Pool 1983b).

The videotape recorder is another important element in the new video diversity. A recording capability allows the individual to record broadcast programming at unusual or inconvenient hours for later viewing, further maximizing the potential for diversity and flexibility (Levy 1987). Furthermore, tape rental outlets and video libraries have sprung up in virtually every community, stabilizing in 1986 at about 27,000 stores. Most of these outlets focus on popular movies, but the potential for greater variety is there. One sourcebook, for example, lists 40,000 video titles on tape and disc available to institutions and individuals. As competition in the video rental business grows, diversity of the available programming will increasingly become a critical competitive factor. The technology of the videocassette recorder may seem a bit mundane, but it is as clear an example as is provided by any of the new media of how technology can give increased control to the user of the medium (Ganley and Ganley 1987).

The print media have not been falling behind either. More than 10,000 periodicals are currently published, and the numbers are steadily increasing. The book industry remains healthy as well, averaging more than 40,000 new titles each year (Compaine 1982).

Nevertheless, the ultimate symbol of the cornucopia probably will remain the home videotex terminal, much like the Memex described by Vannevar Bush. Given a two-way connection by telephone lines, the individual, through a personal computer or terminal, can call up virtually any electronically stored information or data base – the universal Alexandrian library. Originally the idea of videotex was based on connecting a terminal to a central information-providing computer. The early designers imagined a data base of several million frames of information as economically feasible, and that seemed like a lot (Fedida and Malik 1979). But as new systems emerge, their interconnectedness allows the central computer to serve as a gateway to all the others, and so the accessible information base quickly becomes, in effect, limitless, or limited only by the individual's awareness of what is available (Hiltz and Turoff 1978; Tydeman et al. 1982; Barber 1984).

The historical parallel between Gutenberg's printing press and the new media is frequently drawn to emphasize the range of the potential impacts on social life. Thousands of monks working in the medieval scriptoria copying manuscripts by hand could barely keep up with the natural processes of wear and decay, let alone produce new manuscript copies in usable quantities (Smith 1980), and as a result, the total number of books and the number of titles were quite small. Holmes (1952) describes the medieval university education as consisting of some exposure to about a dozen books, mostly Latin classics, with very little else available. A "major" library of that era may have contained as few as 500 books. The invention of movable type and, later in the nineteenth century, high-speed printing made possible the accumulation and dissemination of an immeasurably larger knowledge base. If what characterizes civilization is the ability to accumulate and build on the knowledge of preceding generations, then the technologies of information storage, retrieval, and communications will play a critical role (Machlup 1962; Eisenstein 1979).

Information diversity

The second element of this analysis is a growing social and political pluralism that corresponds to the diversity of the information environment. As Naisbitt puts it in his characteristic prose: "Centralized structures are crumbling all across America. But the society is not falling apart. Far from it. The people of this country are rebuilding America from the bottom up into a stronger, more balanced, more diverse society. The decentralization of America has transformed politics, business, our very culture" (Naisbitt 1982, 103). The key symbol is the demise of the general-interest magazines, such as *Life*, *Look*, and the *Saturday Evening Post*. They were symbols of a common culture. But by the mid–1960s the economics of printing, mailing, and, most important, advertising had forced those giants out of the mass magazine business, to be replaced by smaller, more focused, special-interest magazines that provided advertisers access to various select audiences, more likely to be interested in the particular products they had to sell (Maisel 1973; Compaine 1982). By the late 1970s the same pressures were being felt by the major television networks. Whereas only a few years earlier they could depend on sharing between them at least 90% of the prime-time viewing audience, by 1990 that share had slipped to 65% (*Nielsen Media Research News* 1990). The viewers have not left television, but they are watching other channels, independent stations, and cable programming that have been utilizing a strategy based in part on special-interest appeal.

The diversity of media content, so the reasoning goes, corresponds to a rebirth of social diversity. Naisbitt cites numerous examples of this trend, including new citizen advisory panels for public agencies, a rebirth of interest in states' rights, new regional organizations fighting for local interests, and an apparently explosive growth of citizens' groups to provide neighborhood crime watches, fight local pollution, and lobby for other local concerns (Naisbitt 1982, 121). Toffler describes a similar pattern, a bewildering profusion of new special-interest groups: "Mobile-home owners organize to fight for county zoning changes. Farmers battle power transmission lines. Retired people mobilize against school taxes. Feminists, Chicanos, strip miners and anti-strip miners organize, as do single parents and anti-porn crusaders" (Toffler 1980, 409).

Such popular accounts, of course, tend to argue by example and anecdote, leaving numerous counterexamples unnoted. But single-issue politics, according to almost all accounts, will play an increasingly central role in the political process. Arterton, for example, argues that this will be an outgrowth of the technologies of horizontal communications (rather than vertical communications) empowering those who wish to mobilize their peers, rather than complain to those in centralized positions of authority (Arterton 1987). Where once a group might have relied on a mimeographed newsletter, there are now dozens of tools for political communications. Abramson, Arterton, and Orren (1988) cite the increasing sophistication of computerized mailings that personalize the message to address the particular interests and concerns of the recipient. These are particularly handy tools for direct-mail fund-raising, as the computer unfailingly records which appeals seem to be most successful with which households. They conclude that such developments bring to mind the earliest days of the American republic, when potential political leaders created and sponsored their own small newspapers (Abramson et al. 1988, 58).

A particularly interesting aspect of the new pluralism is the much-heralded decline of the American party system. There has been a dramatic decrease in the number of voters who consider themselves affiliated with the Democratic or Republican party. Even among those who still identify themselves as affiliated with a political party, there are higher levels of cross-party voting. Candidates are increasingly getting their funding from political action groups and from federal campaign financing, which further frees them from the control of the party apparatus. The increasing use of media-oriented state primaries, rather than party-organization-oriented nominating conventions, reinforces these trends (Burnham 1970; Nie, Verba, and Petrocik 1976; Dalton, Flanagan, and Beck 1984).

The party system is far from dead, however. Third-party candidacies are still likely to be symbolic rather than politically viable. Most citizens still feel some bond with a political party, and the parties themselves are adjusting to the changing environment by providing sophisticated advice on computerized fund-raising and media strategies. But the flow of politics does seem to be more fluid, open, and pluralistic. Some analysts have been predicting realignments of various issues and interest groups vis-à-vis the dominant political parties. Perhaps we are in a transitional cycle of party politics that parallels the establishment of the American electoral system in the eighteenth century, rather than an end to the party system and centralized political structures in themselves.

Simon Nora and Alain Minc, in their report to the president of France, explain that the trend toward decentralization is a natural outgrowth of the new information technologies. With increasing electronic connectivity, it is simply easier to provide information where it is needed. The original reason for bureaucratic centralization, they point out, was the need to put decision-making power in the hands of those at the top, who could amass and analyze the flow of information in increasingly large and complex organizations. But with distributed data processing and the ability to access the central data bases instantaneously, such organizational structures are no longer the obvious choice (Nora and Minc 1980, 52).

Geographic pluralism is also reinforced by the structure of the American media system. Although one is accustomed to thinking of network television, for example, as an integrative, nationally oriented medium, the fact of the matter is that the networks themselves own only five broadcast stations each and must rely on independently owned local stations to reach the economically essential critical mass of national coverage (Poltrack 1983). To reach the American population by means of advertising, political or otherwise, one communicates through local stations and newspapers. New newspaper printing technologies are reinforcing this trend further by allowing central metropolitan papers to add individualized sections and even change the news and advertising for different communities (Compaine 1982).

Public participation

The third major trend in the literature on the new media environment identifies a new level of public participation in the political process. It is linked, of course, to the new pluralism:

> The ethic of participation is spreading bottom up across America and radically altering the way we think people in institutions should be governed. Citizens, workers, and consumers are demanding and getting a greater voice in government, business and the marketplace. [Naisbitt 1982, 175]

In most cases, the new communications technologies, often in concert with the old, play a central role. In Hawaii, for example, Professor Ted Becker organized the Televote Project, which provided detailed packets of information for citizens to review before casting votes via telephone. These telephone plebiscites are, in turn, publicized and discussed in the local media. A related project utilized broadcast television to organize an electronic town meeting for the city of Honolulu. Congressman Edward Markey, from Massachusetts, joined a number of his constituents in an "electure," a computer conference on the Source Telecomputing Network that allowed each participant to contribute and react to others' comments. In that case the focus was American policy on nuclear armaments. In Reading, Pennsylvania, the local cable operator, Berks Community Television, set up electronic office hours for community officials to solicit citizen participation on public issues. The same group set up a two-way cable link between a senior citizens' center and the high school to facilitate communications between two groups that ordinarily have little common ground (Arterton 1987).

An even grander vision of the new active citizenry has been put forward by Benjamin Barber (1984). He, too, sees a great potential in the new technologies for facilitating broader popular participation in the political process. It will not happen suddenly, he warns. The trick is that democracy breeds further democracy: As citizens succeed in voicing their views, they begin to change their views of the citizenship role. He puts forward a program of a dozen institutional reforms and initiatives that he believes will help to revitalize the citizen's role, including the establishment of a "civic videotex service" and a "communications cooperative" to oversee the development of new communications technologies and extended electronic balloting on a series of public referenda and initiatives. His model of a citizen-controlled communications infrastructure recalls the earlier visions of Brecht (1932), Habermas (1962), and Enzenberger (1974).

These laboratory and field experiments with new media are yielding some exciting results. The studies are not yet completed, but there are strong suggestions that over time the use of these connective technologies will expand the interests and expectations of those citizens who use them. If these initial findings prove to be accurate, Masuda (1980) argues, they will reflect a fundamental shift from parliamentary to participatory democracy.

The optimism of these projections has a familiar ring. It is an echo of the development theorists, who in seeing an increasingly interconnected and reenergized world around them at the end of World War II sought to rebuild and enrich it. The common denominator in all of this work is the vision of the new electronic communications media as powerful resources for pluralist democracy.

In the balance

Orwell's *1984* offered a vision of enslavement. Bush's Memex focused on the liberating potential of the new technologies, a second industrial revolution as significant as the first. The future of the mass audience, no doubt, lies somewhere in between these two contrasting visions of the future; to find out where will require an examination of social and technological forces in tension. This book focuses in particular on three forces. Figure 1.1 outlines these fundamental dynamics. The first force, labeled the "communications revolution," represents the push of new information and communications technologies. My thesis is that the fundamental characteristics of the new media encourage both a diverse pluralism and increased participation in public life. This is the central argument of Chapter 2. Personal computers and sophisticated electronic communications systems have the potential to give individuals unprecedented powers to access and process information. The centrally controlled one-way mass media, such as broadcasting and print media, are supplemented and enhanced by two-way electronic networks and interactive media. Narrowcasting becomes as viable as broadcasting. People are able to select from an almost limitless electronic library, rather than passively view whatever happens to be on television. Individuals can respond electronically to statements by central authorities or, if they wish, evaluate and discuss public issues through horizontal communications with their peers. If I were a technological determinist, I might stop there and conclude that Vannevar Bush was entirely correct. But I am not, and he is not. There is

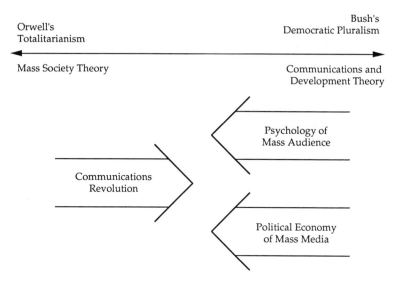

Figure 1.1. Forces in tension.

more to the story. Technological forces do not determine social structure and cultural values, but rather interact with them.

The second force is the inherited culture of mass communications behavior, the social psychology of media use. This force, the subject of Chapter 3, functions in direct opposition to the potentially liberating push of new technology. As evolving information technologies make new forms of education, exploration, and public participation possible, deeply ingrained habits of passive, half-attentive media use constrain that potential.

The third force is the political economy of the American mass communications industry. It is analyzed in Chapters 4 and 5. It, too, constrains the push of technology in fundamental ways. This force represents a combination of regulatory traditions and the economic dynamics of selling information and entertainment for a profit. The American infrastructure of mass communications and telecommunications is unique among advanced industrial nations in that it is entirely privately owned. Europe and Japan now seem to be moving in that direction as well (Hills 1986). Economies of scale push in the direction of common-denominator, one-way mass communications, rather than promoting narrowcasting and two-way communications.

The net result is that although the new media make possible new forms of political and cultural communications, in the main they are not likely to be used that way. Such stories are not new in the history of technology. But because the communications revolution is still very much in progress, it is particularly important to try to understand how these dynamics of technology and society are likely to influence our lives and, in turn, how we might try to influence them.

Orwell calculated that the new electronic technologies would provide the central authorities unprecedented tools with which to control, manipulate, and enslave a powerless mass populace. It was a vision so dark and foreboding that it caught the imagination of a generation. Vannevar Bush's scenario, in contrast, was one of liberation. He saw in the emerging technologies new tools for communication and information retrieval that would give each member of society the power to search out and manipulate information once reserved for princes and presidents. Bush's writings on this topic never became as well known as Orwell's, but his central theme has been picked up and developed by numerous scholars as the Memex he imagined is actually finding its way into homes and offices around the world.

Mass society theory corresponds quite closely to Orwell's vision, and its advocates have found evidence that the mass media and the related large-scale institutions of modern society weaken the vitality of community life and open up the individual citizen to anomie, mass manipulation, and control. The literature on communications and development, on the other hand, is much more optimistic in spirit and tends to define the mass media as a positive force for public communications, national integration, and the development of a participatory civic culture.

Although the contrasts between the two traditions could hardly be more striking, a look back on this body of scholarship from the vantage point of the 1990s can provide a new perspective. I have come to conclude that despite what at first appear to be polar opposite conclusions and emphases, these traditions of research converge on a common insight about the fundamental importance of balanced growth of communications technologies and political institutions. Theories of communications and development focus on the early stages of nation building, primarily in the Third World. Mass society theory, in contrast, draws its historical examples from the potential for political decay in industrialized nations, with the growth of fascism in Europe in the 1920s and 1930s as the central metaphor. Development theory emphasizes the need for a strong and articulate central government able to mobilize the reluctant and traditionalist mass population to confront their critical, common economic problems. Mass society theory emphasizes the dangers when such central voices become too strong and stifle an open debate over public policies.

The two literatures outline the potential pathologies of the political communications process with similar words and concepts. Such terms as "balance," "moderation," "pluralism," "crosscutting cleavages," "gradualism," "equilibrium," "openness," and "institutional flexibility" are shared by the two perspectives. The common concept is one of maintaining balance between forces in conflict through a period of social change. The central issue confronting both traditions is whether or not there can be systemic change without system breakdown. Each literature has its analyses of the need for moderation in the rate of historical change, the optimal sizes of institutions, the acceptable levels of inequality between social classes, and the need for a structured balance between public desires and realistic expectations.

Kornhauser's review of mass society theory, for example, describes historical "disjunctures" and "discontinuities" as the critical factors in explaining a society's vulnerability to totalitarianism. He reviews the statements of aristocratic critics who have bitterly denounced democratization, mass mobilization, and the breakdown of the old class system as the "causes" of totalitarianism:

> It is not democratization per se which produces extremist mass movements, but the discontinuities in political authority that may accompany the introduction of popular rule. Where the preestablished political authority is highly autocratic, rapid and violent displacement of that authority by a democratic regime is highly favorable to the emergence of extremist mass movements that tend to transform the new democracy in anti-democratic directions. [1959, 125]

In the development literature, the theme is much the same and can be traced back to Tocqueville's observation that the areas of France that had experienced the most rapid and profound economic changes were those where popular discontent ran highest (de Tocqueville 1856, 175). Huntington traces nine factors, including the disruptive effects of rapid economic change, geographic mobility, and the displacement of traditional class groups by an insecure and inexperienced nouveau riche, as destabilizing forces (Huntington 1968, 50).

Another component of this concern with balance focuses on the balance of class interests and the degree of economic inequality in society. The growth of a large, vital, and active middle class helps to diffuse tensions between the highest and lowest strata. In a study of 47 countries, for example, Russett (1964) found a substantial correlation between the degree of economic inequality and the level of domestic political violence. These same themes permeate the mass society literature, where the problem is conceptualized as that of direct contact between elite groups and mobilized interest groups, without the moderating effects of intermediating social groups and local institutions. Mass society and development theories both stress the importance of avoiding disruptive political mobilization. Both emphasize the need for nurturance of community organizations and crosscutting political cleavages that will socialize people into the need to accept their political gains and losses gracefully, preventing the kind of ideological polarization and crisis mentality that seemed to characterize the totalitarian demagogues of European fascism.

Mass society is seen as arising from the breakdown of traditional community ties to church, family, and civic organizations, brought about by the homogenizing geographic mobility and dehumanizing organizational scale of urban industrial society. The extremely swift transformations inherent in modern life-styles dislocate, atomize, and alienate individuals from their social and cultural roots. This process makes the individual an easy target for the demagogue or authoritarian leader promulgating abstract symbols and practicing psychological manipulation of the need to belong. Essentially the same argument can be found in analyses of the rapid transitions from traditional to modernizing societies in the Third World.

If this analysis of underlying themes is fundamentally correct, we may now be in a position to formulate a general model of communications technologies and institutions in the process of social change. It is hoped that the model will provide some guidance in understanding the conflict between Orwell's dark pessimism and the naive optimism of the technological futurists. The basic dynamics at work here can be seen as an equilibrium model, as outlined in Figure 1.2.[7] In contrast to Figure 1.1, the political ideal of "democratic pluralism" now stands at the middle of the model, and the process by which communications technologies might facilitate or undermine that goal can be more clearly outlined. As before, the model reflects forces in tension.

The two axes of the figure show the amount of political communication in a given political system (the vertical dimension) and the level of political centralization (the horizontal dimension). As each of the analysts would seem to agree, too much or too little of either can lead to a breakdown of the system. The concern of Orwell and the mass society theorists was that the nature of the new technologies would lead inexorably to a breakdown of democratic pluralism, toward the upper right corner of the figure, an increasingly centralized and intensely political communications system.

In contrast, the starting point for the theory of communications and development is the lower center of the diagram. Developing countries do not yet have political and economic infrastructures adequate to provide conduits for political communication. These dynamics, it turns out, create a triangular diagram, rather than a four-cell table, because when there is virtually no political communication, the dimension of centralization–decentralization is irrelevant. The problem is one of political entropy, a nonfunctioning political system. The emphasis of the development theorists, naturally enough, is the need for more communication, to develop literacy programs, newspapers, a national broadcasting authority, a telecommunications network. Given the divisiveness and the cultural and linguistic differences found in so many emerging nation-states, the assumption is that new communications technologies might provide a powerful force pressing toward the upper left corner

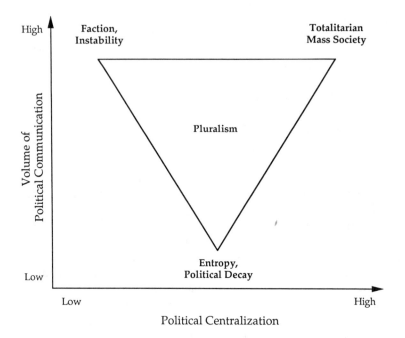

Figure 1.2. The equilibrium model.

of the diagram, toward violent factional disputes and a breakdown of central authority. So the analysts of communications and development emphasize the need for strong, centralized communications institutions.

The political ideal reflected in both the mass society perspective and the development perspective, however, is consistent (Takeichi 1991). The common goal is a balanced pluralism, an open system neither too centralized nor too decentralized, with moderate levels of two-way political communications.

Figure 1.2 thus provides a central organizing model for this book. We focus here on the future of the mass audience in the American political communications system as it enters the last decade of the twentieth century. It is a case study, a bellwether for advanced industrial capitalism. The dramatic technical developments that both George Orwell and Vannevar Bush imagined are just now coming to pass. Although we must take care to avoid crude models of technological determinism, we hope as well not to fall into the trap of assuming that all technologies are politically neutral. The task at hand is to review the fundamental properties of the evolving communications media. How do these properties interact with the forces pulling toward and away from political pluralism? How do the new technologies interact with the economics of commercial, entertainment-oriented mass communications?

How does the potential of the new technologies accord with the casual, semiattentive manner in which most people use the mass media?

The next chapter will review the underlying properties of the new media, examine the impact of the increasing volume of communications flows, and begin the analysis of how each new medium is likely to interact with the forces pulling toward and away from increasingly centralized control. It turns out that these digital electronic technologies do have characteristic properties, but in almost every case the ultimate political impact will be determined in great degree by the way society chooses to structure and control them.

2

The logic of electronic integration

The explosive growth of electronic media has been keeping the patent office busy. The stream of announcements of new computers, enhanced telecommunications, satellite communications, and interactive video is so brisk that even electrical engineers working in those fields admit to some confusion about what exactly is happening. There have been many books and review articles that have attempted to catalog and assess these developments. Unfortunately, it is often difficult to separate the substance from the hype, as many of the review authors have vested interests in one system or another.[1] We are faced with the familiar problem of not being able to see the forest for the trees, with the further confusion that arises because of the overlapping voices of competing salesmen.

The thesis of this chapter is that there is an underlying "logic"[2] behind this cascade of new media technologies. The outlines of the argument have already been introduced. In my view, those who perceive the new media as a growing diversity of unique technologies have missed the point. The key to the new media is their interconnectedness. The terms "integration," "network," and "interconnection" will be used more or less interchangeably in the following discussion in an attempt to identify this important trend. By using the term "logic," I intend to signify a series of technical and economic properties of digital electronics. I use the term "logic" in the sense of a propensity of a technical system. Logics, as I have noted, do not determine outcomes, but making human communications of certain types easier or more difficult is likely to have demonstrable effects on cultural and political intercourse.

The nature of networks

There is a persistent story of the traveling-salesman genre that in its various permutations puts the salesman in the position of asking the old farmer for directions to a nearby town. The farmer strokes his beard and after

48

considerable thought concludes decisively that "you can't get there from here."

What a curious notion. A network of roads has been built, and two points in it are not connected, not just not directly connected, but not connected at all. It would seem to defy the very nature of networks. If the one road is blocked, one might travel a longer and less direct route. If the second road is blocked, one seeks a third, and so on. The nature of networks is connectedness and flexibility. The more evenly spaced and the more frequent the interconnections, the more convenient and flexible the communication between any two points.

The nature of networks has provided the stimulus for rather extensive research and theorizing in policy (Pool 1983b, ch. 5), economics (Wenders 1987), engineering (Techo 1980), and applied mathematics (Stinchcombe 1968, ch. 3). A few key concepts from these various literatures will provide some guidance for this inquiry.

One such concept is the idea of "network externalities." The idea is simply that because the value of a network is communication or exchange of some sort, the more people or places on the network, the more valuable the network is at the margin to the next person who considers connection to the net. If there are two competing and equivalent networks, and one has more subscribers, there is likely to be a tipping phenomenon as more and more individuals opt for the larger network, dropping the smaller one, and thus generating pressure for the smaller network to either connect to the larger one or dissolve. Or, as the economists are likely to characterize it, because there are steadily increasing returns to scale (one universal network is cheaper than two competing and redundant networks), a regulated monopoly or "common carrier" is more efficient and better serves the public interest.

In the domains of both communications and transportation there are technological and economic reasons to maintain redundant and competing networks. For certain types of freight and long distances, the use of redundant waterways or rails may prove an efficient alternative to trucking over roads. Air freight complements rather than replaces land transportation. Furthermore, there is the central advantage that all such systems permit transshipment, that is, interconnection. This is seen in the frequent hybridization of truck trailers attached to railcars and ocean freighters. Containers are increasingly being modularized and standardized to enhance interconnection. Who would ship by rail if the freight were piling up at the train station and could not be moved on to its destination? The key variables are the size of the load, the character of the freight, and the speed of the transmission.

Likewise, in communications, there are overlapping networks of direct-delivery, postal, telephonic, and electromagnetic systems. Each of these technologies has evolved and been optimized for carrying communications of different types. Analog, twisted-pair copper telephone lines do not have the capacity to carry high-fidelity sound or video signals. The economic factors involved in offset printing mandate centralized production of newspapers and magazines, which are then shipped relatively long distances to local distributors, sometimes through the postal system. There are multiple communications networks because interconnection (transshipment) has been technically awkward or impossible. Until recently, there was no way to send a television program through the postal system or deliver a magazine over a telephone line, but advanced electronics have brought rapid change in how individuals and groups communicate. The logic of digital communication is interconnection.

The nature of digital electronics

Those who sit in offices surrounded by a sea of books, reports, journals, memos, forms, newsletters, and newspapers might question the assertion that electronics has become the increasingly dominant conduit of communication. Certainly, paper has not yet lost its place as a medium of communications (Strassman 1985), but the text and images we find on the page increasingly are getting there through electronic processes. More and more we shall have the option to read information from a computer display screen or have it printed out on paper.

Furthermore, electronic mass communications media that involve no printing or paper at all are growing at a much faster rate than are print media. Recent studies in the United States and Japan have documented a growth rate for entirely electronic communications many times that for traditional print. Figure 2.1 shows the numbers of words of communication to which the typical American is exposed during an average day: The electronically delivered component has been growing at a compounded annual rate of over 8%, doubling every 10 years, whereas the print-delivered component has remained stagnant, with no growth at all (Pool et al. 1984). Our era, whether we label it the postindustrial age or the information age, will be indelibly stamped by the increasing dominance of digital electronics in the storage and transmission of speech, text, and images.

The first applications of electronic technology (following the seminal telegraph) were "analog" in character; that is, the recording or transmission medium stored the sound waves of speech or music directly. Edison's "talking machine" was a good example. He simply hooked up a large cone diaphragm with a needle on the end that vibrated back and forth in response to his voice and transcribed the vibrations directly onto a rotating wax cylinder. When Edison put the needle back in the grooves and rotated the cylinder, the cone vibrated as before, reproducing faintly but clearly the words he had just

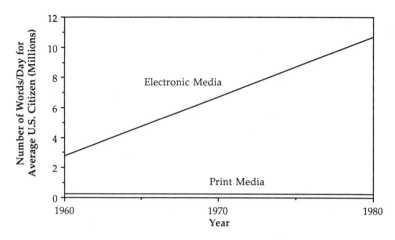

Figure 2.1.The increasing flow of electronic communication. (From Neuman and Pool 1986.)

spoken (Read and Welch 1976). The telephone, radio, television, and magnetic tape use similar electronic analog techniques for audio and video transmission. But video and audio signals can also be stored digitally, as a series of coded magnetic or optical pulses that can in turn be decoded and used to reproduce the original audio or video waveform. For our purposes here, the key question is why digital electronics have become increasingly dominant. The question of why electronic is easy – basically, it is a faster, cheaper, and more convenient medium than its physical predecessors, from stone and clay tablets to typewriters and carbon paper.

The question why the electronics tend to be digital is even more important. The forces underlying the growth of digital information processing provide one of the central themes of this book. Digital communications are preferred because they are easily processed by digital computers. This is fundamental, because it brings the phenomenon of electronic intelligence into the processing and storage of information. Analog media are by their nature passive. An analog record player can reproduce recorded sounds accurately, but the technology has no way of "knowing" what it is playing. Digital recording is different, in that the sounds and images are transformed into digital codes. The codes, of course, can be decoded and redisplayed as reproduced sounds and images, just as with analog technologies, but there is an important difference: The codes serve as labels. Computer-based digital technologies routinely read and interpret these labels and can actively process and manipulate the information as it passes through the system. They can, for example, save copies, forward, reformat, enhance, correct errors, summarize, abbreviate, or encrypt messages, sounds, and images as instructed by the software of the system or directly by the user. Analog communications, for the most part, can be reproduced only as recorded (Baer 1978; Cannon and Luecke 1980; Ide 1983; Dordick 1986).

The phenomenon of a digital medium "knowing" what information it is processing has proved to be a critical factor in the integration of new media networks. The older analog telephone system required a switchboard operator or an expensive and maintenance-intensive physical switch to connect the two parties to a conversation. When the two parties were connected, no one else could use the line, and special messages had to be sent to signal to the system when they had hung up. In digital communications, each message or packet of data is labeled and flows through a common channel at tremendously high speeds, then being received and stored only by the electronic receiver on the system to which it is addressed. Such systems are more efficient, more reliable, and less expensive.

Digital communication allows greater fidelity. Both analog and digital media have properties of noise, interference, and recording errors, but digital technologies can detect and correct errors. In compact digital audiodiscs, for example, if the microprocessor detects a dropout of the audio for a tiny fraction of a second, it interpolates the audio from the preceding instant to fill the gap imperceptibly. In data communications, special "check-sum" bits are included at regular intervals to signal to the system that an error may have occurred. In many systems, the receiver automatically signals the sender to repeat only the segment of the data stream that may have included a transmission error. Digital processing allows for the compression of communications to improve efficiency. Telephone lines, for example, ordinarily permit the transmission of only voice-grade audio. Video images require over 1,000 times the capacity or "bandwidth" of ordinary pairs of copper telephone wire, but with compression techniques, simplified video images can be sent over telephone lines (Techo 1980).

Most important, digital technologies allow for new forms of interaction between the user and the medium (Papert 1980; Lippman 1986). Digital disc and memory technologies allow the user to access any part of the information or any of the stored images instantaneously, instead of forcing the user to follow a predetermined linear path. These technologies can be instructed to provide information at whatever speed, level of complexity, or style a user might prefer and can customize the presentation accordingly.

The important point is that the addition of "intelligence" to the communications process through digital electronics allows for a revolutionary shift in the relationship between media and their human users. The old media (newspapers, magazines, books, radio, telephone, television) were passive, unknowing conduits between human users. Increasingly with the new media,

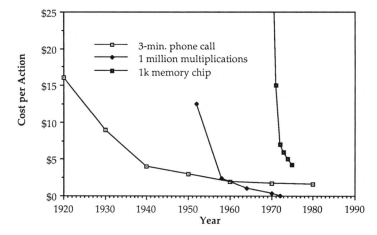

Figure 2.2. Declining costs of electronic communications, computation, and storage. (From Ide 1983.)

however, the medium itself is cognizant of what messages are passing through and indeed is aware of how the user is responding. Videotex and related forms of electronic publishing, for example, routinely format and filter information to fit the expressed interests and previous usage patterns of particular users. These issues will be explored in detail throughout this book. At this point we turn to an examination of nine technical and economic properties of electronic digital communications that in combination reinforce the logic of integration and a convergence of interpersonal and mass communications.

The technological drivers

Decreasing cost

There are three reasons that the new communications media are less expensive than the older ones: The physical part, the hardware, is plentiful and inexpensive; the manufacturing processes are complex, but when large quantities are being produced the processes become much less expensive and less time-consuming than those for the older media; finally, the systems are more efficient, so that more information can pass through a system of given capacity, and the cost per message decreases accordingly.

These patterns are illustrated in Figure 2.2, which reveals the dramatic declines in the underlying costs of transmission, storage, and processing of information since the turn of the century. It should be noted that these were

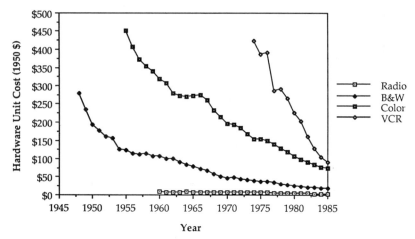

Figure 2.3. Declining costs of mass media technology. (Source: Electronic Industries Association.)

nominal costs, and thus inflation through those years masked an even steeper decline in price. Figure 2.3 tells the same story as it ultimately becomes evident to the consumer, in this case tracing the declines in prices for video equipment since the 1950s in constant-dollar prices. This figure illustrates that as a result of the technological learning curve and the economies of large-scale manufacturing, hardware costs can approach zero very quickly. Again, the steepness of the price decline has been hidden somewhat by inflation. Perhaps the best-known examples of these linkages between microelectronics and product price were the costs of digital watches and calculators, which went from several hundred dollars to less than $10 in the 1970s.

The basic components of computers and communications equipment are silicon and plastic. Silicon is sand, and so we are unlikely to run short of the raw material. It is, of course, highly processed and refined before becoming the basic ingredient in computer chips and microprocessors. Many electronic components still use copper and aluminum, which are relatively expensive. But optical fiber, the newest and most promising of the transmission media, is made of thin glass fibers, and glass is also basically refined sand. Plastics of various sorts are the principal recording media: floppy discs, video, audio, and data tapes, and interactive discs. When first introduced, disc and tape media were relatively expensive, but when they were produced in large quantities after manufacturing techniques had been refined, the prices fell quickly. The raw plastic for an audio recording costs about 25 cents, and that for an audiotape a little more. If one compares the price of the raw photographic film stock for a 16mm or 35mm motion-picture print, which runs in the neighborhood of several thousand dollars, with the five-dollar cassette cost for a videotape copy, one can appreciate the scale of the difference.

In addition to their use of inexpensive raw materials, the hardware items for new electronic media are relatively inexpensive to manufacture, for the basic technique in making microelectronic chips is to print them. Although they are tremendously complex and expensive to design, once the design is finished and tested, copies can be etched by a photolithographic process, basically high-quality printing, for only pennies per copy. In the preceding generation, the state-of-the-art technology had featured tubes and transistors, each with hundreds or even thousands of components that had to be carefully soldered into place by assembly line workers, an expensive and error-prone process. Given that the engineering, development, and testing costs for a single silicon chip can run into millions of dollars, the production process becomes economical only at very large scale. Because most electronic functions can be served by general-purpose microprocessors in combination with specialized software, however, each new application does not require the design and manufacture of a single-use chip.

Increasing miniaturization of complex circuits on smaller and smaller chips is further reducing the price of electronic equipment because fewer chips are needed for the same amount of processing capacity. In the 1960s, the practical limit was about 10 transistors per chip. Now, chips with 10,000 transistors and a total of more than a quarter of a million related components, such as resistors and capacitors, are common (Ide 1983). Data processing will never become costless, but the push of technology has dramatically shifted the costs away from hardware to the human-linked costs of software production and maintenance, as reflected in Figure 2.4.

The other element contributing to the decreasing costs of communications and data processing is that the new technologies make more efficient use of the limited transmission capacity of the existing communications systems. This is reflected in dramatic decreases in the costs of long-distance communications. Thus, rather than go to the considerable expense of buying a new cable and putting it in place, communications companies increase the capacity of the existing cable by attaching sophisticated equipment at both ends, equipment that uses digital processing techniques to increase the cable's capacity to carry data or voice communications severalfold. There is a parallel in microwave communications whereby companies add additional or high-efficiency transmitters to existing microwave towers to avoid the expense of building new towers and obtaining new right-of-way.

Walter Baer, for example, summarizes this pattern by describing the changing constraints under which today's electronics engineers work. He says, in effect, that design engineers treat computation as free (Baer 1978, 65). The average individual sees this cost phenomenon reflected in the way in which

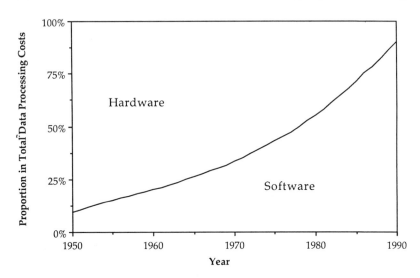

Figure 2.4. Declining proportion of hardware costs in data processing. (From Ide 1983.)

modern electronic equipment is repaired: When faulty circuit boards are replaced, they are simply thrown away. In fact, some firms that repair computers have been accused of not even bothering to do the necessary diagnostic, but simply replacing circuit boards until the unit appears to work. In the smaller electronic appliances, one confronts the ultimate impact of declining hardware costs: It is almost always less expensive to buy a new unit than to try to repair the old one.

Decreasing distance sensitivity

Electronic communications have altered the social meaning of geographic distance as significantly as has the evolution of transportation technology. In both transportation and communication, what were once defined as unconquerable distances have been shrunk: At the outset the going is slow, unreliable, occasionally dangerous, and surely expensive. The ability to span longer distances, however, quickly becomes reliable and inexpensive and thus routine. As in modern air travel, it is sometimes less expensive to traverse longer distances than shorter ones. The result is that the problem of geographic distance quickly recedes. That has not yet been fully achieved in communications, but we are quickly moving in that direction.

One intriguing example of the conquest of distance concerns a sophisticated computer system in Sweden used to provide the fire department information about the number of occupants and construction of a building when a fire alarm is received from that building. The data bank also shows the quickest route from the station to the fire. The irony is that when the system was designed, the Swedes found that the least expensive, most efficient, and most reliable data-processing bid came from a company located in Cleveland, Ohio. So when fire fighters set out to travel the shortest route to a fire in downtown Stockholm, the information provided seconds earlier came from downtown Cleveland (Dizard 1989).

The pace of change in communications cost patterns generates some interesting anomalies. Older telephone users who grew up in an era when long-distance telephony was prohibitively expensive still think of it that way: Overseas calls are simply out of the question; instead, one writes letters. Many younger people are as quick to pick up the telephone and dial directly to Japan or Europe as to the West Coast, and quite correctly so, because the cost differences are not that great.

The key factor here is satellite technology. Satellites are indeed expensive pieces of equipment. As a rough rule of thumb, it costs $50 million to construct a sophisticated communications satellite, and another $50 million to place it in orbit, but the capacity of these new satellites is so great that they are equivalent in cost on a per-line basis to land lines and microwave links. But satellites have a special property; once in place, their effective costs to communicate across the street and across the country are the same. Dramatic improvements in microwave, optical-fiber, and undersea-cable technologies have also reinforced the trend toward insensitivity to distance. Figure 2.5 illustrates this pattern, drawing on domestic long-distance telephone data for the United States. These same patterns are characteristic of data and video communications (Martin 1977; Cannon and Luecke 1980).

Marshall McLuhan popularized the term "global village" to characterize the increasing potential for growth in world communications. Because sounds and images from the other side of the world can be brought into our living rooms instantaneously, he reasoned, our perceptions of geography, cultural differences, war, and world politics will be likely to change. Although his notion of the global village reflects both a bit of wishful thinking and his characteristic impulse to be simplistically provocative, the issue remains important. We need not be put off entirely by his crude determinism, which argues, in effect, that cultural boundaries will irresistibly be bridged by the sheer availability of international communications. The issue can be reframed as a research question: Under what conditions will the availability of inexpensive international communications increase international awareness and international economic activity?

McLuhan's mentor, the Canadian economic historian Harold Innis, had earlier demonstrated the importance of transportation and communications infrastructures in the maintenance of empires and nation-states, from the

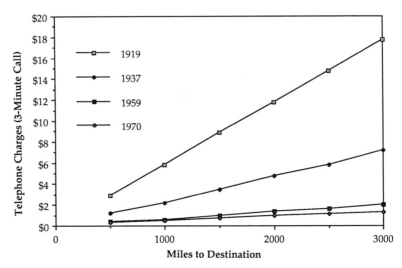

Figure 2.5. Declining costs of long-distance communication. (Adapted from Abler 1977.)

days of classical Greece and Rome, through the messenger systems of the Inca civilization, to our modern postal and telephone systems. He suggested that the chief determinant of the size of a viable empire is the number of days it takes for its messenger system to get information out to the fringes of the empire and back to the capital, as well as the reliability of that system (Innis 1951).

Such issues are not irrelevant to the experience of American national integration. The telegraph, of course, was the precursor of our modern national networks of communications, and its invention was hailed in the mid-nineteenth century as a critical means for drawing the republic together: "Nearly all our vast and wide-spread populations are bound together, not merely by political institutions but by a Telegraph and lightning-like affinity of intelligence and sympathy, that renders us emphatically 'one people' everywhere" (Czitrom 1982, 12).

One can imagine that the relationship between the cost of communications and the flow of national news must have been only a quaint concern in the nineteenth century, but it has become a significant factor. Epstein (1973), for example, cited an example in which the news of the unveiling of a new airplane by Boeing in Seattle was given little notice because getting film from Seattle to the news desk in New York in time for the nightly news was inconvenient and expensive. He asserted that had the debut taken place in New York, it would have been given more prominent coverage.

The fact that distance is becoming a less important factor is not entirely a function of technology. The Integrated Network System (INS) proposed by Japanese telecommunications authorities for the future of the Japanese telephone system, for example, will incorporate a unique and explicit policy to erase the technical and cost distinctions between local and long-distance telephony (Tanase 1985). Such decisions often have important economic ramifications, and it will be interesting to see if similar policies to reinforce the technological trend will be followed elsewhere.

Such communications issues have a lot to do with the balance between local authority and national authority, as well as the balance between concentration and decentralization in complex business organizations (Simon 1976; Malone, Yates, and Benjamin 1987). The issue, as it is most often framed, focuses on which authority is best informed and best able to deal with local matters. Traditionally, the local official quite correctly argues that a central office cannot keep up with the details of local events, but as communications costs become increasingly insensitive to distance, and as volumes increase and communications become more highly automated, such arguments are weakened. It may well be that central decision makers will have received and analyzed data before local decision makers, and the central office will also have the benefit of additional information correlated from other locations. Nora and Minc (1980), for example, argue in their study of the impact of computerization that there is no clear-cut link between distance-insensitive communications and either centralization or decentralization, because the communications flow in both directions. Local decision makers are becoming better informed about central goals and centrally collected information, and thus the traditional arguments for centralized authority are again weakened. As they put it, information flows to where it is needed, and thus the locus of decision-making power becomes an open question (Nora and Minc 1980).

A parallel phenomenon in international relations is reflected in the declining power of the ambassador. In the days of less convenient and less immediate communications, the ambassador functioned more independently, as a delegated representative and local decision maker, but as communications with the home ministry increase in volume and frequency, the need for decision making by the ambassador abroad has diminished.

One can expand that argument to address directly the issue of public participation in political decision making on issues that are not community-specific. The key notion here is the "critical mass." In any number of small communities there may not be enough people interested in a given cause, such as protecting an endangered species, to get a respectable meeting together. But flexible communications can span the geographic chasm and dramatically change the dynamics, economics, and human psychology of achieving a critical mass (Oliver, Marwell, and Teixeira 1985; Markus 1987).

It may also be that such mobilization efforts will bring rural and remote areas closer to the economic and cultural mainstream in regard to other matters (Meier 1962; Dillman 1985).

Increasing speed

For most of human history, the speed of the messenger, traveling either by foot or by horse, determined the speed of communications. People also experimented with communications systems using drums, smoke signals, carrier pigeons, and the waving of semaphore flags from towers and hilltops. But it was not until the perfection of the telegraph in the mid-nineteenth century and the concomitant transoceanic and transcontinental cables that the speed of communications was suddenly and permanently increased many orders of magnitude.

Figure 2.6 shows the delays in communications in the early years of the republic. A number on the map indicates the average number of days between the occurrence of an event in the hinterlands and the reporting of that event in the Philadelphia newspapers. It is difficult for us to imagine a pace of commerce and communications that required two weeks for important news to travel between Philadelphia and Boston, and communications between private parties were even slower.

Electrical impulses travel at the speed of light. Even the most modern satellite or fiber-optic link can communicate no faster than the first telegraph built by Samuel F. B. Morse between Baltimore and Washington in 1844. What has changed has been the availability of high-speed connections for routine communications, which, in effect, has been an outgrowth of decreases in both costs and distance sensitivity. So what in technological terms was a single quantum jump in capability was translated, over the course of a century, into a much more gradual adoption of routine high-speed communications by increasing numbers of people.

Naisbitt refers to this as the collapse of the information "float." Whereas traditionally it had been the economic elite who benefited first from the cutting edge of communications technology, today a professional gold dealer in downtown Manhattan cannot expect to hear about changing prices on the European market any sooner than a hobbyist using a videotex terminal in the Midwest. The Rothschild family reportedly made a quick fortune in the stock exchange because they had received word of Napoleon's defeat at Waterloo by carrier pigeon before anyone else in Paris had heard (Naisbitt 1982, 57). The news of the fall of Veracruz during the Mexican War in 1848 was reported by an enterprising *Baltimore Sun* before the War Department in Washington had received word (Czitrom 1982, 16). Today, when a news story breaks, such as the disaster of the space shuttle *Challenger* in 1986, the president and his

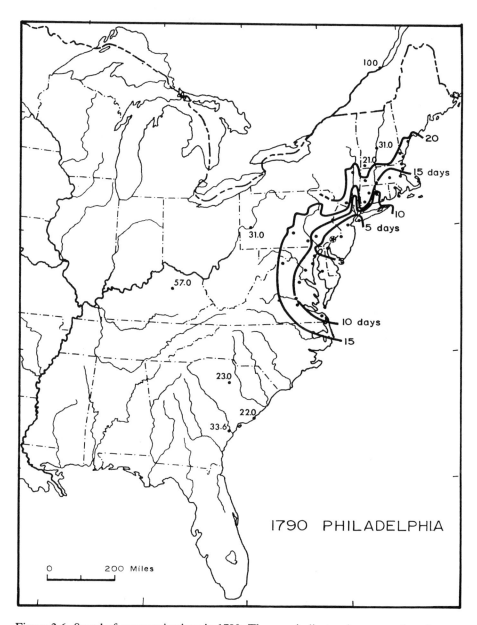

Figure 2.6. Speed of communications in 1790. The map indicates the average length of time between the occurrence of an event in an outlying area and the publication of that event in the Philadelphia newspapers. (From Pred 1973, with permission of the publisher. Copyright © 1973 by the President and Fellows of Harvard University.)

advisers watch the television reports in the Oval Office along with the rest of the nation.

Next-day delivery and express delivery services are increasingly becoming routine. In fact, it is sometimes argued that mail needs to be sent via such services simply to get the recipient to pay appropriate attention to it. It may well be that except for the delivery of physical objects, such services will become increasingly electronic and thus, in fact, immediate. First-class mail could be displayed instantaneously on screens or be printed out by high-quality, high-speed printers in the home or office of the recipient (Pool 1983b).

There is a second sense in which the speed of communications has increased, but it is more closely related to the system's communications capacity than to the speed of electrons: the amount of time required to pass a large amount of information from one point to another. Whereas in Lincoln's time it would have taken longer to transmit the Gettysburg Address by Morse code than to deliver it orally, today it is possible, with large-capacity, high-speed connections, to transmit the entire contents of a 20-volume encyclopedia in a matter of seconds. The limited capacity of the current telephone connections for home computers limits their usefulness; at the rate of only several words per second, the transmission of large information bases, such as newspapers or magazines, for home printing remains impractical. The connect time required to transmit large amounts of information, more than the transmission time to communicate short messages, is experiencing dramatic technological change at the moment. Optical fiber, for example, when connected directly to the home, will permit instantaneous transmission of huge amounts of text or graphics or high-resolution full-motion video (Dordick 1986; Judice et al. 1986). What were once significant constraints and bottlenecks for interpersonal and public communications fade into insignificance as a result of these reinforcing technological trends.

Increasing volume

One of the most frequently noted characteristics of the modern media is the spectacular growth in communications volume, and that, of course, is one of the central elements that leads analysts to characterize this as the information society and to fret over the problems of information overload. Derek Price's analysis of the growth of scientific journals indicates that the number of journals doubles every 15 years, and in some fields the number doubles every 10 years (Price 1963). The explosive growth of technical information means that most of what has been written and published in the entire history of science has been published during our lifetimes. Machlup

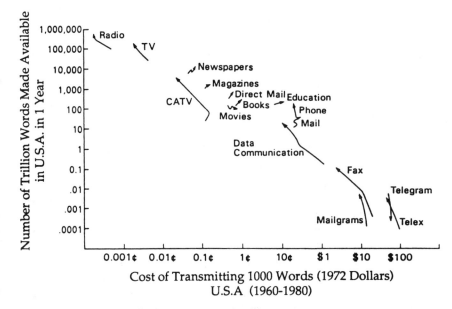

Figure 2.7. Relationships between communications costs and communications volume. (Source: MIT Research Program on Communication Policy.)

estimates that currently there are 50,000 different periodicals and 50 million book titles in the current store of published information (Machlup 1980–4).

The clear lesson is that the communications volume is a function of cost. Pool's data, illustrated in Figure 2.7, demonstrate what appears to be a lawlike functional relationship between communications costs and use. These data are from industry sources and cover the period 1960–80 in the United States. The basic unit is the total number of words communicated by each medium per year. The chart illustrates both the distributions for the different media and the fact that as the prices of individual media change (most prominently, the electronic media), they seem to follow a log-linear curve. We see, for example, that for data communication in 1960 it cost about a dollar to transmit 1,000 words. At that price, there was an average of 0.1 trillion words (i.e., 100,000,000,000) of data communication per year in the United States. As the price fell one order of magnitude over the next two decades, the volume rose two orders of magnitude to 10 trillion words per year (10,000,000,000,000). It is difficult to work with figures of such magnitude, but the general point should be clear enough: The information explosion is all around us.

In 1945, Vannevar Bush envisioned a desktop computer that would give instantaneous access to the entire store of the world's knowledge. He did not predict a precise date, but he believed that the nature of the evolving technology would make such a development inevitable. All the evidence indicates that he was right; it has not happened yet, but the desktop personal computer is here, and there are hundreds of computer services providing information. But electronic information retrieval is still quite expensive, often averaging $100 per hour of search time, and many important documents and resources are not yet on-line. Furthermore, the many information services are not interconnected, and retrieval procedures can be complex enough to require an expert programmer.

The 1980s might be characterized as a halfway house on the trail to Bush's predicted universal electronic information bank. Most of these early services are directed toward professional applications. Thus, for example, there is Lexis, a dial-up service that allows a lawyer at a local terminal to search through the legal code and accumulated case law by keyword for relevant precedents and citations. The Lexis data base contains over 18 million documents (Williams 1985). The On-Line Computer Library Center has accumulated an integrated electronic card catalog for the nation's major libraries. MEDLARS has compiled the latest medical findings for doctors and medical researchers. Dialog is a general-purpose information data base consisting primarily of government and specialized technical reports, a mixture of full text and abstracts. Dialog's main computers store approximately 120 million items of information (mostly bibliographic references) for electronic searching and browsing by its subscribing users. One general-information service is Lexis's sister service, Nexis, which stores electronic files of the entire editorial content of the *Washington Post, Newsweek*, and several dozen general publications and allows the user to search the entire data base by keyword for references to particular people, places, events, or concepts. The system allows the user to display or print out several sentences or the entire article and to search for patterns or particular combinations of keywords. Most of these services are still prohibitively expensive for the casual household user, but prices continue to fall as the data bases grow in size and diversity at tremendous rates. In the mid-1960s there were only a few dozen on-line data bases; that had increased to 2,800 publicly available data bases by 1984. Furthermore, usage has been growing at compound rates of 20% to 30% (Williams 1985).

The increasing volume of communications is perhaps the defining characteristics of our age. It is, at the very least, a central tenet of our models of social change and evolution based on such concepts as the postindustrial society and information society. Whereas in the early years of the republic the great majority of the population worked in agriculture, the farmers were soon replaced by industrial workers, and they in turn by information workers, ranging from clerks to computer programmers and scientists. Agricultural

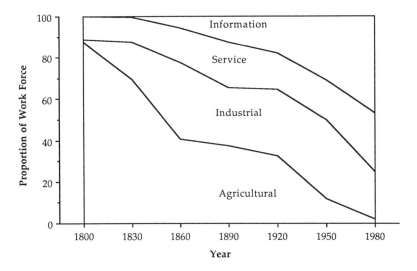

Figure 2.8. Evolution of the information society. (Adapted from United States Department of Commerce 1977.)

work now accounts for less than 3% of the work force, whereas nearly half the work force is occupied primarily with information processing (Figure 2.8). It is difficult to imagine that in 1831 the information management functions of the entire federal bureaucracy (excluding the military) required only 666 employees, including President Jackson (Beniger 1986, 16). Now the scale of government information processing is so large it requires 1.9 million civilian bureaucrats (perhaps equally difficult to imagine) (U.S. Bureau of the Census 1986). Whereas typically workers once earned their wages by manipulating the natural environment, and then machines, today the communication, storage, and processing of words and data occupy their working hours. Such a dramatic shift in the nation's economic life is certain to have significant effects in the social and political arenas. The attempts to assess those effects are still in the early stages of their development (Bell 1973; Machlup 1980–4; Rubin 1983; Beniger 1986; Jonscher 1986).

Increasing channel diversity

Communications volume is one thing; diversity of content is another. In Orwell's scenario of the telescreen, there is no shortage of communications. The fundamental message of the governing elite is repeated and elaborated endlessly, with forceful imagery and stirring music, but there is only one source of communications: the Ministry of Truth. Clearly, the technical capacity to expand the variety of communications is only part of the picture. Diversity will be a fundamental focus of the analysis here. The key is to analyze the relationship between technical communications capacity and meaningful communications diversity. It stands to reason that an abundance of inexpensive, convenient, and effective communications channels is likely to promote diversity. Three factors are at work simultaneously to reinforce the technological trends: more communications through existing channels, development of new channels and increased ability of individuals to use the available communications channels effectively.

There are numerous instances of expanded communications through existing channels – teletext, videotex, dual-channel television audio, low-power television, and subcarrier radio, for example. In the case of teletext, a small portion of the broadcast spectrum assigned to television allows the transmission of text and graphics on each broadcast channel, text and graphics that may be related to the program being broadcast or may concern an entirely different subject. Viewers can display the text or not, as they see fit. In videotex, telephone lines are used to transmit text and graphics to terminals or home computers. In advanced systems, this all takes place over existing lines at the same time and without disrupting normal voice telephony. In dual-channel audio, the capacity of television to deliver stereo audio is used for a second audio sound track that may provide educational information for younger viewers or audio in a second language. Low-power television provides additional television broadcasting stations for smaller geographic areas simply by fitting them in between the existing full-power stations. Subcarrier radio is similar to teletext. It allows the broadcaster to send a second or third signal to specially equipped receivers for audio or data, without disrupting the main signal.

A second factor in our changing electronic technology is the availability of entirely new channels of communications. That includes the capacity to use higher and higher frequencies in the broadcast spectrum on a practical basis. The most obvious example here is the omnipresent parabolic-dish antenna for high-frequency satellite reception. These microwave frequencies are also used for some terrestrial television. In addition, of course, cable technologies, including coaxial and optical-fiber cable, offer the potential to expand the number of channels to the home many orders of magnitude. Coaxial cable, that is, cable television, in the United States is reaching its maximum practical penetration of 80% of residences passed. Those rural areas not likely to be wired for cable will be able to use direct satellite reception on a subscription basis, much like cable and at a roughly equivalent cost.

The third factor is the increasing ability of individuals to take advantage of the existing communications capacity through the use of recording and storage technologies. Thus, for example, video or audio recorders can be

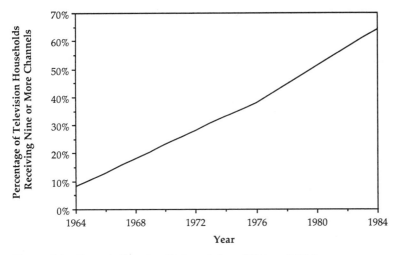

Figure 2.9. Channel diversity. (Adapted from Nielsen 1986.)

preset to record programming delivered over regular broadcast or cable channels, later to be played back at the user's convenience. Also, data can be sent out over telephone lines in the middle of the night, when the system is underutilized, and stored for later display or analysis. In another example, a computer system can send out news information in a slow, steady stream over a broadcast subcarrier, with the information being cataloged and stored in personal computers at the receiving end, later to be displayed on demand as a gigantic, up-to-date electronic newspaper (Schneider 1990).

Currently, the technology that offers the greatest diversity of electronic communications to the home is not some exotic technological refinement, but simply cable television. By retransmitting weak signals from regional UHF television stations, cable has had the interesting effect of strengthening, rather than weakening, the economics of local broadcast television (Baldwin and Mcvoy 1983). So with increasing numbers of individuals connected to cable systems, and others benefiting indirectly from a relatively healthy broadcasting environment, the number of television stations received by the typical household has increased steadily in recent years (Figure 2.9).

Increasing two-way flow

It is the nature of electronic communications to be open to communications in either direction. When one prints a newspaper, book, or magazine, the flow of mass communications is decidedly one-way (Pool 1983b). A reader might send an author or journalist a letter of comment, or a reader might go to the trouble of publishing an article or book in reply, but that would involve working through the entire communications process anew.

With electronic communications, the functions of transmitters and receivers turn out to be quite similar. In practice, of course, there are many more radio and television receivers than transmitters. It is presumed, of course, that the airwaves would revert to chaos if anyone who wanted could simply broadcast at will on any public channel. That was indeed the case in the first decades of this century, when the airwaves became an open playing field for electronic hobbyists and experimenters who talked to each other at will and often obliterated each other's signals, unintentionally or otherwise (Barnouw 1966). Today, with the development of intelligence-based digital processing of communications, the issue of shared, noninterfering, two-way communications again arises as a practical possibility.

The classic example of two-way electronic communications is, of course, the telephone. (With only minor improvements, the first telegraphy systems were also able to send messages simultaneously in both directions.) Each telephone is designed both to transmit and to receive. The key to the viability of the system, of course, is to assign a channel or a connection to only two parties at a time. In the days of party lines, only one household could use the line at a time. But with the advent of digital processing, such constraints lose significance. Many messages can easily and conveniently be sent over a common channel, with only the intended receiver "hearing" a given message. It is all done with labeled digital packets that reliably and efficiently reproduce text, graphics, or speech from shared channels of communications. In fact, most telephone users probably assume that they each have a single, unique line of connection made available to them, when in fact eight or more entirely independent conversations may be taking place over a single pair of copper wires.

The basic principles of two-way digital communications apply to radio transmissions as well as to cable-based systems. One thinks of cable television, however, as inherently a one-way system. Indeed, most systems are designed that way, with special equipment to prevent households from sending video or other electronic signals back up the cable. The amplifiers in the system, for example, are explicitly designed to be one-way amplifiers. But the system could as easily have been designed the other way around, or, at minimal extra cost, as a two-way system, so that anyone so inclined could simply plug a VCR into the cable system and show everyone in town some recent homemade tapes.

One of the most complex and most interesting characteristics of the two-way connectivity of electronic communications is the phenomenon of "interactivity." Interactivity basically means that the system knows what the user is receiving or what the user wants to receive. It is, in effect, two-way communication in an intelligent system. The system is thus able to adjust the content as well as the pace and format of information to the user's needs and interests. The potential benefits and practical considerations that flow from this aspect of electronic communications are just now being explored. These issues will be the primary focus of a later chapter.

Increasing flexibility

The increasing ability of the communications user to select, control, and manipulate the flow of information is, in a sense, a culmination of the factors previously described. One central element of user control and flexibility, of course, is choice from a diversity of inexpensive and conveniently available contents. The more channels, ceteris paribus, the more choices. Channel diversity, in turn, is a function of decreasing costs and the expanding volume and speed of communications.

The term "flexibility" also refers to the increased ability of the user to store, format, edit, and display electronic images and text. The electronic media are becoming more like traditional print media, allowing the reader to browse, scan, reread, skim, or skip any portion of the flow of information. Traditionally, print media occupied the space domain, and broadcast media occupied the time domain: A reader of a newspaper or magazine could move around in space to find the content of interest, but a member of the broadcast audience had to spend time waiting for an item of interest to appear. But now, because of the processing, editing, and convenient recording of broadcast information, such distinctions between these media begin to dissolve. Some television viewers prefer to videotape a program and watch it later, even if it was originally broadcast at a convenient time, simply because that gives them the ability to fast-forward through the commercials or less interesting sections of the program. Such issues as skipping commercials, of course, threaten the entire economic basis of the industry and are being closely watched (Nielsen 1986).

Watching videotaped television with a finger on the fast-forward button is one form of direct control. Another is to allow the intelligent information-processing capacity of the system to do some of the filtering and fast-forwarding, which has particularly intriguing ramifications. Suppose, for example, one were interested only in news about a few sports teams, a favorite movie star, and one or two local issues, and one would like to be able to program the flow of news coming into the home to filter out anything but those highly limited topics. That is what the fundamental technology of videotex can do. Thousands of pages of information are available with videotex, but the only information to appear on the screen will be what has

been explicitly requested. People have been fast-forwarding through unwanted sections of newspaper and magazines since their inception, and so
the basic question of user control is not fundamentally new, but the cumu-
lative impact of expanding and automating such filtering and information-
processing capacity across the full range of information sources remains to
be determined.

Increasing extensibility

"Extensibility" is an especially important correlate of user-controlled system
flexibility: In digital systems it is easy to upgrade and expand the capacity
of the system; the key is to change the software and (within appropriate
limits) continue to use the existing hardware.

This is one of the more positive aspects of the transition from an emphasis
on industrial technologies (hardware-based) to an emphasis on information
technologies (software-based). Imagine the following scenario: As a quintessential industrial-age entrepreneur you manufacture widgets. You purchase
a new, higher-power blast furnace to expedite the manufacturing process,
but to your horror it blows up, damaging other machinery, widgets, and
workers. It takes months to detect and correct the design error and rebuild
the physical plant.

In contrast, as a postindustrial information entrepreneur, you purchase
new data-base software necessary for your consulting business. But its design
proves faulty, and to your horror it "crashes" the system, losing data and
frustrating your workers. No problem; you have backup data. The problem
is identified by internal process-monitoring subprograms. Corrections are
made, the software is reloaded, and the system is up and running with the
correction in place.

The idea behind the extensibility of systems is that they expand their
capacity as they are used, a counterpoint to entropy in mechanical systems.
Organization and self-knowledge accumulate rather than dissipate; with appropriate feedback, information machines get smarter and more efficient the
more experience they have. Furthermore, if someone discovers a new, more
efficient algorithm, everyone else's systems can be upgraded with the new
software without having to be rebuilt.

In physical manufacturing processes or in analog communications, once a
piece of equipment is in place to detect, transmit, amplify, or display information, it will work precisely as it was designed to work until it breaks or
is replaced. In digital processing, the physical equipment in place may well
be used for processes and purposes not even imagined by the engineers who
originally designed it.

We have now reviewed eight of the nine properties that characterize the communications and information media of the post-industrial age. Similar lists have been derived by other analysts with somewhat different vocabularies, but the central ideas are emerging with increasing clarity (Pool 1983b; Rice and Williams 1984; Dillman 1985; Abramson et al. 1988). Two key elements that span all lists are the costs and capacity of the system. The new media can carry more information cheaper, faster, and farther; information will be abundant. Whereas only a few centuries ago secrecy and ignorance pervaded the lives of isolated, parochial, fearful pockets of human existence, today our capacity for connection among communications systems is almost infinite. Scarcity and rules for allocation seem quaint and profoundly inappropriate. Some analysts worry about the dangers of overabundance and information overload, and we shall address those questions shortly. Abundance, however, seems much less of a challenge than scarcity.

A second concept that spans the work of those who analyze the new media is flexibility. The new media are labile and plastic; they can be molded and reconfigured to suit the tastes and needs of individual users. They are more organic in nature than the older media, as they pick up and reflect characteristics of the information that passes through them. The barriers between the various older media of print and analog transcriptions and transmissions were formidable; it was an expensive, labor-intensive endeavor to take information from one format and translate it into another. Mass communications constituted one world, with its own technologies, economics, cultural expectations, and dynamics; interpersonal communications were carried on in another world entirely.

Flexibility is a neutral concept. Its social effects are difficult to predict, because it means that one can do just about what one wants. But there is more to the logic of electronic flexibility, because it leads to interconnection, to the building of networks and a trend toward convergence into a single, universal, multipurpose network. We now turn to the ninth and most important property of the new media.

Increasing interconnectivity

A fundamental property of digital electronics is their ease of interconnectivity. That was not a property of analog communications or even of first-generation digital technologies. Early telegraphy over long distances required telegraph operators at various intervals to transcribe and resend messages manually. Early telephone systems required the intervention of operators to make manual connections on a switchboard, although in time the telephone's interconnections became automated.

In the early days of the newspaper wire services, the wired stories would be printed out on a Teletype machine, perhaps edited a bit by the local editor, and then typed all over again on the Linotype machine to set the characters for printing. Now the whole process is electronic and automatic: The local editor calls up a wire story on a word-processing system, edits the text, if appropriate, and then cues the story for automatic typesetting. If the newspaper has an electronic edition, the story may be transmitted by telephone lines directly to the subscriber. In such cases, a story may move from a reporter's computer to that of the reader in minutes, passing through dozens of computers and connections along the way, being recoded, edited, and reformatted in each case (Smith 1980).

The impact of this technological interconnectivity on the economic structure of the communications industries is significant. Interconnectivity leads to a dramatic blurring of boundaries and a convergence of delivery systems. Media that once were seen as unique, noncompetitive communications industries have now found themselves in direct economic competition. Consider, for example, the yellow-pages industry, which generates revenues of more than $4 billion per year. Local businesses traditionally have found it advantageous to advertise in the yellow pages of the telephone book, where potential customers can find them under the appropriate service and product headings. But when the yellow pages are delivered electronically to a home computer screen, perhaps being updated daily to reflect new sales and promotions, the difference between electronic yellow pages, and newspaper advertisements begins to blur.

Furthermore, when print materials, such as newspapers, magazines, newsletters, and even books, are delivered to the home electronically by broadcast, by wire, or by magnetic recording, to be displayed or printed out there under the control of the user, the traditional distinctions between those media in terms of advertising, frequency of publication, and physical format become increasingly irrelevant. Likewise, in the electronic delivery of audio and video materials, the traditional industry boundaries between radio and records, and between movies and television, become less meaningful.

Thus, for example, if during the course of a television commercial it seems a good idea to provide a discount coupon or a map showing the location of a new store, there is no reason that a printer could not be attached to the set to give the viewer an instantaneous hard copy. One might prefer to go to the store to buy computer software, but it can easily be delivered electronically and automatically billed to one's electronic bank account. One might want to browse through digital recordings at a retail outlet, but a digital recording of equally high quality can be delivered via telephone or satellite connections.

The basic message about the new technology is straightforward and powerful: Audio, video, text, and graphics can be transmitted, stored, and manipulated at will. Because of increased intelligence in the system, information is automatically reformatted to be transmitted and displayed in any of a number of physical manifestations. Although currently many computer users are still encountering frustrating incompatibilities between software and systems components, these are temporary problems, characteristic only of the first generation of each new technology.

A second important factor in the technology of interconnectivity is that it draws on the potential of voice synthesis and voice recognition to become the means by which humans and machines will communicate with one another. At the moment, for text, at least, that communication is primarily via the keyboard and video screen, but as techniques become better refined, computers will increasingly have the option of synthesizing voice for direct audio communication as well as direct voice input. Thus, one may be as likely to dictate and listen to a letter as to write and read one; it will become a matter of personal preference. Given that speaking is generally faster and more convenient than typing, speech is likely to become the typical input to written communications. Given that reading text is faster and more flexible than listening to speech, electronically displayed text is likely to remain the typical output. Nevertheless depending on context, content, and the user's mood, any combination of sound and visual modalities might be chosen (Bolt 1984).

As noted earlier, the long-term effects of such interconnectivity and flexibility would be difficult to predict. Communications developments depend a great deal on costs and convenience. If one had attempted to predict the ultimate market for xerography from the number of sheets of carbon paper sold per year, one would have underestimated the demand for plain-paper copies by many orders of magnitude. Carbon copies represent an awkward, inflexible, and low-quality technology. Xerox copiers made rapid copying in the office routine in the 1960s, and small, inexpensive copiers are now available for the home. High-speed, high-quality photo-electronic copiers are increasingly obviating the distinction between copying and printing. The phenomenon is further compounded by the fact that page images, once copied, can be printed out on-site, or across town, or around the world. Routinely with electronic mail, the receiver of a message can forward copies of the message regardless of length, to a few people or a few thousand people with two or three keystrokes. The dynamics of such interconnectivity and the problems of information filtering and overload have not yet been explored. It is likely that the first experiments will take place in automated office environments, before spreading in time to the homes of the aficionados of high technology (Campbell and Thomas 1981; Rogers 1983; Schneider 1990).

One likely application for interconnectivity is the home information and communications center. One might imagine, for example, the average living room containing a large-screen video display, a high-resolution, high-speed color laser printer, and high-fidelity speakers. These output devices would be connected to a series of digital disc playback units, to cable, broadcast, satellite receivers, and to an optical-fiber-based telephone network. The family members might watch a television show, establish a three-way video conference with some friends, watch a videotape made by a relative, send and receive mail interspersed with graphics and pictures, pay bills electronically, consult a disc-based encyclopedia, or audit a seminar at a nearby college (Parker 1970; Cornish 1982; Tydeman et al. 1982). The various two-way connections might be made via a new form of digital radio communications, two-way coaxial cable, or the telephone network, whichever might be available or least expensive at the moment (Figure 2.10).

A universal broadband digital network

The prospects for historically unique abundance and flexibility in human communications stir the imagination. An open, diverse marketplace of ideas lies at the core of the democratic ideal. But if the logic of the whizzing digits were to grow organically into some singular, universal, geodesic network, that would give one pause. The prospect is cautionary, as we imagine becoming glued together and somehow entrapped by the network octopus – Orwell again. If there is to be a single, universal network, who is going to control it? Could it be manipulated to serve the ends of some dominant interest groups within it?

These questions are important, and we shall address them in later chapters. Before proceeding, however, we need to finish our assessment of the technological properties of the emerging worldwide network. The network is, in fact, now being designed and built, although its social and political functions, its final architecture, and its economic properties are not at all clear to the engineers and executives assigned to the task. Their assignment is simple and straightforward, although all but a few suspect that something more significant is under way.

The backbone of the new network is the current telephone system. The engineering assignment is simply to update and upgrade the system by moving from analog to digital telecommunications. There is an international plan in place and a name for the new system: Integrated Services Digital Network (ISDN). Such upgrading might at first glance appear to be solely the business of the telephone companies and perhaps a few technical staffers at the FCC and the state regulatory agencies. But the stakes are high, the implications are not at all clear, and increasingly the policy and research communities are taking a very close look (Rutkowski 1986; Anania 1989).

The first generation of the ISDN may not appear to make much of a difference. There will be small changes in the traditional telephone service:

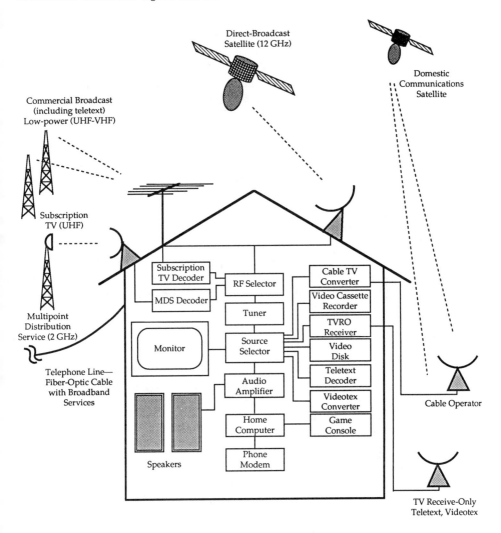

Figure 2.10. Integrated home information center. (Adapted from Kaplan et al. 1985.)

more flexibility, higher fidelity, the ability to forward and filter calls more easily, the capacity to send a data message and a voice message (or two of either) at the same time over a single line. The critical threshold will be reached (if forces do not converge to prevent it) when the system shifts to the second generation: broadband ISDN (B-ISDN). The second step will be expensive and complex because it will require massive redesign of the switching system and a rewiring of the entire network from the central telephone offices to each residence with optical fiber. The costs have been estimated at about $2,000 per household, which sounds forbidding (Sirbu, Reed, and Ferrante 1989), but that would be offset by reductions in the yearly costs of upgrading and maintaining the old telephone system, and such expenses could be incorporated into the day-to-day costs of local and long-distance communications and spread out over the life of the new network (Egan 1991). Furthermore, a great deal of optical fiber has already been installed in the systems' central trunk lines. But what would B-ISDN mean in terms of social and economic impacts?

B-ISDN would mean realization of Vannevar Bush's vision of the Memex. It would mean instantaneous, inexpensive, errorless communication of any body of text, audio, or video of virtually any size from any point to any other. It would represent a complete breakdown of the traditional distinctions between the various media and between different types of human communications. It would be the embodiment of each of the technical properties identified earlier: speed, volume, diversity, two-way flow, flexibility, extensibility, and interconnectivity. But technologies, as noted earlier in some detail, do not spring from a vacuum. They are rooted in and defined by the historical, political, and social context.

The communications revolution as a sociopolitical force

Most of the technological developments that will fuel these proposed changes have taken place over the past several decades, and the changes they will bring in the processes of public communications are beginning to take place now and will evolve further over the next decade. We are at the threshold of a new era.

Although unforeseen developments could yet turn this promising scenario in new and negative directions, the general thrust of the communications revolution is quite clear. As a result of the tremendous growth in digital electronics, the costs of communications are decreasing, and the volume is increasing. The greater ease with which different communications media can be connected with each other, the dramatic growth in new channels of high-quality, two-way communication, and the development of user-controlled electronic intelligence and information processing lead strongly in the direction of diverse, pluralistic communications flows controlled by the citizenry, rather than by central authorities.

Some authoritarian regimes may attempt to ban ownership of personal computers or forbid political communications in the electronic mail system, and surely some authorities will attempt to monitor the electronic communications of individuals and groups suspected of pernicious intent.[3] But the thrust of the new technology works to the advantage of the individual rather than the central authorities. One key element is the volume of communications. If authorities are trying to find a seditious needle in a haystack, the process becomes more difficult as the haystack grows larger. It is easier for authorities to censor a few centrally published newspapers than thousands of electronic newsletters.

To the extent that large corporations or central authorities are doing the communicating, they are provided additional tools to manipulate and propagandize, if that is their intent. But, on balance, the ability of the individual to seek out additional information from other sources through other channels outweighs such factors. Soon after Gutenberg began printing, the government found it prudent to license and control all printing shops; there were few of them, and it seemed unnecessary to let them print any political pamphlet they might want. As printing presses became more advanced, the newspapers they printed were heavily taxed by governments as a further means of control (Pool 1983b). Over the years, a tradition of a free and independent press developed in Western democracies, and such controls abated (Siebert, Peterson, and Schramm 1956). But those were political trends, not technical developments. The economics and technology of large printing presses meant that there would be relatively few of them, and the potential to censor them or shut them down is still very much with us, as evidenced daily in the politics of modern journalism around the world (Gastil 1986). But because electronic communications more easily flow across political borders and through more diverse channels, such control becomes increasingly difficult to maintain.

On balance, then, the new technology tends to shift control of the communications process from the producer to the audience member. Given the basic values of democratic pluralism, that is good news. A further change that results from the communications revolution is that the distinction between producers and audiences begins to break down. Audience members who are so inclined can take advantage of their new ability to store, filter, edit, reformat, and forward information to others, as frequently practiced by those who participate in electronic networks. Already there are thousands of electronic bulletin boards and special-interest mailing lists actively used by computer hobbyists. The new technology significantly enhances the natural two-step or multistep flow of communications from the mass media through various opinion leaders and interested parties to the population at large. It is a critically important, though informal, process of community and group life. Public opinion, it is often observed, is much more than the simple summation of private opinions. Public opinion is as much a process as an entity, and it is greatly enhanced by ongoing discussion and interpretation of public events within the citizenry.

Although it is a time-honored tradition to clip an article of particular interest from the newspaper and send it, along with some comments, to a friend, that can now be done electronically with a few keystrokes, and it can be forwarded to any number of interested parties, friends and strangers alike. The evolving user-controlled network enhances the viability of active intermediate social groupings, the classic pluralist response to the challenge of mass society. Electronic versions of the traditional town meeting or the informal discussions of politics around the cracker barrel at the general store provide positive and hopeful metaphors.

Vannevar Bush's Memex has virtually arrived. It is not a free-standing machine; rather it is part of a complex, interconnected communications system. Some of Bush's intellectual descendants have claimed that we now have the potential to develop an entire generation of scholarly geniuses. They are too optimistic. The future of the mass audience will reveal a gap between that bright potential and how people actually come to use the new technologies (Neuman 1986). That is the message of this book. Those with the ability and inclination to become scholarly geniuses have done so throughout history. Where once they used telescopes, libraries, typewriters, and slide rules, they now may turn to computers. But they represent only a tiny fraction of the mass population. In the language of the industry, they compose a very small market. They may be important to society, but not to the marketplace. The future of the mass audience will pivot on factors of mass psychology and market economics.

3

The psychology of media use

Judging from the new technologies, the future of the mass audience is auspicious indeed. In Chapter 2 we reviewed evidence of the evolving technologies' growing capacity to enhance public communications and political participation. Technological potential, however, is only one side of the story. Orwell, for example, was less concerned with the technologies per se than with the values and cultural assumptions that dictate how the technologies should be used. One fundamental concern underlying Orwell's thinking was the helplessness of individuals caught up in the currents of political forces so much more powerful than themselves. The audience for propaganda is passive, attentive, and gullible. This imagery draws on forces of oceanic proportions: The waves, tides, and currents of mass communications envelop and carry the individual with them.

The other side of the story

Perhaps one of the most telling incidents to support the pessimistic view of the mass audience occurred on the evening of Sunday, October 30, 1938, when the CBS Mercury Theater of the Air presented an adaptation of H. G. Wells's *The War of the Worlds*. The writers were having a difficult time making the story interesting and plausible for the American radio audience. The setting for the novel was England, and the narrative style of the original was difficult to reformulate into an effective radio drama. The rehearsals went so badly that the producers toyed with the idea of dropping the project in favor of *Lorna Doone*. But then they hit on the idea of a simulated news bulletin describing the landing of the Martians at a farm in Grover's Mill, New Jersey. As it was finally broadcast, a musical performance was interrupted by an announcement of the landing of a strange meteorite near Trenton. Police were described as rushing to the scene. The announcer advised listeners to avoid Route 23. The army was said to have been called in, but proved helpless against the Martians' superior weapons. At the end of the broadcast, the host, Orson Welles, explained that the drama just heard had been intended as a Halloween holiday offering, but his words came too late for many listeners.

Hadley Cantril's study (1940) of the panic that ensued described listeners who swamped the police, newspaper, and radio-station switchboards with frantic questions. One woman reportedly called the bus terminal in New York for information, pleading: "Hurry, please, the world is coming to an end and I have a lot to do." People ran out into the streets, huddled and prayed, hid in the woods, drove aimlessly into the country. Even attempted suicides were reported. One listener who tuned in late reported the following: "I know it was some Germans trying to gas all of us. When the announcer kept calling them people from Mars I just thought he was ignorant and didn't know yet that Hitler had sent them all" (Lowery and De Fleur 1983, 77).

The great majority of listeners, of course, understood that it was a radio play. But the spectacular gullibility of millions of listeners became a frequently cited benchmark of mass hysteria and persuasibility. Americans already suspected that the German population was susceptible to Hitler's demagogic propaganda, but here was evidence that the American audience may be no different.

The perception of a helpless mass public was developed further by popular books on the effects of mass advertising, such as Vance Packard's *The Hidden Persuaders* (1957), which described the use of subtle psychological imagery to sell products and politicians. Packard informed his readers of a new and especially nefarious form of subconscious persuasion that he called subthreshold advertising – the flashing of an image on a movie or television screen for an interval so short that the viewer is not aware of having seen it. In the case he cited, theater patrons were unaware of seeing brief images of an ice-cream cone interspersed in a movie, yet ice-cream sales in the theater increased dramatically. Subliminal advertising was widely cited as the ultimate form of irresistible persuasion, and part of a particularly dangerous trend. These images from the beginnings of the era of radio and television have come to frame a coherent and influential research paradigm for understanding media effects.

The helpless audience

Do the new media technologies of the 1990s offer even more tempting prospects for manipulation and control? There are many who strongly believe that this is the case. Even such a prominent figure in American political mass communications as Walter Cronkite, for example, has warned that "without the malign intent of any government system or would-be dictator, our privacy is being invaded, and more and more of the experiences which should be solely our own are finding their way into electronic files that the curious can scrutinize at the punch of a button" (Burnham 1983, vii). Others argue that the new media increasingly facilitate the ability of elites to create and maintain an effective "pseudoreality," including staged press conferences, public events, and ceremonies created by and for the media, the purpose of which is to manipulate rather than reflect reality (Boorstin 1961; Katz, Dayan, and Motyl 1981).

Although the preceding chapter argues otherwise, it is certainly possible to interpret many of the generic properties of the new media as exacerbating the crisis. The decreasing costs of communications lead in turn to the overload problems of high-volume communications. Increasing interconnectivity and two-way electronic communications tempt central authorities to pursue secret monitoring and analysis of the day-to-day communications and economic behaviors of citizens. Sophisticated forms of targeted communications can provide propagandists subtle and effective new strategies and tools.

There appear to be six fundamental arguments that characterize the new media as powerful weapons poised for use against a helpless and passive audience, as summarized in Table 3.1. Many of these authors have developed themes originally used to characterize wartime propaganda; others have emphasized the new factors in the character of the most recent and still-evolving communications technologies. Taken together, as they usually are, these arguments give considerable cause for concern. They are, in effect, a modern reformulation of mass society theory, with a special focus on the psychology of the member of the mass audience.

The quantity argument

The quantity argument draws attention to the pervasive and irresistible flow of media messages. The basic values of the dominant regime, it is argued, become "self-validating" over time through incessant and unchallenged repetition. Marcuse calls this "the hypnotic definitions of dictations" (1964, 14). The theory about persuading the listener simply by repeating the message endlessly has been attributed to Hitler, who mentioned it in *Mein Kampf* (Kecskemeti 1973). It became known as the big-lie theory and was extensively tested by Goebbels and his associates in the German propaganda ministry. One's critical mental faculties simply become worn down and weakened by having to process the endless stream of vivid, coherent propaganda. After lengthy repetition, the words, images, and metaphors develop a taken-for-granted quality, an accepted familiarity that precludes or at least diminishes one's capacity for skepticism.

A related concept is information overload, an imbalance between the amount of information provided and that which an individual could possibly

Table 3.1. *The helpless audience: fundamental issues of new media and manipulation*

Theme	Central issue	Key concepts	Authors
Quantity	Irresistible flow of convergent, persuasive communication	Information overload	Ellul (1964) Marcuse (1964)
Targeting	Messages targeted to needs, weaknesses, and prejudices of individual audience members	Audience segmentation	Frank and Greenberg (1980) Sabato (1981)
Modality	New formats and techniques, especially vivid, visceral, persuasive forms of communication	Medium is message	McLuhan (1964) Schwartz (1973, 1983)
Scope	Increasingly global communications flows; breakdown of national, regional, and local boundaries and sense of community	Communications flows	Tunstall (1977) Schiller (1973)
Addiction	Dominance of contrived, commercial-entertainment-oriented media; distraction from either politics	Pent-up demand; soft persuasion	Habermas (1962) Marcuse (1964)
Subtlety	Increased subtlety and sophistication of persuasive communication	Cultivation analysis; spiral of silence	Gerbner (1972) Noelle-Neumann (1984)

process. The stress and confusion that evolve from various overload coping strategies are hardly conducive to rational political evaluation. In earlier, calmer times, it is argued, there was a natural balance in persuasive communications between the single speaker and the single listener. Now, with the multiplier effect of electronic communications technology, the message can be repeated and magnified relentlessly.

From another perspective, the overload issue can be defined in terms of Gresham's law: With the ceaseless din of commercial messages competing for the attention of the audience member, it is difficult for messages of any other type to get through. It is estimated that the average American is exposed to 1,600 advertising messages per day through the various print and broadcast media (Draper 1986). The question is whether or not commercial communications actually drive out noncommercial communications, in the sense of Gresham's law. Gans (1974) argues that they can do so in more than one way: Commercially oriented popular culture not only distracts the audience member but also may lure away artists and authors who might otherwise be contributing to serious cultural pursuits.

The targeting argument

The targeting argument concerns the issue of increased producer control over communications, the ability to target and adjust messages to the particular interests and backgrounds of audience members through the use of sophisticated information-processing technologies. If an individual is fond of chocolate or imported wines, for example, and has subscribed to a specialized magazine or ordered some imported delicacies from a mail-order firm, that person's name, address, and particular passion will be incorporated into an appropriate data base and sold to other vendors, who will follow up with a stream of tempting offers and promotions. Direct-mail advertising, of course, is as old as the postal system itself, but the increased sophistication of data processing and monitoring of economic behavior complicates the issue. Chocolate lovers may relish being on every chocolate mailing list available. Contributors to an unpopular political cause may be less enthusiastic about the inclusion of their names in a data base the uses of which they cannot control.

The modality argument

The modality argument concerns the increased technological potential for interconnection and new forms of electronic display. "Modality" refers to the way in which technologies act on our senses, particularly the differences between traditional print and newer video technologies. Where once print was print and speech was speech, the electronic interface permits not only communications flows of a higher order but also increasingly sophisticated combinations of imagery and sound. The symbol of Big Brother, larger than life on a huge video screen, staring down at a cowering audience is pertinent. Other examples, less dramatic but equally relevant, include computers (speaking with a digitally synthesized voice) that dial random numbers and conduct telephone surveys, as well as talking vending machines, cameras, automobiles, and two-way video telephones. At the core of this concern is the argument that reliance on television rather than the traditional print media for political news makes a difference in how people understand the political world around them (Schwartz 1973, 1983; Sabato 1981; Diamond and Bates 1984; Neuman, Just, and Crigler in press).

The scope argument

Drawing on the increasing reach of communications around the globe, this argument emphasizes the impact of communications flows across national boundaries. Where once virtually all media were regional or national in character, the nature of satellite and interconnected digital networks is such that political boundaries today are less significant barriers to the communications process. The negative side of this is the limited ability of the local or national entity to protect its indigenous culture and sense of community. To the extent that the electronic global village McLuhan envisioned reflects increased understanding and communications, one finds little fault, but to the extent that it portends an uncontrollable, homogenizing commercial proliferation, it represents a significant problem.

The addiction argument

One premise that seemed to dominate thinking about the new media in the 1970s was the notion of a pent-up demand for new and better entertainment and information media. The videogame craze often was cited as a characteristic model. Enthusiastic entrepreneurs attracted large sums of investment capital for numerous ventures in videotex, two-way cable, and electronic publishing. Each proposal posited that its new medium would quickly become habit-forming, perhaps even addicting, and would generate hours of use. No one seemed to think in terms of what might happen if all the entrepreneurs introduced their new technologies and services all at once, which in a sense they did. Adding together all the market projections for home computers, VCRs, videogames, and other new media uses gives a total of more than 24 hours per day of media attentiveness, with no time for work, sleep, or recreation of any other type. Each new communications delivery system imagined itself as part of the user's daily media habit, and each tried to calculate the magic formula for entertainment, information, and practical application that would motivate the user. To the entrepreneur, that translates into a new income stream; to the communications user, it is an attempt to identify and manipulate the habituating and addictive properties of media communications.

The subtlety argument

Frequently it is argued that the persuasive communications conveyed by the mass media are increasingly subtle and effective. Kris and Leites (1950), in a comparative study of propaganda during the two world wars, concluded that increasing subtlety is part of a broad historical trend. Many Marxists see it as an inevitable result of the competitive pressures on the commercial interests who own the media. Others, such as Diamond and Bates (1984) and Blumenthal (1980), see it simply as a natural outgrowth of increased professional skill in advertising and promotion, applied to the realm of political ideas as well as merchandising.

A point sometimes missed in these analyses of news and public-affairs content is that political messages in the American media are equally as prevalent in the entertainment format (Gerbner et al. 1980). Representing the official point of view in government-controlled newscasts is one thing; it is easily recognized and interpreted by the audience. But more subtle cues regarding what is and is not politically acceptable, carried as part of mainstream advertising, comedy, and action-oriented entertainment, can be more effective (Marcuse 1964; Noelle-Neumann 1984).

These six themes have been identified in thoughtful analyses of the public communications process. Some of that work has drawn on carefully grounded empirical studies. Mass society theory is still very much alive, although it is now evolving a new vocabulary for analysis. These studies have converged on a single point: a concern for the increasingly defenseless and helpless audience member. We have come full circle. How are we to reconcile such work with the standing hypothesis about the potentially liberating force of the new media technologies?

The strategy we shall adopt is to step back for a moment and take a closer look at the communications-effect paradigm inherent in the concepts of mass society and propaganda. If we are to assess the positive and negative social and political effects of the new media in a balanced fashion, we need a balanced starting point.

The paradox of propaganda

The paradox of propaganda is how parties in conflict define it: What one party labels truth, the other defines as pernicious propaganda. As a result, the term "propaganda" finds limited usefulness outside of debate or routine exchanges of diplomatic insults. The paradox of propaganda to be pursued here takes that curious property of the concept a step further: There is an intriguing paradox associated with the scientific study of propaganda effects that works in a manner parallel to the first. The key is how terms come to be defined and to influence the design of the research. The communication of bad ideas is defined as propaganda; the communication of good ideas is defined as education. Communicating propaganda is dangerously easy; audiences can be persuaded and duped with minimum effort. The process is one of infection: Viewers are tainted by pornography, lured by advertisements, infected with false notions by popular music, pacified by television, and stimulated to violent and antisocial behavior by all of these.

Communication as education, however, is frustratingly difficult. The audience for education is inattentive, uninterested, and obstinate. Both in classrooms and in personalized programs of instruction using flashy educational technologies, thousands of dollars per student are spent each year. Yet sub-

Communications Effect

		Strong	Weak
Cultural Value	Negative	Propaganda	Resistance to Education
	Positive	Education	Resistance to Propaganda

Figure 3.1. Strong versus weak communications effects.

stantial numbers of high-school graduates, after 12 years of instruction, are functionally illiterate and unable to perform simple mathematical tasks.

The paradox pivots on differing assumptions about strong versus weak communications effects (Figure 3.1). Such differing perspectives must be confronted if scientific study of the communications process is to progress and lead to a balanced and unified theory and methodology. It is true that some kinds of ideas and information are more easily communicated and grasped by the listener than are others, but entirely separate models of the communications process for good information (education) and bad information (propaganda) are unlikely to be fruitful.

Karl Rosengren has noted that in most cases the introduction of a new communications technology has been accompanied by a moral panic, a concern that the new medium would "debase morals, destroy beauty, distort truth and prevent much useful work" (Rosengren, Wenner, and Palmgreen 1985, 3). Wartella and Reeves (1985) have demonstrated the accuracy of Rosengren's insight empirically by tracing a time line for the introductions of radio, motion pictures, and television and the corresponding sizes of the research literatures concerned with the effects of these "new" media on children. In each case, after a short lag, there was a flurry of studies focusing on the potential negative impact on children. As a new medium is introduced, even though the immediately preceding medium may still be enjoying a substantial audience, attention gravitates to the same fundamental concerns about the new medium: variations on the themes of manipulation, distraction, and addiction, with particular attention to the young, the most defenseless and naive component of the mass audience. It is doubly ironic that the young are also the primary audience for the communications output of educational institutions and all too frequently in that situation prove a resourcefully obstinate audience.

A more balanced assessment of communications effects

The accumulated findings from five decades of systematic social science research, however, reveal that the mass media audience, youthful or otherwise, is not helpless, and the media are not all-powerful. The evolving theory of modest and conditional media effects helps to put in perspective the historical cycle of moral panic over new media. New media are a lot like old media; so are "new" audiences. We need not abandon, but rather can profitably build on, the knowledge about audience psychology and media use that has been accumulated in recent years. The new media, like the old, can be used for propaganda and education alike. It makes sense to move forward from a balanced and integrative theoretical framework that does not focus too narrowly on either propaganda or education.

The original notion about communications and propaganda effects that emerged during the period from the 1930s to the 1950s is sometimes characterized as the bullet or hypodermic-needle model: One need only hit the target (a particular audience member) to have the intended effect. That reflected, in part, the early behaviorist stimulus–response theories in experimental psychology; it also may have reflected the intensity of the moral concern. But as the empirical evidence accumulated, it became increasingly clear that the process was better characterized as an interaction between audience and medium – highly sensitive to situational conditions, audience attitudes and interests, and the nature of the communicated message. Hovland and associates (1953), Klapper (1960), Weiss (1968), McGuire (1969), Kraus and Davis (1976), Comstock et al. (1978), McLeod and Reeves (1980), and Neuman (1989), among others, have published overviews of these findings.

It has been shown, for example, that the social contexts of persuasive communications are critically important. In one study, wartime propaganda directed at undermining the morale of German soldiers was found to be utterly ineffectual for influencing soldiers in a fighting unit, but it had potential to influence soldiers who were separated from the reinforcing social and ideological pressures of the primary group (Shils and Janowitz 1948).

Another classic study demonstrated a two-step flow of information from the mass media, filtered through attentive opinion leaders, who discussed and interpreted public issues informally with their friends and relatives (Katz and Lazarsfeld 1955). That was a particularly important finding because it contradicted the original mass society notion of unmediated, direct manipulative communication between elites and the anomic mass population. Not only were there complex interpretive social networks, but individual opinion leaders developed expertise and influence in areas of particular concern. More recently, the original two-step model has been broadened to incorporate multistep flows and horizontal sharing and discussion of information among equals (Rogers 1973).

Other research has converged on findings regarding selective attention, perception, and retention. The work of Hovland and associates (1953), studying how listeners used a variety of clues to judge the veracity of a speaker, was expanded by Festinger (1957) in a widely cited analysis of cognitive dissonance. It has been found that the effects of persuasion are constrained by the cognitive defenses of those who have already given the subject matter some thought and made up their minds (McGuire 1969). In the realm of electoral politics, the party label has proved to be a critical cue for filtering and judging new information (Berelson et al. 1954, Campbell et al. 1960; Blumler and McQuail 1969).

Although the nature of what motivates cognitive filtering is still subject to debate (Freedman and Sears 1965), the importance of cognitive filtering is not. It is abundantly clear that people do not simply receive messages for storage on a cognitive tabula rasa. That may, in fact, be the most abundantly demonstrated finding from five decades of social psychological and cognitive research. One might trace the intellectual origins of this notion to Lippmann's early work on stereotypes (1922) or the work of Piaget (1930), Bartlett (1932), and Sherif (1935) on schemata and frames of reference. It has reemerged as a revitalized paradigm for research on political cognition (Graber 1984; Lau and Sears 1986; McGuire 1985; Gamson, 1988). Individuals draw on their organized prior knowledge to interpret and construct meaning from incoming messages and information; the audience is actively negotiating with the symbolic culture. Incoming information that does not fit into recognizable categories or schema is less easily remembered and understood (Fiske 1986), and certainly less persuasive (McGuire 1985).

Gamson (in press), for example, has shown how such cognitive schema as "negotiating from strength" can affect people's perceptions and interpretations of international news and how the cultural theme of self-reliance can influence interpretations of news bearing on the issue of equality and affirmative action. Lau (1986) has developed a model to describe how individuals process incoming political information in terms of four schemata, centering on political groups, issues, parties, and candidate personalities, that prove to be quite stable over time for individual voters.

This recent research is reinforced by another tradition of studies focusing on media uses and gratification. "Ask not what media do to people but rather what people do with media" characterizes this perspective (Blumler and Katz 1974; Rosengren et al. 1985). Mass media exposure is fundamentally voluntary behavior. Viewers, listeners, and readers can turn off a channel or put down a publication if they find it objectionable or boring. Individuals find gratifications of various sorts, including the vicarious sense of friendship and familiarity with media celebrities, the satisfaction of being well informed, or simple relaxation and release associated with entertainment materials. The orientation of the audience member will vary with mood, time of day, and type of medium. Although the connection between the audience member's motivation and the media effect is still somewhat unclear, as a result of conflicting findings (Rosengren et al. 1985), the emphasis on interaction between active audience and active media is clearly a more appropriate theoretical foundation for understanding the role of the new media.

The media habit

If we are to understand how the new media will be used, it would certainly seem appropriate to take a long, hard look at how the current media technologies are used in day-to-day life. How much time does a typical American citizen spend with the mass media on an average day? How attentive are people to the messages the media carry? How much do they remember? How often do they learn or change their opinions in response to what they hear and see from the media? Does the weight of the evidence point toward addiction or active selectivity?

Abundant media exposure

One thing is clear: There is a lot of exposure. The media are heavily used by virtually every segment of the population. Television is the dominant medium in terms of time use, representing about 50% of media exposure per day for the average citizen (Neuman and Pool 1986). A. C. Nielsen estimates that the average household television set is on for an average of a little over 7 hours per day, with the average adult watching for about 4.5 hours (Nielsen 1990). At the peak of "prime time" (about nine o'clock in the evening), some 60% to 70% of American households are viewing. There is some variation among different demographic groups, but even those in the lowest viewing category (teenage girls, who may have a number of other things on their minds) watch 3.5 hours per day. Radio is next, with well over 2 hours of exposure per day. A fair amount of that exposure takes place in cars (97% of cars sold in the United States have radios); the peak exposure times for radio are in the mornings and evenings as commuters commute and many others listen as they attend to personal tasks and prepare meals.

Estimates of newspaper reading per day, depending on research methodology, vary from 18 to 49 minutes. Estimates of magazine reading vary from 6 to 30 minutes per day per person (Hornik and Schlenger 1981). Those substantial variations in estimates are due to the difficulty people have in recalling their behavior over the past 24 hours. The broadcast data are in large part derived from electronic viewership meters and thus are a bit more reliable. Book reading is estimated at about 18 minutes per day, and that includes pleasure reading as well as work- and school-related reading for appropriate segments of the population (Neuman and Pool 1986). Taking the rather conservative estimates, all that still adds up to a rather impressive 6 hours and 43 minutes of media exposure per day.

Information overload

The television set presents 3,600 images per minute per channel. Radio, on average, generates just under 100 words per minute, totalling between 3,000 and 5,000 words broadcast by radio each minute of each day in the typical urban area. The average daily newspaper contains 150,000 words and several thousand graphic images. Magazines and books add to the flow on a similar scale. Are we beginning to press up against the psychological limits of human ability to process information? Are there unanticipated effects of media abundance? Indeed, some analysts conclude that overload may result in intrapsychic trauma and conflict, withdrawal, confusion and frustration (G. A. Miller 1956; J. G. Miller 1960; Deutsch 1963; Milgram 1970; Lipowski 1971; Klapp 1978; Malik 1986).

Miller (1956), for example, has demonstrated through experimental tests that the human mind has a limit of about seven factors that it can process simultaneously. The increased complexity and speed of decision making would seem to threaten this physiological barrier. Studies of battlefield commanders, business executives, and air traffic controllers have provided further evidence of significant psychological pathologies (Raymond 1962; Van Gigh 1976; Toffler 1980).

It appears, however, that media audiences have developed considerable skill in organizing, filtering, and skimming information through coping strategies of partial attentiveness. Most people do not feel bombarded or overloaded by an expanded array of available mass media. On the contrary, for the most part they seek out more media and respond enthusiastically to expanded choices. Media behavior is voluntary behavior. People choose to be exposed.

On reexamination of the overload literature, we find that the bulk of the studies have reviewed the work setting rather than the home. Indeed, executives, battlefield commanders, and air traffic controllers are in positions of high-salience decision making under extreme time pressures, precisely the opposite of the casual, entertainment-oriented mass media consumer. Although there may be social pressure to be informed or to keep up with bestsellers and popular television shows, the parallel with the work setting is decidedly weak.

The fact of the matter is that the human capacity for selective attention is indeed well developed. The average individual is bombarded with 1,600 advertisements per day, but responds (not necessarily positively) to only 12 (Draper 1986, 16). The mind, medical authorities remind us, has a remarkable capacity to filter signals. The brain responds consciously to only one sensory stimulus among each million stimuli being sent (Blumler 1980, 231). Although new cable systems provide a cornucopia of available channels, it has been found that tripling the number of channels available leads typically to regular viewing of only two or three additional channels (Lemieux 1983). The concern about information overload, at least in the context of mass communications would seem to be overdrawn.

The casual use of multiple media

There is an inherent contradiction in the media use statistics. The media exposure studies indicate a total usage of 6 hours and 43 minutes per day. But other, independent studies of time use indicate that only 5 hours and 43 minutes per day are available for all leisure activities, many of which, of course, do not involve media at all. It appears that a considerable portion of leisure time is devoted to media use and that media use will overlap with other household activities or the use of other media, typically reading the newspaper while the television is on. This overlapping use of media is an important clue to understanding the nature of the media habit. It indicates that use of the media is active and selective, but casual, habitual, and only semiattentive, a picture rather different from Orwell's portrayal of the attentive and transfixed audience for Big Brother's orations.

Modest recall of media content

Given the massive flow of media messages and the casual attentiveness of the typical audience member, we might expect that a rather small proportion of the communications flow will be remembered. That is indeed the case. In the middle of election campaigns, for example, only rarely are as many as half of the adult population able to name any of the candidates in their congressional districts or any of the candidates in the senatorial races. This is true despite the fact that frequently one of the candidates is an incumbent and has been receiving extensive press coverage as a prominent political official. Such commonly used terms as "tariff," "private enterprise," and "NATO" can be defined by less than half of the population. The Bill of Rights, a fundamental concept of American government frequently cited by journalists and public officials, can be correctly identified by only one in five citizens (Neuman 1986).

In a study of recall of network news programming on television (Neuman 1976), subjects were called at random in the evening and asked if they had watched the news that evening, and if so what they could recall of what they had just seen. On average, respondents could recall only one news story out of 20 without additional prompting. When they were read a list of headlines from the news programs they had watched, they could recall four additional stories and provide details about those stories. They claimed to recall another four stories, but could not remember any of the details. So as a rough rule of thumb, 5% of the stories are recalled unaided, and another 45% with prompting, only half of which are substantiated with supporting details. These general parameters have been supported by subsequent research (Katz, Adoni, and Parness 1977; Gantz 1978; Gunter 1981; Robinson and Levy 1986). Robinson and Levy, for example, focused on only the most prominent stories and found that the accumulative impact of all media over the course of a week led to recall and comprehension of roughly one-third of the stories examined (Robinson and Levy 1986, 92).

The extensive research on recall of commercial messages reveals similar conclusions. Jacoby and Hoyer (1982) found that only 17% of their sample who were watching television commercials within the especially attentive circumstances of an experimental setting could correctly answer six "relatively simple" questions about a commercial they had just seen. Only 4% got all 12 answers right for the two commercials they saw. Burke Marketing Research has been conducting telephone-based and more naturalistic "Day After Recall" research for some years, providing advertisers with information on how well their commercials are remembered. On average, only one in four commercials seen can be recalled the next day, even with prompting from the interviewer. What is more revealing is the range of recall rates. Some commercials are recalled by as few as 2% of the people who saw them whereas others are recalled by 77% of the viewing audience (Burke Marketing Research 1974). A great deal depends on the character and quality of the commercial. The relationship between the audience member and the television set is complex. Recalled impressions vary greatly as a result of selective attention and selective memory. There is a media habit, but not a pattern of helpless addiction. Far from a pattern of information overload, we find that for the most part the audience handles the flow of communications casually, successfully, and enjoyably.

Media and behavior: even more modest effects

The limited ability of typical media consumers to recall much of the information flow hints that they may not be heavily conditioned and manipulated by the flow of messages. Is there evidence that the media can induce the public to buy products they do not want, change their fundamental beliefs, or vote for highly advertised political candidates? Although most people assume otherwise, the answer, based on the accumulated results from systematic research over several decades, is no.

This is indeed ironic, given the massive investment of some $50 billion per year in advertising in the United States. McGuire (1986), for example, suggests that hardheaded American business people would be expected to keep their eyes on the bottom line and to have good evidence that advertisements pay off, that, at the margin, a dollar invested in advertising will generate at least that much in additional sales. His conclusion, however, based on an extensive review of the behavioral literature, is that there is no evidence of persistent or substantial advertising effects. Other recent analyses have come to the same conclusion (Comstock et al. 1978; Schudson, 1984 Lodish 1986). Schudson concludes, for example, that "most firms resort to rules of thumb . . . and rely on 'essentially illogical' approaches to determine their advertising budgets" (1984, 17). Schmalensee's carefully conducted econometric analysis (1972) would seem to support such a conclusion. He found that advertising budgets were more closely correlated with sales in the preceding quarter than with current sales or sales in the following quarter. This would suggest that advertisers are spending the available funds on advertising, but are not boosting sales. In other words, the causal arrow may point in the opposite direction: successful sales leading to expanded advertising, not the reverse. What an irony.

There have been widely cited examples of particular advertisements or advertising campaigns that have seemed to capture the public's fancy and dramatically boosted product awareness. A million-dollar television campaign during the 1972 summer Olympic Games telecasts, for example, reportedly raised the Northwestern Mutual Life Insurance Company from 34th to 3rd place in public recognition of insurance company names (Comstock et al. 1978, 363). But, ironically, those advertisements that are most successful in attracting public attention, such as the series of popular ads for Alka-Seltzer, often are found not to be particularly successful in boosting sales of the product.

One of the most detailed experimental field studies yet published (Naples 1979) reveals that, at most, a 2% increase in sales will be associated with multiple exposures to an advertising campaign under ideal conditions. Lodish (1986) reports that more recent and more refined studies of the advertising–behavior link are even more sobering in revealing how seldom and how unpredictably measurable increases in sales can be attributed to advertising exposure. Study after study reveals no effects, highly conditional effects, or very small effects of advertising (McGuire, 1986). But because of the vested interests of advertising executives connected with the media, the agencies, and the manufacturers themselves, and because of the persisting fears and suspicions of the critics of advertising, the myth of pervasive advertising effectiveness perseveres.

The nature of information-seeking behavior

There have been many theories put forward in an attempt to make sense of how individuals seek out, filter, and store information about the world around them. Most such theories characterize an active, rational, purposive media user. Atkin (1973), for example, describes media behavior in terms of an instrumental utility theory: "To the extent that an individual perceives that environmental objects may personally affect him, he will want to achieve a criterion level of awareness and understanding of them. . . . Basically the individual desires to formulate precise cognitive orientations toward those stimuli that potentially or currently impinge on his well-being" (1973, 208). Such a formulation, however, is fundamentally misleading.

Although typical television viewers and newspaper readers are not passive, dumbfounded, and effortlessly persuaded by each and every message, neither are they, for the most part, attentive and alert information seekers. The day-to-day accumulation of information and ideas from the media is a casual, semiattentive process. People do not approach a television set, a radio, or a magazine with a clearly articulated game plan for what they want to learn and how they are going to learn it. Although research in the tradition of uses and gratifications attempts to make a great deal of the distinction, people do not separate the information and entertainment components of their habitual newspaper reading and broadcast use. It is true that people will answer questions about their relative interest in news and entertainment in polite response to a survey, but their responses probably reflect more their sense of what they perceive as socially acceptable than real distinctions associated with differences in behavior.

Perhaps the classic caricature of media behavior is Paul Klein's Least Objectionable Program model of television viewing (1975). He describes the viewer as seldom deciding on a particular program. Rather, the process for the great bulk of viewing is stepwise: First, the decision is made to watch television. One flips on the set and spins the dial to find out what is on. Whatever is least objectionable is watched. Occasionally, nothing whatever attracts the viewer's attention, and the set is turned off, but that is rare. His speculations turn out to be supported by a great deal of research and apparently are characteristic of other media as well (Comstock et al. 1978; Good-hardt, Ehrenberg, and Collins 1980; Barwise, Ehrenberg, and Goodhardt 1982; Television Audience Assessment 1984; Bower 1985; Levy and Windahl 1985).

Another clue to understanding the media habit is to examine the amounts of other household activities that take place simultaneously with media exposure. Much of the work in this area has focused on television, but the pattern is true for radio and print media as well. Researchers in England and the United States have put cameras on top of television sets to record attentiveness and physical behavior during viewing (Bechtel, Achenpohl, and Akers 1972; Anderson and Lorch 1983), and what has become clear is that media use is part of the fabric of daily life around the household. At least a third of the time, television viewing is a secondary activity while individuals talk, read, answer the telephone, eat, or take care of household chores (Robinson 1972; Comstock et al. 1978). These researchers have found that the eyes of viewers frequently stray from the television set to other objects and activities in the room. Radio use takes place so frequently as a background activity that individuals dramatically underestimate their recent exposure when recounting their activities over the past 24 hours, in effect forgetting that they had the radio on (Robinson 1977).

The notion of individuals staking out a daily set of specific information needs is not supported by research on actual behavior. Only 5% of the population, for example, report consulting an encyclopedia or dictionary in the preceding six months. The estimate is that the average individual spends only 35 seconds per day consulting non-news information resources. The list of information resources consulted is also rather mundane in character. The telephone book is the most often consulted (21% of the population, on average, per day), followed by cookbooks (18%) and product catalogs (9%) (Sharon 1972).

Some people claim that they hardly ever watch television, and then only news and sports, but diaries of viewing behavior for such individuals usually reveal otherwise. The great majority of these self-proclaimed selective viewers watch as many action adventures and comedies as everyone else, or only fractionally fewer (Bower 1973). Often these are lawyers, accountants, and professors who claim to have little time for media use, and because of their work schedules, they may indeed watch television less often, but when they watch, they follow the same entertainment-oriented pattern that characterizes everybody else (Wilensky 1964). Those who call for more public-affairs programming on television do not tend to watch it when it is made available (Bower 1973). Those who claim to attend to the media for purposes of acquiring information do score slightly higher on tests of learning and recall, but the differences are surprisingly small (Garramone 1983; Neuman et al. in press).

Perhaps it is appropriate to draw on the insights of such classic analysts as Herbert Simon (1976) and Anthony Downs (1957), who emphasize the psychological costs of obtaining and processing information. Even though one might wish to explore all the variables before selecting one product from among many, often people "satisfice" rather than maximize their information. They get enough information to make a reasonable decision, rather than the most information to make a maximally rational choice. They act that way with media, too. It is not so much information seeking as doing some filtering on the flow of information and entertainment that comes one's way. It has been said about television, in particular, that "people don't get what they want from TV, they get what they get."

The social context of media use

Another important point about the media habit is that the accumulation of information and ideas from the media takes place in a social context. The choice of medium, the definition of appropriate use, and the interpretation of information are all very much influenced by the cultural and social milieu of the media user. The thrust of mass society theory, for example, posits that media use substitutes for social interaction, but the accumulated research reveals that the relationship between social isolation and media use is weak, and in many cases social integration increases media uses of various types (Johnstone 1974; Levy 1979). There is ample evidence of extensive discussion of news and public-affairs items (Katz and Lazarsfeld 1955; Robinson 1972; Rogers 1973); the fact is that people rely heavily on others to help make media choices and to interpret content. The image of a helpless, isolated individual might be appropriate for framing a good novel, but it is a naive and inappropriate basis for a serious scientific investigation of political communications and media technology.

A theory of low-salience learning

A more appropriate model for proceeding should be based on accumulative learning from the mass media under conditions of limited attention and interest (Neuman 1986). Such a model will help to put the research on habitual media use in perspective and guide our analysis of the impact of new media. The basic dynamic of the model is that media exposure is substantial, but its impact is not. This fundamental fact of media use today is likely to be even more central to the new media environment. There are many hours of use, but the psychological salience of any one element in this massive flow of information is correspondingly low. We tend to value things that are expensive and rare. The media are neither. They are taken for granted. They become comfortable household companions. They share the attention of the individual with numerous other activities in the household. Attentiveness is casual, not like in the workplace or classroom. The media user is not passive, but is somewhere in the middle on a scale from passive to active. The user's behavior is voluntary, and individuals actively scan, select, and interpret the flow of information that comes their way.

McLuhan's hunch

Marshall McLuhan (1964) popularized the phrase "the medium is the message" in the mid–1960s, and the cliché is still with us. As such slogans go, this one is prone to misinterpretation and misuse even more than most. In its extreme formulation it asserts that the entirety of what is communicated results from the technological characteristics of a communications medium, rather than from the "content" it transmits, that is, the words and images usually assumed to convey meaning. In its less deterministic mode, the phrase is simply taken as an important and appropriate reminder that often there are interactions between the nature of ideas being conveyed and the nature of the medium of communications.

McLuhan's formulation of the issue is of particular interest because it frames the matter in historical terms: Because of our increasing reliance on particular technologies of public communications, especially electronic and video technologies, those technologies are increasingly interacting with changing cultural and political beliefs. McLuhan focused attention on the relationship between the sense modality of communication and the psychological complexity of decoding and interpreting messages. Although he emphasized other concepts and terminologies, the notion of persuasion and propaganda were central to his thinking. McLuhan, for example, was particularly interested in how the nature of television coverage of the war in Vietnam influenced public opinion. It was, he argued, our first television war, and the vividness of the nightly television coverage from the battlefields may have constrained the ability of the political elite to characterize the war in the usual positive terms of nationalism and individual bravery.

McLuhan's interest in the physiological characteristics of human uses of different media led him to speculate wildly on the different ways we learn about the world from print and broadcast media. He made a distinction between "hot" and "cool" media that also seemed to attract a great deal of public attention. Television is supposed to be a cool medium because it provides relatively little visual resolution and requires the viewer to participate and, in a sense, fill in the gaps between the flashing dots to make the picture a whole, interpretable image. A cartoon image is a cool medium, compared with a high-resolution photograph, for the same reason. He associated hot (high-resolution) media with the fast pace and uniform homogeneity of the industrial age. Radio, in McLuhan's terms, is a hot medium. It provides high-resolution, high-quality sound to the listener. Radio also tends to be fast-paced in its presentation, and it is symbolic for McLuhan of the period of intense industrialization of the mid-twentieth century. By providing all the information, he argued, hot media leave less room for contemplation, individual involvement, and interpretation.

The distinction between hot and cool media is indeed an intriguing if somewhat elusive notion. It mixes in concepts from artistic communication, cognitive psychology, and mass society theory. Cool media are more relaxing, personalized, more characteristic of the preindustrial age. Because he saw television as a cool medium, McLuhan hypothesized that it would bring about a new form of postindustrialism, a retribalization, a participatory global village. Print is supposed to be a hot medium because it provides information in "high resolution." In this case, McLuhan's analogy is particularly forced, because the processing and interpretation of the alphabet certainly requires considerable cognitive participation on the part of the reader. But his underlying concept is important – the relative involvement, mental effort, and interpretation required of the audience members to process messages in different media.

McLuhan never conducted any field studies or experimental research to test these hypotheses. It was simply not his style. But I suspect he would have been quite intrigued by such an undertaking. Although he was able to attract public attention with his dramatic pronouncements, the research community was not impressed (McGuire 1969). What was lacking was a theory, a set of testable hypotheses that might link the characteristics of the medium to particular effects on the audience. There have been some fragmentary and narrowly focused studies, yielding, for the most part, conflicting findings. More recently, however, thanks to the work of Salomon, Gagnon, Tsuneki, and others, the beginnings of a unified theory have begun to emerge. The connection between media-effects experiments and the broader issues of media use and social change is an important issue that I shall try to address here. Does the accumulated research give us any insight on whether or not the new media will be particularly effective persuaders or educators? Is it clear how media technologies influence the balance of control between communicators and audiences? Will changing media influence the type of information or entertainment people will seek out?

Puzzling findings on channel effects

McGuire (1969), drawing on the traditional distinction between the communications source, channel, and receiver, dubs this the channel-effects issue. Hundreds of studies have been conducted over the years on various aspects of channel effects. Reviews of the literature have come up with a unanimous and dramatically counterintuitive verdict, and that verdict is the same for advertising effects, educational impacts, and experimental tests of attitude change: There is no evidence of consistent or significant differences in the abilities of different media to persuade, inform, or even to instill an emotional response in audience members. Given the strong intuitive sense held by many that vivid film and video media are more effective tools for manipulation and persuasion, this finding deserves close examination.

Surveying the literature in educational (as opposed to persuasion) research, we find a unanimous verdict. Strickell (1963) reviewed 250 studies comparing television to face-to-face instruction and concluded that there were no differences. Chu and Schramm (1967) examined 421 separate comparisons of different media of instruction and came to similar conclusions. Dubin and Hedley's count (1969) for video versus traditional media of instruction in higher education was 89 studies favoring classroom instruction versus 102 favoring instructional television. The no-difference finding held up across a number of different academic fields.

The accumulated experimental research on the persuasive effects of identical (or nearly identical) messages in different media was reviewed by McGuire (1969, 1985). No clear-cut or consistent persuasive capacities were found for any of the media examined. He concluded that the issue of which medium would be more effective would depend in complex and conflicting ways on various characteristics of the communicator, the message, the situation, and the audience member. Video, for example, was found to be more effective for speakers characterized as highly credible, whereas print was more effective for low-credibility speakers (McGuire 1985, 283). Others have found that print is more effective than video when the audience members are of high cognitive ability, whereas the reverse is true for those of low cognitive skills (Marantz and Dowaliby 1973; Salomon and Leigh 1984). Some scholars have concluded that the phenomenon most likely to be at work here is an interaction effect between the modality preferences of a particular individual and the characteristics of different media (Salomon 1979). Some people may prefer to hear information rather than read it, and others may prefer video. But it turns out that although people will express such preferences, those preferences are weak, they vary with subject matter, and they are not highly correlated with the effectiveness of different media. One clear-cut finding, however, is that more modes of communication are not necessarily better. In numerous studies it has been found that when multiple modalities are providing additional information not necessarily consistent with that from the primary modality, learning and impact go down (Cronbach and Snow 1977).

Further puzzling findings on the vividness effect

One of the most intriguing findings of all is the absence of a vividness effect. It has long been assumed that the more vividly presented materials, that is, messages that are emotionally interesting, concrete, and imagery-provoking, will be more persuasive and more easily remembered. The notion, of course, is that video media have special properties of vividness. Such notions are integral to the mass society theory in general and to the modality and subtlety arguments in particular. Vivid characteristics are presumed to be more fully encoded by the audience member, leaving a stronger memory trace that will be more easily and more fully recalled later. It is such an intuitive notion that it has been accepted by some psychologists as a given (Nisbett and Ross 1980).

Nevertheless, in carefully controlled experimental studies, no evidence of an enhanced vividness effect has been found. Study after study has revealed that dry, abstract, and more straightforward presentations are as persuasive and as easily remembered as more colorful ones (Taylor and Thompson 1982). Frustrated experimenters even began to distrust their own judgments of what, in fact, represented a more vivid presentation. But further research revealed that the subjects did indeed agree: The more vivid versions were indeed more vivid, but they were not more memorable or persuasive.

The findings are conflicting and confusing, and the connection between these systematic experimental studies and the broader themes of mass society have not always been made clear. The summary conclusion is that for varied materials and varied audiences there simply are not sustained or significant differences in the effectiveness of different media or modalities. What is missing is a theory or at least a strategy for sorting out the intervening connection between qualities of messages, audiences, and media.

A theory of channel effects

The mixed findings and muddled conclusions regarding McLuhan's hunch represent a special irony of the experimental method. There may well be significant differences, differences of direct relevance to the evolution of new public communications technologies, but any such differences have been masked by the careful controls of experimental design. McLuhan indeed focused attention on a central variable – psychological involvement – but he had the technological linkages confused. He made a single, one-dimensional distinction – hot versus cool – but he included two dimensions in defining it: level of resolution and psychological involvement. His implicit theory was that the low resolution in a particular sense modality required the individual to be more involved, to participate by interpreting and filling in the missing information. But experimental research has shown that a great many other factors affect involvement, and the simple equation of resolution level and involvement is misleading.

The key intervening variable is attention. If channel variables, such as the use of sound, color, or motion, attract attention, then the potential for communications effects is enhanced. The irony of most experimental designs is that the subjects, although they may not be aware of which variables are being manipulated, are certainly aware that they are participating in an experiment, and thus the situation is entirely unlike that of low-salience learning in the home. In the laboratory there are no competing media or other household distractions; the orientation of the subject is toward the demanded attentiveness of work or school. The subject matter is not expected to be particularly interesting or involving, for the subjects have not selected the material they are reading or viewing. So with attention level more or less fixed, potential effects mediated by attention are masked.

There are several clues in the literature that support this interpretation. The research on the elusive vividness effect, for example, comes to a similar conclusion. In reviewing this literature, Taylor and Thompson (1982) discovered a paradox. They found that although there was no strong evidence of a vividness effect, there was strong evidence of a salience effect; that is, in situations where the attention of the subject was experimentally manipulated, forcing the subject to pay more attention to one portion of the environment, clear-cut effects in differential learning and persuasion were evident. In reviewing the few studies in which a vividness effect was demonstrated, they found that those studies were uniquely characterized by the fact that they had allowed vividness to affect attention as well as learning. Such studies contrasted with the usual design, which held attention constant while varying the perceived "vividness" of a message.

A parallel finding was uncovered by Television Audience Assessment (1984) in a study of advertising effects. This group was sponsored by the Markle Foundation to examine whether or not the programming context for advertising on television made any difference in the effectiveness of the commercials. It was thought that perhaps more intellectually stimulating or more involving programs would provide a more effective vehicle for advertising. It was an intriguing strategy by the foundation to try to encourage diversity and quality in programming through research, rather than through direct investment in programming. Television Audience Assessment, however, reviewed the literature and found disappointing results. The more involving programs did not seem to have any measurable influence on the effectiveness of the ads within them. But the researchers recognized that, once again, the intervening role of audience attentiveness might prove to be the critical factor, and so they conducted a set of parallel experiments. In one case, subjects were taken, along with other friends and family members, to a living-room setting, with food, magazines, and other distractions. Television programming of varying levels of psychological involvement was available, but subjects were not required to pay attention. In a parallel study with the same programming and commercials, subjects watched in a theaterlike setting. As the researchers had guessed, in the simulated home environment, distinct programming effects on advertising effectiveness were demonstrated, and in the theater environment, no effects were evident (Television Audience Assessment 1984).

Another element contributing to a theory of channel effects that gets lost in experimental research is media preference. In the laboratory, people are assigned to watch a videotape, listen to a speaker, or read a message. It is a task assignment, and subjects simply accept it as such. It has not been part of the traditional design to give subjects a choice. But choice is in fact a critical element of media behavior in day-to-day life. People have to choose among competing media. Most people rely on a mix of the available media, but behaviorally and attitudinally there is a clear-cut preference for video. Ceteris paribus, people prefer watching television news to reading newspapers or newsmagazines. They prefer entertainment television to reading fiction.

There are two reasons for this. Video is perceived to be more enjoyable and emotionally involving, and it is perceived to be less demanding. Thus, although it is not necessarily either more or less effective in communicating a message, the video domain is likely to be chosen. One particularly well designed study was carried out by Teruo Tsuneki at the Research Institute of Telecommunications and Economics in Tokyo. He focused not on persuasion or learning but on audience perceptions of communications through different media. Individuals were exposed to print, audio, or video versions of five programming segments: weather, news, local events, cooking, and a commercial for a car radio. Subjects were asked to evaluate the media experience on an extensive battery of items, including interest, depth of impression, liveliness, elucidative power, complexity, and intellectuality. He discovered that two fundamental factors of evaluation were enjoyability and ease of communication. Figure 3.2 summarizes the results of his research. For each content type, video was perceived as most enjoyable, with audio a close second, and print a more distant third. The findings for perceived effectiveness of communications varied somewhat from one content type to another and did not demonstrate consistent differences by media (Tsuneki 1988).

Those findings were reinforced by Salomon's work with students and educational media, from which he evolved the concept of AIME ("Amount of Invested Mental Energy"). People perceive print as requiring mental effort to decode, and video as somehow requiring less: Print is hard, and television is easy. There is no supporting evidence that this is in fact the case, that television really requires less mental activity to decode (Reeves and Thorson 1986), but the perception nevertheless influences choice behavior. Salomon and Leigh (1984) studied learning patterns from comparable messages in text

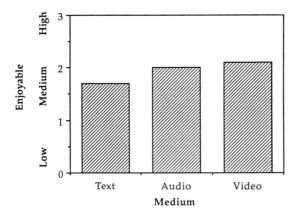

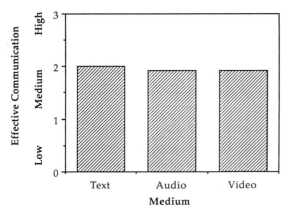

Figure 3.2. Subjective impacts of different media. (Adapted from Tsuneki 1988.)

and video format and found that subjects consistently perceived video as requiring less concentration and thought, although they actually had higher factual recall scores for the video version (Fig. 3.3).

The key finding from the realm of research on educational and advertising effects that must be dealt with candidly if we are to understand the nature of low-salience learning in regard to politics and culture is simply that people are attracted to the path of least resistance. For knowledge acquisition in general, and for public-affairs knowledge in particular, people are not inclined to give such matters a great deal of effort. They prefer to rely on existing schema and the worldviews they have developed, rather than go through the effort of defining new ones. McLuhan had the right question, but the wrong answer. The key factor for understanding how the new media technologies

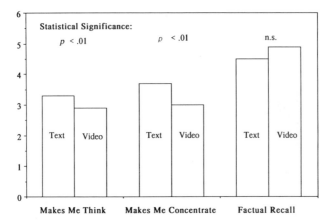

Figure 3.3. Effort required by different media: Salomon's index of amount of invested mental energy. Higher index scores for "makes me think" and "makes me concentrate" indicate agreement with item. Factual recall index based on communications content available in both media. (Adapted from Salomon and Leigh 1984.)

will affect the flow of political communications has more to do with the nature of the media habit than with the nature of the media technologies.

Interactive media

A quite different way of looking at the emergent properties of the new media is to focus on the concept of interactivity. The fact that mediated communications among humans have the potential to be increasingly "interactive" in the coming decades has been a source of irrepressible optimism. We shift at this point to issues of media psychology that have been raised primarily by Vannevar Bush's spiritual descendants, the technological optimists. They focus, of course, on educational potentials rather than propaganda and on individualization rather than homogenization. My theme, as before, is that interactivity offers great promise, but that its growth will be more evolutionary than revolutionary, and that especially in the setting of the home, where low-salience learning dominates, its use and potential will be constrained by the passive psychological approach and limited energies of the average user.

What is interactivity?

Interactivity is the quality of electronically mediated communications characterized by increased control over the communications process by both the sender and receiver. The prototypical interactive process is a simple conversation between two people, a mutual, reciprocal process. Either party can interrupt the other, change the subject, raise new ideas. Most traditional mass media, electronic or otherwise, are not interactive. Their communications are predominantly one-way from producer to large audience, with only limited and crude forms of feedback, such as letters to editors, ratings, and circulation figures. Once a newspaper, book, or motion picture is produced, it becomes a single, unchanging product to which audience members may or may not pay attention. Although different people take quite different messages away from a particular program or article, the communication content remains unchanged by those who choose to watch, read, or listen.

But five of the generic properties noted in the preceding chapter push the new media in the direction of interactive, personal conversations: increased speed, interconnectivity, the two-way character of electronic communications, and the increased control over the process by both producer and audience member. Thus, a video game represents a form of electronic communication rather unlike most forms that preceded it. There is no single script for the game; the script varies depending on the behavior of the audience member. The author of the game and the player of the game interact electronically, interpreting and anticipating each other's behaviors. A video game is, of course, a limited genre: The vocabulary of action and ideas is quite limited, and the player often is limited to such behaviors as up, down, back, forward, and shoot (Gagnon and McKnight 1983). The ability of the author to communicate complex ideas is limited. But these are not permanent or inherent constraints. Several new games that allow the players to choose from among the strategic alternatives for nuclear deterrence and international relations are capable of communicating quite sophisticated political messages.

A fundamental quality of the process, not previously present in print or broadcast communications, is that the medium itself monitors, stores, and reacts to the behavior of the audience member. Thus, in text-oriented computer games, the computer may respond, "You've tried that ploy before, it will never work." Or an electronic news delivery service may prefilter and feature information similar to that which a particular user has previously requested. Or an educational medium may adjust the rate and level of instruction based on what it "knows" about a particular user. Such information about preferred learning style or level of knowledge can be programmed in from other sources or "intuited" by the machine as it monitors the user's differential success in learning.

One can imagine that the communication of text and images through intelligent electronic media might well stimulate a great deal of excitement among artists, educators, and others, offering the promise of an entirely new medium with a new and evolving grammar and cultural genre. The author can offer the reader the option of influencing the plot, selecting alternative outcomes, participating in the writing process. The artist can allow the viewer to alter shapes or colors in selected ways. The author of a text or videodisc-based game can allow the player to move around a previously designed space, manipulate objects, interrogate characters, and be acted upon by the characters themselves.

Early experiments in such areas have had modest results. Many authors and artists would prefer to control the characters and the colors themselves, rather than defer to the tastes of the public. Others have understandably felt constrained by the technical limits of the first generation of such media, which have offered very limited formats of communications and have been extraordinarily difficult to program. But these technologies represent only the first generation of interactive media. To condemn them as limiting so soon would be like condemning the telegraph as a fundamentally limiting factor in electronic communications.

Interactivity as educational promise

The power and flexibility of interactivity offer unprecedented potentials in the field of education. Seymour Papert, for example, drawing on Piaget's analysis of active learning, argues that computer-based media allow the student to manipulate and experience basic principles in action, thus making the learning process both more effective and more enjoyable. His widely used Logo program gives youngsters the ability to draw and explore basic mathematical relationships by manipulating an electronic "turtle" on the computer screen. The phosphorescent trail of the student-controlled turtle can be used to illustrate geometric forms and relationships or simply to explore motion and playful geometric art. Although his program arises from a very different tradition of research, it converges on the same fundamental concept of psychological involvement and active learning. The computer allows the student to manipulate and actively experiment with fundamental concepts. Learning takes place not from mere exposure but from active experience (Papert 1980).

Additionally, the use of computer-based learning environments allows the student to take greater control in the pace and style of learning. It may be that one student finds a portion of the curriculum of special interest and wants to study it in depth. Unlike a "linear" textbook, which provides exactly the same material to every reader, videodisc and electronic text systems are "layered," and in response to the queries of the student or the guidance of the teacher, they can provide materials of additional depth to the curious. Or if a particular component of the curriculum is especially difficult for a student, additional practice and instruction can be provided. It may also be that a given type of lesson or exercise will work particularly well with a subgroup of students. Again, flexibly and naturally the system responds with examples and types of instruction tailored to work best with each individual learner.

Computer-based learning is not a panacea. The introduction of the power of the computer to the classroom in the 1960s, originally dubbed CAI (computer-aided instruction), was foreseen as a true revolution. But the actual software developed frequently was less than ideal and often added frustration to the learning process along with the individualized instruction. Furthermore, some teachers felt threatened and were confused by the new machine in the classroom, a frequent recipe for disaster. Interactive media, like filmstrips, language labs, and workbooks, represent a tool, a powerful tool, for educators, not a panacea for the difficulties of the educational process or a replacement for the thoughtful and talented teacher (Oettinger 1969).

Interactivity as diversity

Another way of looking at the potential of interactivity is that it provides a stimulus to cultural and political diversity. Although it has always been true that the experience of watching a television newscast or reading a novel will have quite different effects on two individuals, each bringing their own beliefs, experiences, internal mental images, and selective attention to the common experience, by giving the individual audience member more control over the format, pace, and even content of the communications experience, that natural potential for diversity is enhanced.

The most clear-cut example is that of interactive fiction, in which the audience member selects among alternative paths as the plot proceeds. There have been experiments with books, plays, and movies in which the audience has voted or otherwise influenced the outcome (Backer 1986); the limitations of the media, however, usually have constrained both the opportunities for choice and the number of alternatives available. Typically there is a choice between two endings, or with carefully contrived movies there can be a choice among 16 outcomes. The new media, however, are beginning to feature programmable, nonlinear technology of almost limitless flexibility.

Perhaps the most important aspect of diversity in the flow of electronic communications is the ability of the system to complement or work against the prejudgments and cognitive schema of the user. One recurrent theme addressed in this book is the danger that sophisticated videotex systems will allow a user to filter out important but unwanted information and, in effect, become less well informed by being more narrowly informed. But the fact of the matter is that with appropriate programming, the system can be designed to have just the opposite effect.

Herbert Gans, in his thoughtful *Deciding What's News* (1979), concluded his analysis of the sociology of news-gathering and the economics of news

institutions with an unusual exhortation. He called for a new structure, a foun-
dationlike entity to provide what he called multiperspectival coverage of news
events. He observed that the economic nature and professional norms of journalism lead to a distinct worldview, one that is not inherently wrongheaded,
but is monolithic and serves to filter out information and styles of presenting
events that fall outside that worldview. His proposed "endowment for news"
was to be an institutional response to that problem. The new interactive media
could complement this impulse to diversify news coverage. An electronic news
service could also be programmed to bring in complementary and contradictory commentaries on those of the day's events that interested a particular user.
The editorial opinion page of the daily newspaper serves this function in part,
but it could be extended through interactivity so that each news article would
be accompanied by the equivalent of several editorial pages of commentary
from worldwide sources on the topic in question.

Interactivity as social context

Another intriguing element of the shift to electronic communications is that
it does more than change the structure of vertical communications between
political elites or journalists and the mass citizenry. It influences the pattern
of horizontal communications within the citizenry. Among those who have
studied the differential effects of different media, much has been made of
the different psychological effect of viewing a play or movie or hearing a
speech in a public setting within the context of audience laughter, applause,
or skepticism, as compared with the privatized, anonymous experience of
most mass communications. The nature of flexible interactive media blurs
that distinction. Two-way electronic bulletin boards and computer confer-
encing allow the individual to simply observe the ongoing commentary or
add to it. Electronic mail systems allow the user to comment on and forward
news items or messages with a few keystrokes.

One of the most intriguing applications along these lines is Theodore
Nelson's hypertext (1974), which allows people to comment in a flexible
environment on what has already been said. It is a bit like an electronic
bulletin board. A professor may assign a poem and draw students' attention
to particular ideas and passages by means of electronic marginal notations.
The students can access this central data base and are free to add their own
comments or ask questions of the professor or each other. The process need
not take place in real time, but allows the flexibility and openness as well as
the personal involvement of classroom discussion to flow into learning associated with reading assignments and exercises done outside.

Equally important is the broader implication of the sense of the group and
community awareness made possible by facilitated horizontal communica-

tions. Rather than being a substitute for human involvement, as some had feared, computer communications may well enhance involvement.

Interactivity and thought-provoking media

One of the most interesting studies of modality effects was conducted on subjects' responses to ads for new food products (Wright 1974). The unique aspect of the study was that the subjects' open-ended responses to the ads were carefully coded and analyzed to see if print or broadcast messages were more thought-provoking. Wright's approach to measuring thought-provokingness was to assess whether or not subjects weighed both positive and negative factors in evaluating a product. The study demonstrated that print media were more thought-provoking. Those subjects who were allowed to control the pace of reading and could pause to evaluate the arguments being put forth were better able to articulate the original thesis and to articulate possible objections than were those who had been shown the video presentation in a fixed time frame. That was especially true for subjects highly involved in the subject matter.

Such findings parallel Papert's and Piaget's arguments that when subjects are allowed to manipulate, control, and, in effect, think about the issues at hand, that increases their ability to internalize those issues. It has been demonstrated that people can better remember their reactions to a communicated message than the message itself (Petty and Cacioppo 1977). Thus, the distinctions between print and broadcast media will diminish as the individual is allowed greater control over the pace and format of the presentation, and accordingly the social definition and reality of its thought-provoking and involvement potential.

The disjuncture between low-salience learning and interactivity

These commentaries on interactivity have been, on the whole, quite sanguine. Although not revolutionary or deterministic in effect, the prospects for increased control over the communications process will, at the very least, allow those who are so inclined to draw more information and enjoyment from the media around them. There is, however, a significant qualification, and it is a central theme of this book: The reality is likely to fall far short of the potential. The lesson from the mass psychology of media behavior is that learning is partial, for the learner is selective and semiattentive. The mass citizenry, for most issues, simply will not take the time to learn more or understand more deeply, no matter how inexpensive or convenient such further learning may be.

The great bulk of research on persuasion and learning has taken place in controlled, worklike environments in which subjects have had a task orientation and have known full well that they would be asked to recall information and answer questions at the end of the communications event. Day-to-day exposure to the media is so unlike that attentive task orientation that the basic findings in the research literature are of dubious relevance.

There has been an intriguing pattern of failure in the mass market for the new information technologies that have been introduced over the past decade. These failures can help us put in perspective the balance of forces between the potential and the psychological reality. We reviewed the curious failure of videotex services. Despite numerous attempts and heavy subsidization from entrepreneurs, systems for electronic news delivery to the home have simply flopped. The level of activity required for the individual to log on and then keyboard through layers of topic menus and keywords to locate a desired fragment of information simply does not jibe with the casual browsing and monitoring behavior that characterizes the accumulation of information from news radio, television, and print media (Greenberger 1985).

The video-game craze, when it started in the early 1980s, had all the earmarks of a whole new medium of entertainment. Within a few years, 20% of American homes had a unit for playing video games, and many more people were frequent players in the public arcades. The growth of the phenomenon was faster than the growth of television in the early 1950s. But in 1983 there was a sudden drop-off, in fact a reversal, as what had looked to be a new medium turned out to be a fad. The mazes and shooting games that had been developed offered only limited variety, and as quickly as the fad had begun it ended, with the attentions of the youthful audience turning to other pastimes (Lazarus and McKnight 1983).

The interactive videodisc offered similar promise for the home. *Murder, Anyone?* allowed users to accumulate clues and manipulate the story line to try to uncover the culprit in an interactive murder mystery. Numerous how-to discs and children's game discs have also been offered, but the primary use for the videodisc in the home has been much like that for videotape: uninterrupted, linear playback of movies and entertainment programming.

One of the most frequently cited examples of interactive media is two-way cable television, notably the QUBE system of Warner Communications in Columbus, Ohio. The system Warner installed there in the late 1970s was unique and quite flashy. Virtually all of the other cable companies had talked about the prospects for taking advantage of coaxial cable's inherent two-way capability, but none had invested the managerial and technological resources to make it happen. QUBE subscribers were given a numeric keypad the size of a desk calculator. The keypad was used to select the channel and to respond to queries from the system's head-end computer. No one really knew how interactive television would work, so Warner hired the former programming chief of CBS, Mike Dann, to move to Columbus and dream up a variety of new applications. They staged a football game and allowed the viewers to call the plays for the local team by pushing buttons and picking one of four options. They conducted numerous quiz and game shows that allowed viewers at home to compete for prizes. Public-affairs programs were created that would allow civic leaders to debate an issue and at regular intervals allow the viewers to register their agreement or disagreement. The percentages from the instant opinion poll would flash on the screen several seconds later. Educational programs allowed viewers to test their knowledge and allowed the teacher to ask if the pace was too fast or if a particular point should be explained in more detail.

Some cynics in the cable industry griped that Warner was not interested in interactivity as anything more than a competitive gimmick for securing contracts in towns and cities that were not yet franchised for cable. It appears in this case that the cynics were correct. Warner did distinguish itself in competition with other cable companies and won a number of attractive cable franchises in the early 1980s, including Pittsburgh, Milwaukee, and Houston. But it turned out that the expensive two-way system did not bring in sufficient revenue to support the locally produced two-way programming. So the two-way capacity was not fully installed in the new systems, and the Columbus system, its economic purpose served, sits idle. QUBE in Columbus is still used to allow subscribers to select premium movie channels. No one seems to have noticed that viewers are no longer asked their opinions or asked to call the plays for the local football team. History will record that the one time the audience actually called the plays for the local team, it lost.

A key finding concerning the psychology of two-way entertainment media can be found in the carefully protected data on how many subscribers in Columbus actually took the trouble to touch their keypads during the heyday of QUBE. Warner was willing to report only the percentages of those responding who expressed different choices, never the percentage of those watching who responded, a figure the system could easily compute. Former Warner employees have reported that with the exception of game programs on which prizes were awarded to viewers, the number responding from among the relatively few who opted to watch the interactive programming tended to be very small, usually only one in five viewers. Given that responding was costless, that the program was explicitly geared to solicit the votes and opinions of viewers, and that the tiny audience was already self-selected to those interested and curious, such figures pose an appropriate caution for those who would predict a revolutionary impact for two-way entertainment video.

Further supporting evidence comes from data on remote-control channel selectors for television. There was a flurry of concern in the advertising industry when it came to light that remote controls for television sets and

VCRs gave viewers a convenient way of switching channels or fast-forwarding when a commercial came on. Given the economic reliance of the television industry on commercial support, one can understand the broad concern with the impact of this technological development on viewing behavior.

It is true that given the convenient opportunity, viewers will opt to skip some commercials, but such an initiative is still relatively rare. The key test appears to involve the commercial break in the middle of an ongoing program, usually at a quarter past or a quarter before the hour. The average figure for viewers who switch or "zap" now stands at about 3%. In households with remote controls, the average is about twice that. Such statistics could, over time, have some economic effect at the margin, but they provide convergent evidence that for the majority of viewers the television experience is predominantly passive, and even the simplest intervention of changing the channel has thus far been a curiously seldom-used capacity.

Optional interactivity

This overview of the reality of low-salience monitoring of the flow of information and entertainment in the media prompts a revision of the originally enthusiastic prospect for user-controlled, two-way entertainment and informational media in the home. People like the option of interactivity. They like having the ability to voice an opinion, to skip a commercial, to select from a diverse offering of channels, and to call up specialized data and information. But they would prefer not to have to interact. Media monitoring does not have to be like driving a car, where a moment's distraction from control can have serious consequences. Reading newspapers and watching television are associated with relaxation and amusement. The distinction between seeking needed information and browsing or being entertained is blurred, and the two behaviors are intertwined.

Few adults expect to be quizzed on current-events information. As a result, they satisfice rather than optimize when it comes to monitoring and internalizing information about distant and complex events that may or may not have any direct influence on their lives. If new interactive media allow people to learn in greater detail about the economic and political events that may affect their lives, and if that involves some extra effort and expense, the uses and advantages of such a technology are likely to be unequally distributed through the society. Those strata that have already distinguished themselves by expending extra energy and taking initiative are likely to be differentially advantaged by the new information technologies in the home.

Such conclusions must be qualified, however. The examples and systematic studies that can provide the basis for such judgments were based on the earliest, relatively crude prototypes of interactive information and entertainment services. It is also likely, given the declining costs for the technology involved, that interactivity, much like color television, will only at the earliest stages be differentially received on the basis of the economic resources of the early adopters. Furthermore, the behavior of the average television viewer is largely culturally reinforced. It should not be surprising if most households react hesitantly to two-way television. The preceding 40 years of experience have engendered a different set of expectations.

One might conclude, then, that the prospect for interactive media in the home is heavily constrained by the traditional psychology of the mass audience. To the extent that fundamental changes are in the offing, they are certain to be more evolutionary than revolutionary.

Persuasion in perspective

In the early pages of *1984*, Orwell describes a scene in which Winston Smith is in a small group watching Big Brother hold forth on the telescreen. Big Brother's extreme pronouncements strike Smith as absurd exaggerations, but, Smith muses, perhaps not so extreme that someone less alert and intelligent than himself might be taken in. Such a perspective lies at the core of the concern about propaganda. Few people perceive themselves to be brainwashed. It is, instead, a magnanimous regard for others, in other countries, or the youth of one's own country, that energizes concern over the power of the media to persuade. Although the term "propaganda" itself has fallen somewhat out of fashion in the past several decades, the underlying issue is as hot as ever. The helpless audience is all too frequently perceived to be overwhelmed by the quantity, targeting, multiple modalities, scope, and subtlety of presentation. Furthermore, the seductively entertaining quality of the media is seen to be destructively addictive. Is there fire beneath the smoke?

I conclude, for the most part, that there is not. The new media will provide no more tempting tools for mass manipulation than did those available to the playwrights of Periclean Greece or the orators of the Roman Senate. Trying to reinforce the persuasive power of words with music and moving images on a flashing screen in the home changes the process in surprisingly small ways. It is not at all clear that such reinforcement really makes the message more persuasive or the audience member any less sensitive to the fact that he or she is being propagandized. In fact, there is clear evidence that inappropriate content in parallel modalities can diminish and distract from the persuasiveness of the message, whatever it might be.

Occasionally a member of a Roman orator's audience may have bravely spoken out with a question or retort. I suspect it happened rarely. The primary feedback to the orator was crudely aggregated data, as in applause, laughter, or the size of the crowd. Ironic as it may be, such crude dynamics are likely to remain the best guidelines, even when sophisticated electronics make articulate feedback at a distance easy and inexpensive.

Theories of education and mass communications have been troubled by a naive distinction between information and entertainment. Although in common parlance we all routinely make such distinctions, in the practice of day-to-day mass communications the two elements are inextricably intertwined. Neither the communicator nor the audience can meaningfully determine which element of a message or which characteristic of the delivery medium is most successful in attracting attention or in amusing or informing the audience. Both those who write research questionnaires and those who answer them pretend to be able to make such distinctions. That is primarily a cultural artifact, and its continuance distorts our ability to build and test reliable theories of propaganda and of education.

The audience member is both passive and active at the same time. The mind is such that new information, ideas, and impressions are taken in and evaluated and interpreted in the light of cognitive schema and the accumulated information from past experience. Given how little we remember of our daily experiences, it should not be surprising to find that the accumulated research of the past several decades confirms that the average audience member pays relatively little attention, retains only a small fraction, and is not the slightest bit overloaded by the flow of information or the choices available among the media and messages. The problems of selectivity and guarding against information overload are no more difficult in the evolving media environment than in the multiple and overlapping conversations in a crowded room.

As new electronic techniques for manipulating and transmitting sound and images provide striking new examples of the seductively persuasive powers of the media, there will continue to be concern. Such skepticism is healthy. There may even be a temporary cultural lag as the producers of messages labor a few steps ahead of the mass audience in disguising the message and intent. But in a competitive media environment, with communications flowing both horizontally and vertically, such victories of the propagandist (or the educator) are likely to be short-lived. The force of the technological communications revolution will be significantly constrained by the partial attentiveness and limited energies of the mass audience.

4

The fragmentation of the mass audience

Although the spectacular technological break-throughs in communications tend to move the potential of public communications in the right direction, there are significant constraints on both the direction and speed of social change. In Chapter 3 we reviewed the psychology behind casual media use and low-salience learning. The key issue was the intensity of the media experience, the vertical dimension, if you will, the connection between the individual audience member and the communications medium. The connection turns out to be weak, the intensity, for the most part, quite low. That is an important constraint.

We turn at this point to the horizontal variable: the diversity of audience interests. If the number of available channels expands 10-fold, should we expect new topics of public discussion and new formats of presentation to evolve? Or, on the other hand, should we expect to see simply more of the same, mass-audience, common-denominator fare simply multiplied by 10?

The fragmentation hypothesis

The "new age" has arrived. We are reminded of it daily by the media. The business and trade press drive the point home with graphs and charts demonstrating how new life-styles, work schedules, and values are changing the marketplace. The popular press has a parallel and equally insatiable appetite for human-interest articles on the "new working woman," the "resurgence of ethnicity," the "new politics," or some such conceptual hook for characterizing change. Common to many of these analyses, and of particular importance for the future of the mass audience, is the notion of a central underlying trend in America toward social fragmentation and a divergence of life-styles and leisure interests (Frank and Greenberg 1980).

The increase in higher education frequently is noted as a critical factor in this process. As Richard Maisel (1973) notes, the education system is the most important of all specialized media systems. At its core is the school system, a mammoth medium for the communication of specialized information. . . . The product of the education system, particularly of higher education, is a stratum of individuals who both in their work and private life, are consumers of specialized communications.

In 1960, 61% of Americans aged 25–29 had graduated from high school; by 1972, the figure had risen to 80%. Now, about half of high-school graduates go on to college, and many of the others seek alternative forms of post-secondary education and specialized training. Of all the traditional demographic variables, education most strongly predicts the breadth and depth of specialized interests and cultural pursuits (Hyman, Wright, and Reed 1975).

Even among the less well educated strata of the population it appears that we are seeing a rebirth of pride in social differentiation. Social historians characterized America in the early twentieth century as a cultural melting pot. Immigrants changed their names, studied English, and struggled to provide an Americanizing education for their children. Frequently they were embarrassed and uneasy about their Old World origins. Many of the next generations, however, sought to change their names back, to reassert their ethnicity and pride in their roots. That pattern was reflected in the social movements of the 1960s and the persistently vocal minority communities of the 1990s. Although the matter is somewhat less clear, it has been argued that regional pride and differentiation are on the upswing as well. Increasing consciousness of the unique cultural traditions of, for example, the South, California, and Yankee New England is reinforced by new media, particularly the specialty regional magazines of the major metropolitan areas.

One of the most widely cited social phenomena of the post-industrial era is the changing character of the American family. That categorization, of course, involves a number of significant and interrelated shifts in social life. Women are entering the work force in greater numbers. In 1965 there were 26 million women in the labor force, representing 39% of women aged 16 or older. Within two decades 40 million women were employed – 48% of women aged 16 or older. Young adults in greater numbers are pushing back the age of marriage, and when married, they are delaying or forgoing parenthood in order to pursue their professional lives more aggressively. Families are smaller, thus decreasing the number of years that a parent must be home to care for small children, allowing the parent, most often the woman, to return to the workplace or pursue other interests sooner.

What impact the changing roles of women will have on social fragmentation is not entirely clear. It appears that expanded participation of women in the workplace, especially in professional roles, will broaden their interests and leisure pursuits. These new activities most often are added on to their traditional interests and responsibilities for homemaking and raising children. Also, of course, the additional income from a second worker in the household tends to increase discretionary spending. The larger cohort of unmarried young adults entails an expansion of an especially active market, whose members have diverse interests, great energy, and the necessary discretionary income to pursue those interests.

All things considered, the theory of the fragmented society is more diffuse than one might like. The theory identifies a number of recent social trends that are real enough – the expansion of the information and service sectors of the economy, rising levels of education, the renewed salience of ethnicity, the changing family – but it is not clear that they hang together as a coherent whole. In fact, the postindustrial, fragmented-society scenario is an attempt to make sense out of some confusing and at times contradictory trends. For example, the professionalization of work life runs counter to the prediction of expanded leisure time. A recently reported decrease in the average work week to 35 hours was widely and proudly hailed by the leisure industries, but a follow-up report that the decrease was an artifact of unemployment, underemployment, and recession, rather than voluntary leisure, was less widely cited. The average citizen is getting older, and older people are much less adventurous in the variety of their leisure pursuits. Affluent individuals may purchase more books and magazines, but because of their busy schedules they are less likely to read them.

Media historians have developed a general theory of media evolution that predicts a pattern of specialization (Merrill and Lowenstein 1971). It is, in effect, a three-stage model, progressing from (1) the elite stage to (2) the mass stage to (3) the specialized stage, and it attempts to characterize the evolution of and competition among newspapers, motion pictures, radio, and television in twentieth-century America. Figure 4.1 summarizes the pattern. When a new medium is introduced, it is adopted first by an educated elite who have the cultural skills and financial wherewithal to become early adopters. As the price of the new medium falls and it becomes more widely accepted, it increasingly emphasizes mass-appeal content and becomes dominated by the economics of the mass audience. But when a new, competitive medium arises, the old medium must specialize and take advantage of its unique technological appeal in order to survive. These trends are summarized in Figure 4.2. The bottom axis of the figure represents the historical time line. The vertical axis represents the percentage of penetration of the medium into the marketplace. It is difficult to compare the patterns of use of different print and broadcast media. To facilitate comparison, the maximum household penetration for each is defined as 100%. On the scale in Figure 4.2, 100% equals 1.4 newspapers per household, 2.5 weekly attendances per household at motion pictures, 7 hours per household per day for television, and 4 1/3 hours per day for radio. The decreasing

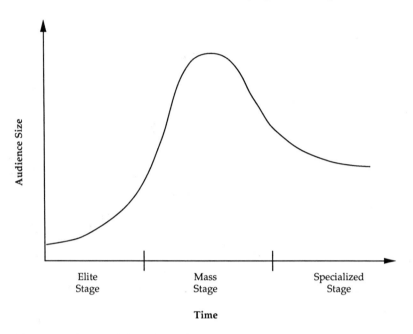

Figure 4.1. A model of media specialization. (Adapted from Merrill and Lowenstein 1971.)

curves for the specialized stages of the older media reflect their decreases in exposure due to competition from new media. Thus, we see that motion pictures have fallen to 40% of their historical peak in the 1920s and 1930s, the most dramatic decline being due to competition from new media. Radio listening has fallen to 2 1/3 hours per day, 54% of its historical peak before television. Newspapers have declined to 75% of their peak, averaging just over one newspaper per household, although that probably is due as much to declining competition among urban dailies as to competition from other media. Network television viewing has fallen from 90% of viewers in the 1970s to 65% in prime time in 1990. In 1990, VCRs have penetrated to 70% of American homes and cable television to 60%.

The newspaper strategically emphasizes its portability (especially for mass-transit commuters), its availability to be consulted at any time, its local coverage, and its ability to cover events and routine information such as stock prices in greater depth and breadth. Radio, when it had to begin to compete with television in the 1950s, switched to music and news formats and moved out of the living room into the car, bedroom, and kitchen. The motion-picture industry seems to have been least successful in surviving the competition from broadcasting, especially television. The movement toward wide-

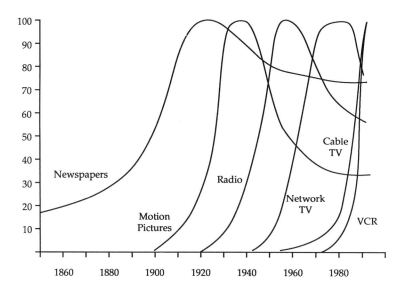

Figure 4.2. Evolution and competition of American mass media. (Adapted from De Fleur and Ball-Rokeach 1988 and Feldman 1985.)

screen spectaculars in the 1950s met with rather limited success. The primary target for out-of-home movie attendance turned out to be the youth market, and the industry restabilized at a somewhat lower level than before. Because most movie studios produce television programming, they have adapted well to the changing marketplace.

It is not at all clear, however, that the elite–mass–specialized pattern will repeat itself as television begins to face competition from even newer media. Although cable television and especially "pay television" have cut into the network share of prime-time viewing, network television, perhaps in a modified format, is likely to remain the dominant, low-cost, mass-audience medium.

The diversity of human interests

One of the most frequently repeated claims of the new media entrepreneurs is that audience members have become impatient and dissatisfied with the currently dominant medium – commercial television. Whenever there is a dip in the viewership levels, or video-game use goes up, or prominent celebrities comment that they no longer watch television, several theories about the demise of television will be trotted out. They revolve around the notion that the audience has grown weary of the familiar television formats, has overdosed on commercials, and hungers for more control and selection among program options. It seems difficult to read a dissatisfaction interpretation from viewership levels that now extend beyond seven hours per day per household, but such arguments are frequently made and perhaps are worth exploring.

The research of McHugh and Hoffman (1983), the Washington news consultants, is characteristic of this school of thought. Their study of television trends concluded that the television audience has finally "come of age"; the audience has "grown more mature and sophisticated in the value judgments it sets for the medium and more demanding that the medium serve its needs – rather than they serve the medium."

Their study found that 64% of the audience defined television as a prominent source of news and information, as well as entertainment, up from 28% in the 1960s (although the survey items were not strictly comparable). They concluded that

this expansion has resulted from a growing comprehension on the public's part of a "need to know" which grew out of the Vietnam War, Watergate, inflation, recession, etc. . . . Today, as never before, television serves the dual role of entertaining and informing the majority of Americans. And, it is in terms of this dual need that the public judge the medium.

They found that 39% of respondents claimed to be viewing less. McHugh and Hoffman surmised that this is less a measure of actual behavior than an indicator of growing dissatisfaction. Their findings have been confirmed by recent network studies. They found as well a broader and more complex set of categories that respondents used to characterize entertainment programming, further evidence, they argue, of a sophisticated and demanding audience. More recently, the spectacular growth of prerecorded videocassettes and home video in England has been taken by other analysts as confirming evidence of dissatisfaction and unmet demand for a greater diversity of programming than the English four-channel system could provide.

Could it be that the marketplace for television and mass communications has matured and diversified beyond the ability of the networks to meet the demand? Are Toffler and McHugh and Hoffman correct? Are audiences dissatisfied, impatiently waiting for multichannel narrowcasting? Will national network television soon become as inconsequential as network radio has become?

There has been surprisingly little basic research on audience interests. (For the exceptions to the rule, see Frank and Greenberg 1980 and Bower 1985.) Given the potential for spectacular profits acknowledged to reside in the ability to catch the pulse of public taste through appropriate market research, one might expect these issues to have been well researched and well understood. There has indeed been a great deal of research, but most of it has focused quite narrowly on evaluation of magazines or television "pilots." Audience interests are exceedingly difficult to measure meaningfully by the usual techniques of social and marketing research. This chapter addresses the issue of the delicate balance of media supply and demand and the prospects for narrowcasting by focusing on a few of the available studies. Such data provide some clues, but as yet no clear answers regarding the extent to which different audience segments have different content interests.

A study conducted by Jack Landis of Marketing Evaluations Inc. examined a massive national sample in an attempt to determine how people evaluate television programming – not just which shows they watched, but why (Landis 1979). The data allow us to answer two questions. First, do different demographic groups evaluate programming in distinct ways? Should we expect to find, for example, that different sectors of the "fragmented audience" (say grammar-school-educated versus college-educated groups) perceive different qualities in a particular action-adventure or public-affairs program? Second, are these perceptions related to differential viewership? For example, should we expect to find that younger viewers are especially attracted to action-adventure programming, or that college-educated viewers harbor an "unmet demand" for informative programming?

Another relevant survey was conducted for the Newspaper Advertising Bureau's "Newspaper Readership Project" (1983). The study included a unique research technique to answer this question: If people edited their own papers, what features would they carry? Respondents were given a wide range of topics from which to choose and were instructed to put together "a paper tailor-made to your own interests." The data allow for an analysis of the diversity and fragmentation of audience interests in newspaper content directly parallel to the television study by Marketing Evaluations Inc.

The television study

The research in this case consisted of extensive, in-depth interviews and survey pretests in an attempt to determine what vocabulary people used to describe and evaluate television programming. The analysts wanted to avoid biasing the results by forcing their own vocabulary on respondents or by omitting unanticipated dimensions of evaluation. The extensive pretest interviews generated a list of more than 1,000 commonly used words and phrases. Those results were further analyzed and combined into a primary list of 68 descriptors and phrases.

The respondents were asked to rate a set of 74 prime-time programs with the battery of descriptors. The data provide a rich resource for assessing both the perceptions and behaviors of the American public with regard to program diversity in television.

There were two stages to the analysis. The first stage attempted to determine if different social groups perceived programming in the same terms.

For example, were men more likely than women to perceive sexual- or adventure-oriented content in programs, and, as a result, more likely to check off those descriptors? Or were college-educated viewers more likely to perceive public-affairs content as educational or informative? A review of the evaluations for each of the 74 specific programs did reveal significant differences. But on reviewing the patterns as a whole, we see that the programs were similarly perceived by different social groups. The summary results are reported in Table 4.1. The "Overall average" column summarizes the typical response of the sample as a whole to the average program. The results across demographic groups were strikingly similar. Although women were twice as likely as men to note pathos as an element (6% to 3%), and although there were consistent differences for younger viewers, who seemed to find each element present more often than did their elders, the differences were consistently small. The patterns were also quite similar across reported motives for viewing and aesthetic dimensions.

A more critical question was addressed in the second stage of the analysis. We reviewed not only how people perceived programming but also how such perceptions were correlated with viewing. Even if those of different educational levels equally perceived "60 Minutes" as information-oriented, perhaps that perception would be more likely to lead to viewing for the college-educated. Correlation coefficients between perception and frequency of viewing were calculated for the different demographic categories. The results are reported in Table 4.2.

There are several interesting summary results. It seems that although humor was not perceived as the most prominent element in prime-time programming, it clearly was the element most highly associated with viewing. Also, in comparing Tables 4.1 and 4.2, it becomes apparent that although only 19% of the sample described the average program as relaxing, relaxation clearly was the attribute most highly associated with viewing – a correlation of .45. Interestingly, perceiving programs to be informative or sophisticated was negatively correlated with viewing. These should not be surprising findings for those familiar with television research.

Again, the pattern by demographic groups was quite consistent. People liked for television to be funny and action-filled. That was true for the teenager and the grandmother, the construction worker and the tax lawyer. There were a few small-scale surprises. One might have expected sex and violence to have been more highly correlated with viewing for men, but the opposite was found. Also, informational programming was less consistently avoided by lower-income viewers than might have been expected. But the overwhelming pattern was one of rather uniform motivation and choice (Wilensky 1964).

Table 4.1. *Audience diversity: perceptions of television programming* (%)

Demographic Groups	Sex		Income			Education		Age				Overall average
	M	F	Low	Medium	High	High school	College	12–17	18–34	35–49	50+	
Program elements												
Adventure	23	26	26	26	23	25	25	29	27	23	22	25
Humor	16	17	19	17	14	17	17	19	18	17	14	17
Violence	13	15	16	14	13	14	15	18	17	14	10	14
Suspense	12	14	13	15	11	14	13	16	15	11	11	14
Fantasy	14	13	12	14	13	13	14	14	15	14	11	13
Sex	6	8	9	7	6	7	8	9	9	7	5	7
Spectacle	5	6	8	6	4	6	5	10	6	5	4	6
Pathos	3	6	5	5	5	5	5	5	7	5	3	5
Motivation												
Relaxation	18	20	21	19	18	18	20	19	21	19	17	19
Value reinforcement	13	15	15	14	12	14	14	18	16	13	11	14
Information	13	14	14	14	13	13	14	16	16	12	11	14
Identification	9	11	12	10	9	10	11	12	13	9	8	10
Aesthetics												
Sophisticated	11	12	13	12	11	11	12	15	14	11	8	12
Imaginative	10	10	11	11	9	10	11	12	12	9	8	10
Realistic	8	9	9	9	5	9	8	11	9	7	7	8

Table 4.2. *Audience diversity: patterns of television viewing (Pearson correlation coefficients)*

Demographic Groups	Sex		Income			Education		Age				Overall average
	M	F	Low	Medium	High	High school	College	12–17	18–34	35–49	50+	
Program elements												
Adventure	.13	.15	.14	.15	.14	.15	.17	.06	.19	.13	.16	.16
Humor	.36	.33	.37	.34	.32	.35	.35	.33	.34	.39	.39	.35
Violence	.09	.17	.14	.13	.12	.12	.18	.07	.16	.15	.11	.13
Suspense	.07	.11	.14	.08	.10	.13	.06	.00	.10	.14	.08	.10
Fantasy	.09	.04	.01	.11	.00	.07	.05	.03	.06	.11	.10	.07
Sex	.17	.30	.30	.29	.18	.22	.30	.21	.18	.22	.31	.27
Spectacle	.09	.09	.16	.07	.05	.08	.13	.15	.11	.07	.11	.09
Pathos	−.04	.02	.01	−.02	.05	−.02	.05	.00	.04	−.03	.00	.00
Motivation												
Relaxation	.45	.44	.47	.43	.43	.44	.45	.39	.44	.34	.49	.45
Value reinforcement	.10	.12	.09	.07	.20	.12	.10	.20	.11	.09	.09	.11
Information	−.22	−.23	.03	−.25	−.25	−.20	−.23	−.35	−.20	−.23	−.22	−.22
Identification	.13	.25	.26	.22	.16	.24	.19	.19	.14	.21	.23	.22
Aesthetics												
Sophisticated	−.26	−.21	−.04	−.24	−.28	−.24	−.24	−.37	−.20	−.27	−.22	−.24
Imaginative	.13	.00	.11	.01	.05	.02	.10	.10	.06	−.01	.07	.06
Realistic	.00	−.04	.04	−.04	−.03	.01	−.07	−.13	−.13	−.17	.09	−.03

The newspaper study

It may be that people's interests in television programming can provide only an incomplete test of the interest-fragmentation hypothesis. After all, the social definition of television as a large-audience, mass-appeal medium is widely accepted, and the pattern is continuously reinforced by the economics of the Nielsen system. Newspapers, however, continue as a competitive mass medium through the technique of internal diversification – appealing to a wide variety of interests, from financial listings to home repairs, recipes, and astrology, all within the same newspaper. Perhaps the study of people's newspaper interests will provide a more complete measure of diversity.

The study was part of a comprehensive analysis of media use conducted by the Newspaper Advertising Bureau. Respondents were asked about their use of and attitudes toward various media, which stories they had read in yesterday's paper, and, most important for this analysis, what they would choose to include in a newspaper tailor-made to their interests.

Respondents were given an alphabetized list of 34 subjects (not including local, national, or international news) and were asked in each case if they would allocate a lot, some, a little, or no space to that interest category. There was a great deal of variation across categories, the most popular being allocated a lot of space or some space by 78% of the sample, the least popular being given a lot or some space by only 22% of the sample. But the analysis of interests by different demographic categories revealed a pattern of consistently similar interest preferences. The tailor-made newspapers, for male or female, for high-school- or college-educated, for young or old, for black or white, were, with only a few predictable exceptions, almost identical. The data are summarized in Table 4.3. The 34 topics are listed in order of their overall popularity. One can see the relative importance of each topic (the percentage who would allocate a lot of space or some space) for each demographic group simply by scanning the rows horizontally. Or one can get a rough sense of the similarity between any two demographic groups simply by scanning a pair of columns vertically.

As one might expect, there were several predictable, stereotypical differences. Women were more likely than men to be interested in "Best food buys," "Recipes," "Women's fashion," "Weddings," and "Beauty tips." Men had greater interest in sports. The college-educated had more interest in politics and book reviews. Older readers were more interested in obituaries and less interested in movie reviews. Nonwhites expressed greater interest in fashion, music, and religion.

But all things considered, the levels of agreement among different demographic groups on what they were interested in were overwhelming. The average difference in interests between each of the demographic groups and

Table 4.3. *Audience diversity: personalized newspapers (preferences for types of newspaper information)* (%)

Topic	Sex		Education				Overall average
	M	F	Some high school	High school	Some college	College	
Best food buys	72	84	78	81	79	74	78
Health	63	82	74	77	77	72	75
Human interests	71	78	71	77	80	73	75
Consumer news	73	73	65	72	80	85	73
Environment	71	73	60	63	82	81	72
Editorials	69	72	62	71	78	79	70
Political figures	69	66	61	65	76	76	67
Sports	72	47	57	61	60	59	59
Home maintenance	58	57	62	60	56	51	58
School news	51	61	57	59	54	47	56
Letters to editor	53	54	51	55	55	56	54
Personal finances	53	56	49	54	51	61	54
Hobbies	53	54	50	56	52	59	53
Religion	43	56	58	51	46	34	49
Celebrities	56	44	54	51	48	39	49
Home furnishings	41	56	49	52	48	41	49
TV reviews	48	51	60	48	43	39	49
Book reviews	37	50	34	39	55	63	44
Obituaries	34	50	53	44	35	27	43
Travel	42	41	39	42	43	43	41
Comics	44	38	43	41	39	38	41
Recipes	22	52	45	39	32	27	38
Hunt/fish	52	26	44	41	31	29	38
Women's fashion	24	50	43	39	34	28	37
Personal advancement	27	44	46	37	29	21	36
Music	32	36	37	33	36	30	34
Movie reviews	32	33	34	32	30	33	33
Pets/animals	30	36	43	33	28	21	33
Weddings	23	37	37	32	25	19	30
Beauty tips	16	39	31	32	24	17	28
Psychic predictions	28	29	31	29	30	17	28
Men's fashion	29	26	31	30	22	21	27
Crossword puzzles	19	26	25	23	20	20	23
Astrology	16	27	31	24	15	9	22

the overall national average was 4.8%. Yet the difference between the most popular and least popular interests for the population as a whole was 56%. There were only five topics with more than a 20% difference between men and women, only eight with that great a difference when comparing the some-high-school and college-educated groups, only three comparing the 18–24 and the 55 + age groups, and only two reflecting racial differences.

Consider the finding that women exhibited greater interest in reading about "Best food buys." The difference was only 12%. One might have expected that section of a newspaper to have had two to three times as many women readers. The less well educated strata tailor-made their newspapers with more sports and comics, but the difference was small: only 2%, compared with 5% for the better-educated. These are not numbers that are likely to stir the souls of targeting marketeers or those whose financial investments are based on the narrowcasting concept.

Diversity within mass society

The accepted wisdom, both among professionals in the communications industries and among the scholars who study them, is that the content of the media is determined by critical economic and technological variables. Within the mass of mass society there is a vital diversity of interests and tastes that are frustrated by the processes of aggregation and homogenization practiced by the major media industries. The new electronic conduits for text and video, it is believed, may finally come to serve that diversity. There is surely much truth to that perception. Spanish-speaking citizens welcome the Spanish channels that cable can bring them. Younger Americans have distinct musical tastes and have responded positively to MTV and VH1, the 24-hour music video channels. Black Americans do prefer programs prominently populated with black performers and black culture.

But in pursuing the matter of different cultural and informational tastes one step further to the question of different motivations, perceptions, and worldviews, one finds reason to pause. The elements of adventure, humor, violence, sex, and pathos have been consistently predominant in our primordial myths, nineteenth-century novels, and modern media fare (perhaps in roughly equal proportions). On close examination, the drama and comedy of the Spanish and black networks look surprisingly similar to the equivalent genres in network television. The topics that college-educated and non-college-educated people read in their newspapers differ only by small degrees. Neither group has an exclusive interest in international news or sports and comics.

The data on audience interests are only part of the equation. The changing economics of print and video production, distribution, and marketing are also critically important. Furthermore, there are subtle dynamics of supply and demand in response to which audience tastes and interests may evolve gradually as new media technologies explore new areas and genres in search of a viable economic niche. The future of specialized media and the possible fragmentation of the mass audience remain unsettled questions.

5

The political economy of the mass media

The economics of mass communications do not promote diversity. There is a curiously powerful centripetal force in the marketplace of ideas that leads to what economist Harold Hotelling some years ago labeled "excessive sameness." Hotelling's work (1929) focused on a very general mathematical characteristic whereby markets tend to oversupply products whose properties are centrist and modal. His article, ironically published just before the great crash of 1929, has become a true classic and has spawned numerous lines of research, including the study of product differentiation in marketing (Scherer 1980), the centrist dynamics of multiparty political systems (Downs 1957), and spatial modeling more generally (Enelow and Hinich 1984).

Economies of scale are more pronounced for the production and distribution of information than for most other consumer goods. Furthermore, if in the mass marketing of washing machines or cereals we find that despite different labels most products look the same or taste the same, that is a relatively minor aesthetic disappointment. But in the domain of political communications and culture, as mass society and critical cultural theory emphasize, the powerful market dynamics that reinforce homogeneity pose a significant threat to the democratic ideal of pluralism and diversity.

This chapter continues the strategy of analyzing the forces that are likely to shape the new media, by focusing on the structural properties of the current American media system. Thus far we have reviewed the accumulated evidence on the psychology and habitual behavior of the mass audience. We begin here with an analysis of structural factors in capitalist communications systems that alternately constrain and enhance diversity and mass participation and that are likely to continue to play such a role in the new media age.

Citizens of liberal capitalist democracies pride themselves on the openness and intellectual diversity of their political culture. They ridicule the stiff and stuffy bureaucratese that traditionally dominated the controlled press in the communist systems on the left as well as the systems of one-party ruling elites on the right (Siebert et al. 1956; Merrill 1974; Fascell 1979; Martin and Chaudhary 1983; Gastil 1986). Yet they are puzzled when the same criticism of cultural homogeneity and elite-ideology domination is leveled at the commercially controlled press of capitalist systems (Marcuse 1964; Schiller 1973; Williams 1974; Bagdikian 1983; Grachev and Yermoshkin 1984). Most liberal democrats shrug off such criticism as irrelevant propaganda. Perhaps that is because critics on the left tend to weave stories of outrageous conspiracy. For the most part, the conspiracy notions are simply wrong. *New York Times* reporters and editors do not call up Wall Street barons for permission to publish a story as a reporter at *Izvestia* might have cleared a story with the Kremlin.

But despite the proud independence of the fourth estate, and the entertainment industry more generally in the United States, the net result is that what most people hear and see in the mass media is remarkably uniform in content and worldview. That uniformity is not the result of a nefarious ring of scheming conspirators; it is structural. It derives from the critical-mass mathematics of the marketplace. Nefarious, perhaps, in its own way, it is, nonetheless, likely to be a critical constraint on the development of new media and new expectations for political communications.

The structure of the American communications industry

There are three defining characteristics of the American mass communications system: The media are privately owned. They are lightly regulated by public authorities. They are, in general, extremely profitable.

Private ownership

The tradition of commercial mass communications in the United States stands in rather stark contrast to the situation in most of the rest of the world, where, for example, most of the broadcast systems are directly or indirectly run by the government and are supported largely by tax revenues. By one estimate, 66% of the world's newspapers and 76% of the world's broadcast systems are subject to some form of direct government control over their content (Gastil 1986, 103). Most nations treat the broadcast media, and often the print media as well, as a public service, like the postal service or the rail system. Broadcasting generally has not been seen as an appropriate domain for private enterprise.

The evolution of government-controlled public media around the world has followed a straightforward logic: Having an informed citizenry is seen, naturally enough, as a worthy public goal. The government has information it legitimately needs to communicate to the populace. Like education, public communication is a public service that merits the government's direct involvement and support. National communication is too important to be left to chance (Siebert et al. 1956; Deutsch 1963; Smith 1980; Pool 1983b). In the case of multiparty democracies, a diversity of voices and an independent press free to be critical of government are desired. Accordingly, legal and constitutional guarantees are put in place to protect the independence of journalists and artists within the context of a government-dominated communications system. Often an insulated government board or agency is set up, such as the British Broadcasting Corporation (BBC) in England or the NHK, the public broadcasting entity in Japan. Sometimes the legal structure explicitly provides a means for a government channel to be managed by political parties or interest groups, as is the case in Holland (Smith 1973). Some governments permit independent newspapers and broadcast channels to compete with the government's own media under the constraints of a press law or oversight commission of some sort, as is often the case in Latin America (Martin and Chaudhary 1983).

It is a bit more difficult to explain the logic of a privately controlled, commercially dominated communications system. Both the system and its rationale evolved in the United States through what might be characterized as a series of rather unusual historical circumstances. In effect, the monopoly rights to provide telephone and broadcast services were simply handed over to commercial interests who happened to be at the right place at the right time. In the 1920s, radio-station licenses that guaranteed the exclusive permanent right to broadcast on one of the few available frequencies in a given geographic area were simply given out by the secretary of commerce, Herbert Hoover, to the first people to ask for them. (A few years later, after he became president, Mr. Hoover's economic philosophy would become even more well known.) Thereafter, those broadcast licenses could be sold and transferred to the highest bidder, and they are now worth tens of millions of dollars in the major urban areas. Television licensing followed a similar pattern in the 1950s. Most of those who applied for television licenses already had radio licenses; they apparently knew a good thing. Television-station licenses now trade in the hundreds of millions of dollars (Barnouw 1966; Levin 1971; Shooshan 1977; Pool 1983b).

The telephone network was handled a bit differently. Samuel F. B. Morse and his colleagues presumed that the government would build the first telegraph network based on their invention, but when the government declined to do so, they took the initiative as private entrepreneurs. It is not clear why the government failed to act (Brock 1981; Pool 1983b; Schneider 1988). Some have hypothesized that given the novelty of the medium, no one was sure where it would go, and risky ventures were best left to private capital. In later years, when governments in other countries faced a similar choice, they had the advantage of the American experience. Others have argued that protection for private enterprise simply was more important in the American political culture than was public service, and they note that some of the congressmen who voted to assign telegraphy to the private sector then became major investors in the new companies. In the early years of telegraphy and telephony there was wild competition among rival companies, which raced to be the first to wire up an area. There were stories of sabotage and high jinks that mystified the staid bureaucrats in other countries' postal and tel-egraph authorities. At the turn of the century, however, Theodore Vail, the brilliant chairman of American Telephone and Telegraph (AT&T), proposed to accept some government regulation in exchange for a government-guaranteed monopoly franchise and exemption from antitrust restrictions. The industry then stabilized under limited government supervision (Brock 1981).

An equivalent monopoly in local newspaper service evolved some 50 years later, as a once highly competitive marketplace, with up to a dozen news-papers in many urban markets, gradually eroded. For reasons that will be discussed later in more detail, the smaller-circulation papers could not con-tinue to bear the fixed costs of newspaper production and distribution, largely because mass advertisers were migrating to the larger, locally dominant papers in order to reach the widest possible audience with their advertising (Com-paine 1982).

A curious tradition of public regulation

One important effect of the privatized network of communications is that the nation conducts its business of public communications on borrowed time, literally at the discretion of a rather odd assortment of financiers and large corporations. The freedom-of-the-press tradition, drawing on English com-mon law and the classic works of Milton, Locke, and Mill, was applied with fervor and success to the evolving printing industry in the United States. That philosophy, of course, had evolved in a preindustrial era, when presses could be bought and operated economically by individuals of modest means. There was also a rich tradition of pamphleteering and the gentleman printer-publisher who operated a weekly paper as a side business or hobby. The local newspaper publisher frequently was the postmaster. The large-scale print media of newspapers and magazines made possible by the steam-driven cylindrical presses of the 1830s were simply treated as the smaller publishers had been. They were seen as independent voices in an open marketplace of ideas and information, despite the fact that because of their size they over-whelmed the smaller competition, and the costs of entering the marketplace skyrocketed to exclude all but the wealthiest industrialists (Tebbel 1974).

The fact that broadcast media were using the electromagnetic spectrum put them in a different category from the start. They were defined as private entrepreneurs, but also as public trustees who had a special obligation to perform public services as a condition of keeping their licenses. The Communications Act of 1934 set up the Federal Communications Commission to oversee the process of license renewal and to ensure that broadcasters continued to serve the public interest (Shooshan 1977; Krasnow, Longley, and Terry 1982). The act specifically prohibited the FCC from censoring speech, but it put forward rather vague guidelines about serving local interests and protecting diversity and a free and open marketplace of public opinion. Over the years, a series of magic numbers evolved, representing nominal percentages for public-service programming, news, and local and religious programming. The FCC was never very specific, perhaps for fear of being unable to justify in court how it defined how much diversity or how much local programming was sufficient. The critical irony of the whole process, however, was that the FCC almost never revoked licenses; there were a few exceptions when owners flagrantly violated technical restrictions or failed to file appropriate forms. It might be argued that the mere threat of revocation has had positive effects, but there have been only a few instances among a hundred thousand renewals in which substantive cases of failing to serve the public interest in terms of programming or fairness have been addressed. It has been a curiously minimal constraint (Levin 1980).

Critics have labeled the FCC a classic case of a "captured" regulatory agency, populated by people who either have come from or soon will be employed by the industry they are supposed to regulate. Furthermore, Congress and the president, recognizing the potential political power of the electronic fourth estate, are noticeably reluctant to displease the industry that has now established itself as a powerful political player (Mosco 1990).

Publishers versus common carriers

The 1934 Communications Act makes a fundamental distinction between two elements of the overall communications system: broadcasters and common carriers. Broadcasters, as publishers, are responsible for the content their medium conveys. It is presumed that there will be many broadcasters, competing in an open marketplace of ideas. Common carriers, on the other hand, are required by law to provide service at the same price to all comers who care to use their medium of communications. The telephone system is a classic example of a common carrier. It would seem wasteful in the extreme to have multiple telephone companies, each running wires down the street and competing for the business of each household. If such companies were not interconnected, one could speak only to people subscribing to one's own telephone company. One would have to have multiple telephones, one from each telephone company, in order to be able to communicate with everybody. Clearly, there are economies of scale in having a single, universally interconnected telephone system, just as there are for providing other utilities like electricity and water. Such enterprises often are labeled "natural monopolies." Other such natural monopolies, usually managed directly by the government itself, are the postal service and the highway network (Sharkey 1982; Pool 1983b).

In order to prevent the common-carrier monopolist from charging excessive prices for a needed service, the rates are regulated by a public commission that examines the costs of maintaining service and computes a reasonable rate of return on invested capital for the monopolist. In granting common-carrier status, the public authorities also protect the monopolist by forbidding others to offer potentially competitive services. In return, the common carrier, by law and by tradition, must not refuse service to anyone and must offer the same rate to all who request service.

Common carriage works best for bridges, taxicabs, water, and electricity, where the services provided are evident and unambiguous. It is a bit more complicated in the domain of communications because of the potential power of the monopolist to control what is supposed to be an open and pluralistic marketplace of ideas. In the case of the telephone system, the role of common carrier appears to be straightforward: The telephone company establishes a connection between two locations. What is said over that connection is of no concern to the telecommunications company. In the case of mass communications, however, what a particular vendor offers, in large measure, is the reputation and editorial judgment of the management. Thus, the *New York Times* or the CBS television network represents much more than a simple conveyer of information and entertainment held open for any who might like to communicate through the medium. There is a tension between the editorial character of mass communications and the open-to-all characteristics of the common-carriage tradition. Broadcasting is clearly a special case in which the distinction is finessed. The public airwaves are a limited resource. Therefore, broadcasters are caught between being defined as a regulated common carrier and being defined as a completely unregulated free-press competitor in an open marketplace of ideas (Noam 1985; Tunstall 1986; Newberg 1989a,b; Garcia 1990; Lichtenberg 1990; Smith 1991).

These tensions, however, become increasingly important as the evolution of the electronic network blurs the distinction between telephony and mass communications. The local telephone companies, still regulated common carriers, now function in part as publishers, providing audio information services such as weather and sports information and increasingly text and data information services (Neustadt 1982; Garcia 1990). Cable television, however, which is granted an exclusive franchise to wire up a local area in much the same way as the telephone company, is defined as an unregulated competitive private business. It is not defined as a monopoly because, at least in theory, one can receive video services from competing terrestrial broadcasters or from one's own satellite dish. Cable is not regulated like broadcasting because it does not utilize the public broadcast spectrum (O'Donnell 1989). Newspapers, of course, in the strongly defended tradition of a free and open press, are not regulated at all. Yet, for economic reasons that evolved in the middle of the twentieth century, newspapers enjoy much greater monopoly powers in most urban markets than do broadcasters.

Market power, competition, and profitability

Each of the major American communications media is privately owned, for what are, in essence, separate historical reasons. That is to say, as the technology for each evolved, a debate ensued about how it should be developed, who should control it, and how best to serve the public interest. But in each case the result was the same. Clearly, the American political culture puts a great deal of faith in the value of the marketplace and competition among profit-seeking, self-interested venturers for allocating scarce resources.

Because the character of the public communications system is of such central importance to the political process and the maintenance of national identity, and because communications systems frequently have some or all of the characteristics of a traditional common carrier, the decision to leave them to private enterprise was never taken lightly. In fact, the courts and the regulatory agencies have monitored the performance of the media with particular concern. Nonetheless, with the exception of rate-of-return regulation in telecommunications, the behavior of the media is constrained, for the most part, by vague threats of potential regulation and only in extremely rare instances by the real thing.

The net result is what business entrepreneurs are trained to seek: the bucket of gold at the end of the capitalist rainbow. Business schools call it sustainable competitive advantage (Porter 1985). Others might call it sustained high profitability, or perhaps protected legal monopoly. Those in the communications industries are puzzled by such caricature. For them, such profits are the results of a great deal of hard work. They would point out that although there may be only one newspaper in town, it certainly is not the only advertising medium in town; the media compete with each other for the limited attention of the audience and the limited advertising dollar. Although entry into broadcasting, for example, is limited by the number of slots in the electromagnetic spectrum, usually there are a dozen television stations and three dozen radio stations competing head-to-head in most major markets. Executives gaze with furrowed brow at the horizon, as cable, satellite broadcasting, and VCRs significantly threaten their livelihood. Furthermore, they complain, some competitors are required to get regulatory clearance to develop new services and test out new technologies, whereas other players with different technological histories, such as the print media, never are.

Whatever one's view of the theory of competition, one fact is beyond dispute: The communications business tends to be profitable, in fact, very profitable (Vogel 1986). Television provides an interesting case in point; its profits traditionally have run at a rate of 20% of sales, whereas the overall average for American manufacturing is 8%. The profit rate on the book value of tangible broadcast property has hovered around 73%, which is more than three times the average for other industries (Noll, Peck, and McGowan 1973, 16). The median profit for publicly held newspaper groups in 1980 was twice the average for other industries (Compaine 1982, 46). The figures depend in part on how calculations are made, but profits from motion pictures, publishing, newspapers, and broadcasting tend to run 1 1/3–2 times the national average (Compaine 1982, 34).

If there is any doubt about the value of the monopoly access right inherent in television and radio licenses and newspaper monopolies, one has only to examine the prices paid for them. Newspapers provide the clearest case. One can expect to pay over a hundred million dollars for a newspaper in one of the medium- or larger-size markets. (That in itself is an indication of the resources necessary to enter the marketplace.) But perhaps the most revealing number results from computing the price per newspaper subscriber; that runs between $200 and $500 for newspapers dominant in their markets. Thus, for example, when the Gannett chain bought the *Shreveport Times* and two smaller papers in Monroe, Louisiana, in 1976, with a combined circulation of 141,000 readers, it paid $61 million, that is, $464 per existing subscriber and newsstand reader. The figures for similar sales have been even higher in recent years. Such prices are no measure of the cost of the printing presses or the editorial talents of the staff; they represent the value per subscriber of the newspaper reading habit. Given that the average subscriber may pay no more than $60 per year to subscribe to the paper, that might seem like quite an gamble. But it is not a risky or imprudent investment, of course, because for local advertisers, there may be no other advertising outlets, or few others, that have the audience reach of the local newspaper. It is the established medium of local communications, and advertisers pay appropriate premiums for access.

Television stations cost similar sums. Again, the value of the buildings, studios, and transmitters will be in the tens of millions of dollars, but the sale price for the station as a whole will run in the hundreds of millions of dollars. A station in Boston, for example, recently sold for $240 million, which represents about $120 per household in the receiving area. In that case there were almost a dozen other television stations broadcasting in the region. Television is not a monopoly, but it has functioned as a guaranteed oligopoly, and that translates into substantial profits. Cable television systems frequently sell for prices in the range of $1,000 to $2,000 per subscribing household, which reflects the substantial additional income from cable subscription and pay-television charges.

The concentration curve

Economists have, over the years, derived a number of helpful techniques for measuring and understanding social and economic inequities. A factor of particular interest in this study of diversity and pluralism is the process by which the natural inequities of the marketplace seep into the presumed egalitarianism of the political realm via the economics of mass communications. The principle of an equal vote and an equal voice for every citizen in the polity is almost universally acknowledged as desirable (Wolin 1960; Rawls 1971). So is the economic notion that unequal rewards are necessary to motivate hard work and to reward risk-taking and innovation (Bendix and Lipset 1966). If mass media and communications networks were seen as serving purely political functions, perhaps they would be entirely egalitarian in their distribution of resources. Every political or artistic voice, being equally worthy of attention, would get equal access to public media, an open and rigorously balanced marketplace of ideas. No one would be permitted to speak louder or longer than any other.

But the American communications system, although it is infused with politics and embedded in the political system, is private and commercial. Dollars buy space in the marketplace of commercial entertainment and information, and bigger dollars buy more space, longer speeches, and louder voices. There are many voices, and one can listen to whichever strikes one's fancy, but if there is a voice in the air or a printed document at hand, almost surely someone paid up front to put it there.

There is fairly wide recognition that some level of market failures of various sorts is inevitable in commercial systems, and accordingly numerous government agencies and some private foundations supplement the mix of commercial print and video by means of public libraries, arts subsidies, public television, postal subsidies, and public forums of diverse character. Nonetheless, the great bulk of what is seen and heard is filtered through the structures and profit motives of a commercial marketplace. Many have argued with considerable success that such filters are much to be preferred over government-determined editorial regimes (Smith 1980; Abel 1981). In the American setting, it is the character of the commercial marketplace as a filtering mechanism that draws our attention. How well does it serve the goals of diversity and pluralism?

Not very well. All things considered, the open commercial systems of liberal democracies probably are the best that one is likely to find, in the real world, for maintaining an open, competitive, and vibrant marketplace of ideas. They remind one of Churchill's famous comment on democracy.[1] But there is ample room for improvement. The common-denominator pressures of the market render the flow of information and entertainment almost as homogeneous as that produced by the most attentive government-run media systems in single-party states. It is a spectacular irony. We shall focus here on the character of the marketplace mechanism. Policy alternatives will be reviewed in the final chapter.

The general form of the concentration curve

We have observed a disjuncture between the potential for diversity in information and ideas in the mass media and what is routinely seen and heard by the average citizen. It is an issue of concentration, sometimes anecdotally said to follow Pareto's law, which states, in effect, that 80% of what is purchased in the marketplace represents a concentrated core of only 20% of what is offered. There are numerous techniques for measuring concentration, and they reveal a great deal about the marketplace dynamics in mass communications.

Perhaps the best-known tool is a graphic device known as the Lorenz curve (Figure 5.1). In this technique, one arrays the units (which may be people, firms, or ideas) from the smallest to the largest along the horizontal axis. If we wish to measure the degree of economic equality, we array the population of households from the poorest to the richest on the horizontal axis and record their actual wealth (or percentage of total national wealth) on the vertical axis. Thus, in the case of perfect economic equality, if there are 100 families in a nation, each with the same household income of 1% of the total national income, the Lorenz curve will be a straight line at a 45-degree angle (labeled the equity line in Figure 5.1). If, on the other hand, the richest 10% of the population have accumulated 20% (curve A) or 80% (curve B) of the aggregate wealth, the curve dips farther below the equity line, representing an increased concentration of wealth. One can use the same technique to study the structure of an industry, measuring the dominance of a few successful firms in the marketplace. Thus, if each of 10 firms has exactly 10% of the market, there is no concentration. If 2 of the 10 firms garner between them a 50% share of the market (which is typical in American industry), that situation looks more like the curve labeled A in Figure 5.1. There are also single parameters, such as the Gini coefficient and the Herfindahl-Hirschman

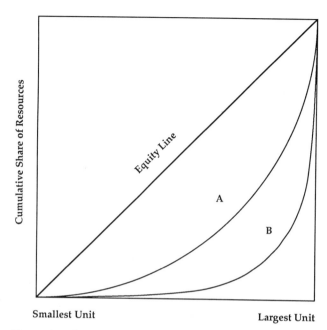

Figure 5.1. General form of the concentration curve.

index,[2] that allow for convenient summary of the Lorenz curve and convenient comparisons of levels of concentration.

There is a great deal of concentration in American mass communications. We shall focus initially on simply describing it, before turning to its multiple causes. American communications are concentrated in terms of their (1) products, (2) formats, (3) markets, and (4) firms.

Product concentration

Product concentration refers to the general property of cultural markets whereby a few individual works become extremely popular, often universally known within a culture, while the great majority of works recede into permanent obscurity. Stock analysts refer to the communications industry as a "hits" business: Many titles are produced, but most of the money is made on the few that catch on and become hits. The figures vary in different domains of publishing, but the rule of thumb that 80% of the income is derived from 20% of the published works is not far off the mark.

Figure 5.2 shows the concentration curve for theatrically released motion pictures. These data have been averaged over multiple years, but it might be more helpful to think of the pattern for a single year. Reviewing the

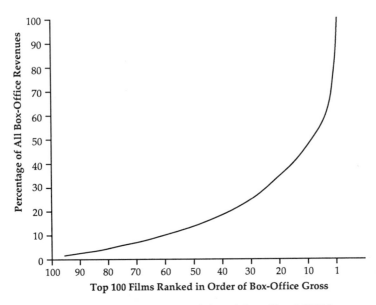

Figure 5.2. Product concentration. (Adapted from Vogel 1986.)

top 100 films released and distributed through primary channels in the United States each year, we find that 10% of the films generate 50% of the box-office revenues, and 20% of the films generate fully 65% of the revenues.

It is not unusual for a single hit film to make up in profitability for the losses suffered by a dozen other films. That was dramatically illustrated in the case of *Star Wars*, released by 20th Century-Fox in 1977; the film was credited with saving the financial fortunes of the company. *Star Wars* cost just under $10 million to produce, the industry average at that time, but within two years of release it had earned $235 million in box-office revenues. Although industry insiders like to pretend otherwise, they have no way of knowing in advance which "product" will be a hit. In the case of *Star Wars*, for example, the studio had assumed that it would be a minor release, a fantasy-adventure film, with no major stars, perhaps of interest to only a subset of the teenage market. It was distinctly unlike other recent hit movies. It was not until *Star Wars* began to be previewed that the executives at Fox realized it might be more than a throwaway (Earnest 1985).

There are similarly dramatic examples from the other side of the coin. *Heaven's Gate* cost $40 million to produce and reportedly has earned less than $1 million at the box office (Bach 1985). Such steep curves for profits and losses lead to roller-coaster careers in the industry, and only the lucky or the very talented (or those who combine the two) survive for very long.

A studio that goes a year or two without a "blockbuster hit" is likely to be in financial trouble. A great deal of the energy of any participant in the movie industry is unavoidably held captive by the concentrated economics of the hit movie.

The curves for the economics of best-sellers in the book industry are even more dramatic. Whereas there may be only 400 new films each year, usually there are more than 30,000 new book titles released each year, many of which sell only a few hundred or a few thousand copies (Compaine 1982). Similar curves characterize the sales of magazines and records.

Format concentration

Not only do we have the pattern of a few titles dominating, but also it is generally true that a very limited number of styles, genres, or formats preoccupy the commercial media. This is a little more difficult to illustrate, because categorizing titles by genre is by its nature a more subjective enterprise, but by utilizing the vocabularies that have become dominant in several industries, we find evidence of concentration much like that characteristic of individual works. Figure 5.3 illustrates the pattern for radio programming. It is a particularly telling example because radio is frequently cited as a very competitive marketplace, with some 30 to 50 stations in most major markets. That competition, presumed to lead to a diversity of content, was the basis for a substantial deregulation of the radio industry in 1982.

Certainly the increased diversity of musical and news/information formats in American radio in most major markets is a welcome development. Where once only amplitude-modulation (AM) stations had audiences of a critical mass, and where news was available only in five-minute chunks at the top of the hour, now the industry proudly boasts a variety of full-time call-in and news formats. But, in perspective, the pattern of concentration on popular music still leaves unserved, in many markets, those who would prefer classical music, jazz, or news commentary.

One of the most interesting phenomena has been the appearance of what seems to be a lawlike dynamic whereby, over time, fads in the popular genres and formats rise and fall, but the domination of a few popular formats is a consistent organizing principle. One study of the relationship between the amount of violence in a program and program popularity found a four-year cycle. At the low point in the cycle there are relatively few programs (usually in the action and police-drama categories) in which violence is predominant. At that point, when new programs from those genres are introduced at the margin, being relatively rare they are valued and frequently viewed. This pattern encourages the introduction of new programs of similar character until there is an oversupply, and such programs at the margin are least likely

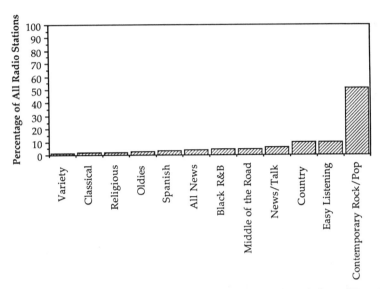

Figure 5.3. Format concentration. (Source: National Association of Broadcasters.)

to succeed in the Nielsen sweepstakes. The pattern reverses itself back and forth approximately every four years (Gerbner 1972).

Overall, however, despite an expansion in the number of channels available, the diversity of program offerings apparently has declined. The available data extend back only to the 1970s, but indicators of the dominant share of a few genres in prime-time programming and measures of the similarity of the three networks both indicate a decline in diversity (Figure 5.4).

Market concentration

Geographers, demographers, and historians have labored long and hard to study the phenomenon of urban concentration and its origins. Urbanization is one of the critical defining characteristics of industrial society. Built originally around navigable ports and rivers, or sources of water power and, later, railroad junctions, cities evolved as social, cultural, and commercial centers in their own right. The growth of suburban belts around cities following World War II had fairly dramatic effects on the character of the cities themselves, but relatively little effect on the media that serve them. The cities and their surrounding suburbs represent aggregated metropolitan markets around which television and radio broadcasting and newspapers are organized.

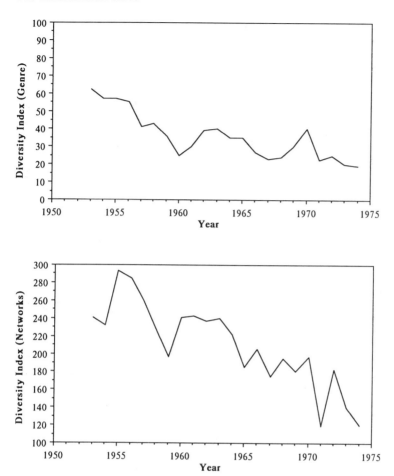

Figure 5.4. Trends in format concentration. (Source: Dominick and Pearce 1976.)

One result of this urban concentration of the population is that with only five well-selected metropolitan television stations (one-half of 1% of the total stations), one can reach one in five Americans. This is true for each of the networks, and until recently each network had been permitted to own outright only five of its affiliated stations. The overall concentration curve for the largest 65 television markets is shown in Figure 5.5. (The corresponding pattern for newspapers is quite similar.) This curve, on the whole, is strikingly similar to the others we have seen, even though this one is entirely the result of population concentrations in urban areas, rather than being a result of actions taken by the media themselves.

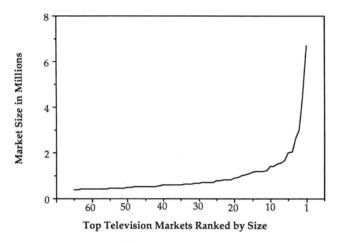

Figure 5.5. Market concentration. (Source: A. C. Nielsen Company.)

Firm concentration

The fact that a few large corporations dominate the American communications industries has been the focus of a great deal of concern, and as a result it is probably the best-known aspect of industrial concentration in this field (Barnouw 1975; Schiller 1989; Compaine 1982; Bagdikian 1983; Picard et al. 1988; Picard 1989). The ownership of the American mass media is concentrated, but not significantly more concentrated than ownership in other industrial enterprises. Figure 5.6 shows data drawn from statistics on book publishers: In 1977, the 4 largest publishers accounted for 16% of the total earned by all 1,500 book publishers in the American marketplace; the top 8 publishers earned 29% of the total, the top 20 took 54%, and the top 50 took 73%.

What makes industrial concentration important to economists is that if a few firms corner a large share of a particular market, the temptation to exercise that power and behave monopolistically or oligopolistically to raise prices and reduce true competition may prove irresistible. Such behavior is, of course, inefficient. In the political realm, however, there is the added and perhaps even more important potential problem of bias and monopolistic control of public debate and discussion. The question of the linkage between ownership and editorial control of mass media is subtle, and the equation is not as simple as some critics who see a media conspiracy are likely to assert.

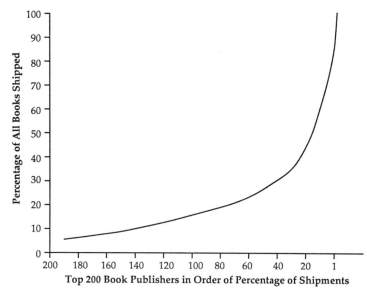

Figure 5.6. Firm concentration. (Source: Compaine 1982.)

Economic pressures toward homogenization

Thus far we have reviewed some important background factors, such as the evolution of the current ownership and regulatory structure, and taken an overview of concentration and homogenization. We turn at this point to the core of the argument: the question of the sources of these powerful forces tending to counteract diversity and pluralism. There are, in fact, many over-lapping and reinforcing factors at work. Some of them derive from the psychology of low-salience attention to the media and the convergence of mass tastes, as documented in earlier chapters. They will be reviewed briefly here under the rubric of demand-side dynamics. The effects of these factors are reinforced by equally strong supply-side dynamics having to do with the economies of scale and scope that are characteristic of information commodities. Hotelling's theory of common-denominator economics will be used to put these factors in perspective. Finally, the special role of advertiser-supported media will be examined.

Demand-side dynamics: a brief review

Those who defend the idea of commercial markets as the best way to organize mass communications rely heavily on the argument that the public gets exactly what it wants through open market competition. What could be more fair? What could be more efficient? If public tastes aggregate around sensationalist tabloid newspapers, corny game shows, trashy romance novels, and violent and simplistic movies, so be it. Complain about public tastes, not about the media system that caters to them.

Critics of American mass media rely heavily on just the opposite assumption: The public does not get what it wants; it gets what it gets. There is a presumption of a largely frustrated body of rich and diverse tastes and interests that are simply ignored by the media moguls because responding to them would be unprofitable.

The evidence collected over the years by both qualitative and quantitative methods reviewed in the preceding chapter tends to provide more support for the former view than for the latter. Although there are numerous and important exceptions, on the whole most people within a given cultural setting display remarkably homogeneous tastes. Stories of romance and adventure and news of war and peace are universally valued. The forms of competitive sports vary from culture to culture, but rarely does the centrality of sports competition. Blame it on the human condition, but people generally prefer to read about sex, food, or murderous villainy, rather than philosophy, poetry, or mathematics.

People are passive and only partially attentive to what they see and hear from the media. For most of the people most of the time, the psychological costs and inconvenience of finding special-interest information and entertainment outweigh their desire to find it. Most people have been conditioned to pay a great deal to buy access to special-interest materials, even though mass-interest, advertiser-supported materials are abundantly available for free. When most people sit down to read a book or to watch television, they are in a mood to relax and enjoy themselves. They want to spend some time with something they enjoy, and the most popular book or television show is as reliable an indicator of what they might enjoy as anything else. Searching through obscure and unpopular titles and genres is the obsession of a tiny avant-garde elite, not the great bulk of the populace.

When it comes to the marketplace for information and culture, the population as a whole is quite satisfied. Widespread cultural frustration and unmet demands for new ideas and new media are, for the most part, favored fantasies of a small artistic elite and wishful thinkers (Gans 1974; Becker and Shoenbach 1989).

Supply-side dynamics

The key to the profitability of mass communications is close attention to economies of scale. Henry Ford's development of mass production, interchangeable parts, and the assembly line itself for the manufacture of industrial goods has become legendary. It is intuitively obvious and, of course, has been widely documented that the cost per unit declines as the number of units manufactured increases. Development and overhead costs can be spread out over more units. Management and efficiency improve over time as more and more units are produced and the manufacturing operations progress down a learning curve. Complex processes can be broken down into simplified, repetitive tasks performed at maximum efficiency by specialized labor or by specialized machinery whose development is justified by the scale of production. The pressure toward homogeneous products from the day of Ford's Model T to the present is fundamental.

Economies of scale in information commodities. The returns to scale are dramatically higher in information and communications than in most industries. The effort and expense involved in writing and performing a symphony or a play are substantial, and it is also extremely expensive to record or publish such works in record or book form. But once the work is captured, the manufacturing costs for the second and third copies are but a fraction of the cost for the first (Figure 5.7). The master plates for printing books and stamping records, or the master negative for a movie or video, or the master copy of a computer program may cost several millions or tens of millions of dollars to produce, but copies cost only a few pennies or a few dollars each, and that will be increasingly the case for the new media. The raw materials for books and records are paper and ink or plastic. The raw material for a phonograph record or compact disc costs about 25 cents. Stamping, packaging, and shipping may raise the total manufacturing costs to about a dollar per copy, with retail prices running from $8 to $15. The raw materials and printing costs, in quantity, for a typical hardbound book may be several dollars, with the list price ranging from 5 to 10 times that amount. Such differentials between first-copy cost and the cost of subsequent copies generate strong incentives for illegal, bootleg copying of works for general sale, as well as for personal copying of borrowed works, as in the case of computer software or books, whose retail price may be several times the cost of photocopying and binding one's own pirated version.

Economies of scale in production. The production process is the traditional locus for achieving economies of scale, and that is particularly true for video and film media, where the fixed costs of the existing studios and the specialized talents of large production crews permit lower costs per production for the larger studios. This is true as well for periodical publications like newspapers, for a small paper will be saddled with the fixed costs of a relatively large staff of journalists in order to be competitive, even if its circulation is

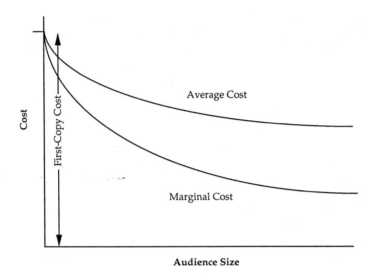

Figure 5.7. Economies of scale in information commodities.

substantially less than that of other papers and its staff costs per subscriber are accordingly much higher. Such publications also enjoy traditional man-ufacturing-scale economies in the production of the physical print product, such as a newspaper or book.

Economies of scale in distribution. Here we confront again the issues of dis-tribution networks, economies of scale, and natural monopolies. The postal and telephone services provide for relatively efficient distribution of infor-mation across a common network, and also in the fields of motion pictures, books, and television, the distribution channels benefit tremendously from economies of scale and scope. The basic issues here are the fixed costs of a physical network, whether it be a fleet of trucks or an installed electronic infrastructure, and the increased efficiency of transactions when retailers deal with a syndicate rather than with thousands of individual authors, artists, or publishers.

Critical mass. Each of the previously cited forms of scale economy diminishes the likelihood that there will be many small competitors, but they do not preclude that possibility. Efficiencies due to large scale mean that, ceteris paribus, large-scale producers will be more efficient and accordingly more profitable than small-scale producers, but not necessarily so much so to exclude a potentially larger number of smaller players. There are several other factors, however, that further tend to diminish the number of firms and occasionally the diversity that their presence might provide. The key is a critical-mass entry barrier to potential new participants in the marketplace.

One aspect of the concept of critical mass is the capitalization necessary to enter the marketplace as a publisher or communications provider; it varies for different media, but is in general quite substantial. For broadcasting and newspapers, buying into an existing property requires millions or tens of millions of dollars. Book publishers need not be printers; they may simply subcontract printing operations to a large and efficient specialist. Thus, as one might expect, we have large numbers of small publishers, many of them publishing no more than one or two books per year. Likewise, in magazine publishing, Compaine cites a number of recent examples in which entrepreneurs' original investments were less than $20,000, but given the promotional expenses required to draw attention to a new periodical, such low critical masses are the exception to the rule. It is more often the case that magazine start-up expenses will be $2–4 million (Compaine 1982, 173).

This may all sound quite contradictory to the thrust of Chapter 2, in which it is argued that both the costs in general and the minimum viable scale of operations are declining. The contrast merits comment. What is declining in cost is the technology, but in a commercial venture, the critical factor is the size of the potential market. The value of a radio or television transmitter is a function of how many receivers there are, and for television and radio, 100% of the population have receivers, and so the values of the media are high. In the case of the new media entering the marketplace, there is a catch–22 if a receiver is required. The initial audience is virtually zero, and given the diversity of media already available, a new medium must provide a fairly unusual and high-demand service in order to entice potential early adopters of the new technology to invest in receivers. Thus, we confront an irony that has important economic consequences: There is considerable technological potential for a variety of new and inexpensive electronic highways to the homes of the citizenry, but until unique historical circumstances and substantial economic resources can establish a new audience of critical mass, these will remain highways that lead nowhere.

There is a further issue concerning the concept of critical mass. In this case it has to do with the volatility of selling individual communications products. The motion-picture industry provides an appropriate example. The average commercial film currently costs about $25 million to produce. The costs of prints, distribution, and promotion add another $12 million to bring a picture to the marketplace. At that point it is the concentration curve, the hit-movie phenomenon, that plays a critical role. As noted earlier, one can expect, on average, that a given movie will be a flop. The great majority are. In fact, only a very few make a profit. Those that do, of course, make substantial profits, explaining why, under such circumstances, businesses still opt to invest in movies. But given the volatility of movie profitability, the only way one can expect to break even is to make a substantial number of movies each year, relying on the statistical probability of producing one hit along with the many that are unlikely to be popular enough to earn back their invested capital. A number of well-financed, experienced entertainment companies, including CBS, ABC, and the General Cinema Corporation, have tested the waters around the approach of making only a few movies, and all have retreated.

Scarcity. A central theme of Chapter 2 is that the explosion of new media for the storage and transmission of information will present an unprecedented opportunity for new channels of communication. Some have argued that such a technological push is fundamental and literally signals an end to scarcity in the domains of information and communications (Masuda 1980); subsequent chapters, however, have counseled caution. One's view will depend on what one saw as scarce in the first place.

The economic and political power wielded by those entrepreneurs who have captured the few bottleneck facilities that can provide a connection between a would-be public communicator and the mass audience appears to be threatened by the new media, but that threat will be hollow unless the new media can in fact attract substantial mass audiences. So what is scarce is not the technical means of communication, but rather public attention.

The irony, of course, is that although there is some grumbling among the general public to the effect that all the movies and all the television shows are the same, what reliably attracts public attention is not the fresh, new, and different, but rather the familiar. Thus, it is the well-known broadcast journalist and the movie star who, although they could not have gained their fame and public status without the media, represent the ultimately scarce commodity, rather than the medium itself. This fundamental economic fact is reflected in their typical salaries. There is an instructive contrast between the salaries of the talented technicians and artisans who make the communications possible and the salaries of the celebrities who attract the audience.

Thus, the typical approach to finding the key to success in getting a new communications service off the ground has been to look as much as possible like the ones that already exist, including hiring away some of the old media's familiar faces. That was evident in the sports world when the United States Football League tried to attract a critical mass of attention by investing a great deal of its extremely limited financial resources in a few football stars from the National Football League.

The same approach is evident in the reliance that cable television has placed on repeating the familiar genres and famous faces from television and the motion-picture industry. The economic plan behind cable television, from the first, has been to give the consumer a convenient package of old movies and reruns and, on pay television, recent movies. The exploration of new forms and formats for cable television has been, from an economic standpoint, at least, a minor distraction.

Promotion thresholds. We have already addressed the issue of information thresholds from the standpoint of the psychology of the audience member. The effort required to monitor all the available media for a snippet of information or entertainment that will resonate with one's tastes and interests usually is more than most are willing to invest. The result is that the average audience member satisfices, following primarily the most widely publicized best-sellers in each medium. This has important economic ramifications in the aggregate. It translates into a critical threshold for advertising and promotion of new information products.

One of the clearest cases is found in the motion-picture industry. It is not unusual for a new release to be accompanied by $15 million of advertising and promotion. In some cases those expenditures will be more than was spent in making the picture itself; in every case they will represent a substantial portion of the total cost of bringing the picture to market. It is well known that a provocative advertising campaign by itself will not sell a movie. Indeed, after several weeks of release, the primary determinant of box-office volume for a picture is its word-of-mouth reputation. The public is quite capable of ignoring even the most intense promotional blitz. But on the other hand, industry wisdom dictates that even a very promising picture needs to be jump-started by heavy up-front advertising. Needless to say, the tradition of large-scale promotional efforts is an impediment to a studio or distributor who might be offered an independently made film or one from overseas and would otherwise be inclined to take a chance on it. Such a film might well be experimental, or off the beaten track; most important, the film would already have been completed, financed by other sources. To release such a film to a few screens not otherwise occupied in order to see how it would play would be technically and organizationally feasible, but that is seldom done. It would rub industry traditions the wrong way; it would sidestep the traditional hoopla and promotion of the usual new-product rollout.

One finds parallels in the introduction of new magazines, as well as the many special programs and miniseries in television. The promotional-cost hurdle imparts a conservative influence, tilting programming decisions away from one-shot programs in general, and risky gambles on unfamiliar formulas and new faces in particular. It is taken as given in product marketing generally that one does not simply introduce a new product. In order to get retailers to make scarce shelf space available, they must be convinced that the new soap or cereal will be accompanied by an appropriate advertising and promotion campaign to ensure that at least some of their customers will try it. These critical threshold costs of introducing a new product are substantial. In cereals and soaps, however, if the new product catches on there will be substantial repeat sales over the months and years to justify the up-front investment. In the case of an information product, such as a book, a movie, or a television program, all those promotional costs must be borne by the single product itself, as consumers will buy only one. Such economic constraints are inauspicious for the cause of pluralism and diversity in the commercial marketplace of ideas.

There are some exceptions. Books, for example, often are introduced with elaborate fanfare, in store promotions and traditional media advertising; however, because of the nature of the book trade, including production costs and profit ratios, sometimes it is possible for a publisher to serve limited and specialized markets with short-run titles. In such cases, advertising will be either nonexistent or minimal and highly targeted; the promotional threshold is low. Books, it turns out, are the distinct exception to the rule.

Industry culture. A final consideration in mass market economics involves the norms of the various communications industries. One might argue that fads and fashions that dominate the executive suites of the media industries do not represent an independent causal factor, but simply reflect the bottom-line economics of the product in question. Perhaps. But it is also possible that industry culture reinforces and exaggerates pressures toward homogeneity and mass market popularity.

The most vivid example of the role of fashion in commercial mass communications is the me-too pattern that is so predominant in book publishing, television, and motion pictures. If there is a breakthrough hit with some unique characteristics, there will soon be an overflowing supply of very similar copies and spin-offs on the market. When *Jane Fonda's Workout Book* became a success, a dozen movie stars and sports celebrities quickly followed, all with similar insights on the benefits of eating less and exercising more. Similarly, after the unexpected box-office success of the summer movie *Animal House*, which featured the high jinks of a college fraternity, by January each of the three television networks had introduced a half-hour situation comedy based on fraternity life with similar situations. One of the three even featured many of the cast from the original movie. Given the rush to bring those instant copies to prime time, it is not surprising that none survived past the spring. A number of analysts have remarked that this fad mentality is reminiscent of the manic behavior of lemmings, not shrewd economic judgment. In any case, such industry traditions reinforce the already heavy pressures toward homogeneity.

The economics of common denominators

This chapter began with a brief discussion of Hotelling's classic theory of market behavior. Hotelling (1929) attempted to explain the general tendency of markets toward homogeneity and centrality, and his case studies and approach to modeling have provided inspiration to analysts of these issues for 50 years. It is appropriate at this point to return to that theoretical base to try to put the particular case of information and entertainment markets in perspective.

Hotelling was primarily concerned with the case of how two competing merchants, each trying to maximize profits, determine what price to charge and where to locate their stores. He took as his primary example the existence of Main Street in a small town, with the population of consumers equally distributed around the center of the street (Figure 5.8). He noted that if the first store were located at one end of the street, it would be advantageous for the second store to locate as close to the first as possible, but closer to the center of town, so that the new store would be more convenient than the old for the greatest number of customers. All other things being equal, the first store would then be patronized by only the small number of customers who lived at that edge of town closer to the first store. There would then be an incentive for the first store to undercut the second by moving to a location on the other side, again a bit closer to the center of Main Street. Given these dynamics of store location and the potential for leapfrogging each other down the street, one can quickly see that the stable equilibrium is to have the two stores located next to each other at dead center. In this case, neither has a geographic advantage or an incentive to move. This general phenomenon helps to explain the clustering of automobile dealerships on an "auto row" and other similar commercial clusterings.

As an aside, Hotelling noted that the dynamics for retailers on Main Street may well apply also to political parties. In this case, Main Street represents a policy continuum from extreme left to extreme right. Parties in a two-party system (and in a number of conditions in a multiparty system) have incentives to capture the largest number of voters. This results in centrist pressures on political platforms, much like the retailers locating to maximize their numbers of customers. Hotelling expressed concern that this does not seem to be politically optimal, because it appears to reduce the political alternatives available to the electorate. Our interest here is in pursuing this logic further to examine the diversity of political voices in a commercially oriented public communications system.

An explicit application of this genre of economic theory to television programming was developed by Peter Steiner in 1952 and elaborated in the following years by Rothenberg (1962), Wiles (1963), McGowan (1967), and

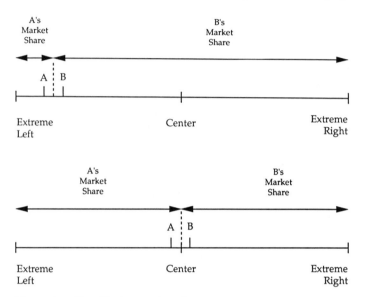

Figure 5.8. Hotelling's centrism theory.

Owen, Beebe, and Manning (1975). Steiner posited a set of viewing groups, each with a preferred type of programming and no interest in any other type. In the simplest case, one might imagine three groups and three networks, as indicated in Table 5.1. Each group in this formulation prefers only one type of programming and will watch nothing else (e.g., Viewing Group 1 will watch only Program Type 1). Each network can provide only one type of programming. Networks have an incentive to maximize income by maintaining the largest possible viewing audience, given audience preferences and competition from other networks. These are, of course, quite limiting assumptions, but they are helpful in illustrating the dynamics of the model. The economists who followed Steiner have explored the implications of relaxing these assumptions.

The first network, of course, opts for Program Type 1, to try to attract the maximum possible viewers: 5,000. The second network reviews the option of offering Type 1 or Type 2 and selects Type 1, because half of the larger (mass-audience) group is larger than all of Viewing Group 2. Let us say the two networks are equally skilled producers and divide the audience evenly, thus securing 2,500 viewers each. The third network considers offering Type 1 or Type 2 programming. If it feels it can do no better than the other two networks, and all three end up sharing the audience equally, it will have 1,667 viewers. Suppose it opts for a sure thing and offers Type 2 programming for a guaranteed audience of 2,000. In that case,

Table 5.1. *Steiner's application of the centrism model to media programming*

Group	Network A	Network B	Network C
Viewing Group 1 (5,000)	Program Type 1 (2,500)	Program Type 1 (2,500)	Not served
Viewing Group 2 (2,000)	Not served	Not served	Program Type 2 (2,000)
Viewing Group 3 (1,000)	Not served	Not served	Not served

as illustrated in Table 5.1, although three networks could satisfy the interests of the full audience perfectly, the smallest audience group remains unserved.

If we return for a moment to the decision of the third network, we can easily see how the outcome could have been even less pluralistic. Let us say the aggressive management of the third network felt they could do a bit better than the competing networks and could win 50% of the total audience or more, perhaps 2,500 to 3,000 viewers. That would represent substantially higher revenues. They might well choose to offer Type 1 programming, the same as the other two networks, and in doing so leaving two significant minority audiences totally unserved by the system. If one thinks about the likely career benefits to broadcasting executives, one can imagine that the pressure is consistently in the direction of making optimistic forecasts about winning large portions of the mass audience, rather than retreating from a possible position of industry leadership to serve smaller minority audience tastes.

Thus, the relationship between the variety of audience interests and what providers will offer in a public communications system depends on two critical variables: the number of networks and the relative sizes of the audience groups. In the current example, if there were 10 networks permitted, and still only three viewing groups, one would imagine certainly that the smallest viewing group would be served. However, if the smallest viable audience size was 1,500 viewers, only four networks would survive, none serving viewing Group 3. It turns out that relaxing the various assumptions of the Steiner model does not significantly reduce its central dynamic toward homogeneity. Allowing them to allocate their programming time to various program types, for example, which would more closely correspond to the real marketplace for television, would reproduce the Steiner dynamics all over again, with each network providing only token representation of minority audience interests.

Advertising markets versus real markets

The basic dynamics of the Hotelling and Steiner models work the same if individuals pay directly for communications services or if such services are supported by advertisers wishing to communicate their commercial messages to the public. There are, however, some additional factors that reinforce homogeneity and the maximization of audience size, and they are due to the culture and economics of the advertising industry itself.

Advertisers pay fees based on audience size, in effect, a fixed sum per viewer or reader. Because the numbers are so critical to the economics of the industries, audience sizes for various media are carefully monitored by independent agencies such as the Audit Bureau of Circulations for newspapers and magazines and Nielsen and Arbitron for broadcasters. The key term in the industry is "cost per thousand audience members." We note from Figure 5.7 that there is an inherent motivation for information producers to gravitate toward serving larger audiences, and the economics of advertising reinforce that incentive, generating an even steeper gradient tilted toward maximally large and homogeneous audiences.

One element is the "Nielsen slope." In the domain of television, advertisers prefer to advertise on the most popular programs. It is a point of status on Madison Avenue to boast to one's client that through special arrangements, time has been purchased on the number-one, highest-rated program. The special arrangements, in effect, represent paying a premium, that is, a higher cost per thousand, to advertise with the more popular programs (Figure 5.9). Thus, for one of a dozen run-of-the-mill situation comedies with average ratings, advertisers typically pay $10 per thousand viewers for the airing of a 30-second commercial. But for the hot show of the season, they are willing to pay a dramatic premium, perhaps $15 per thousand. The reverse is true for public-affairs programs, controversial programs, or simply unappealing programs with typically low ratings, for which advertising is sold at discount prices at the last minute (Poltrack 1983).

Another related element is what is known in advertising as "reach," which refers simply to the percentage of the total audience reached by a single advertisement. "Cume" refers to the accumulated size of the total audience reached by a series of ads. Executives in the industry gossip and strategize about reach and cume tirelessly. It is the essence of their business.

As with most phenomena of this sort, there are declining returns to scale.

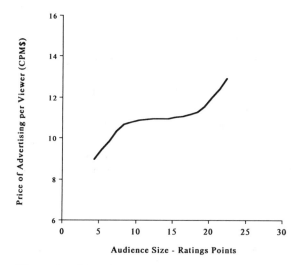

Figure 5.9. The Nielsen slope. (Source: CBS, Inc.)

One might reach 30% of the desired audience of young homemakers with the first ad, but only 5% more with the second ad, and so on, such that the cume advances by only a fraction of 1% with each additional and equally expensive ad placement. Repeated viewings of the same commercial are likely to be of limited value, especially after two or three exposures; so there is a premium on a large reach with the initial exposure. This works out quite well for the television networks, for television is the only advertising medium that regularly reaches tens of millions of viewers. To reach an audience of similar size with newspapers would require the substantial additional transactions costs of contracting with hundreds of urban dailies, rather than just three television networks. To establish a substantial reach by combining ads in a variety of special-interest magazines would be nearly impossible to accomplish or to calculate, because of complex patterns of overlapping readerships and extremely high transactions costs. Special-interest publications, accordingly, tend to rely most heavily on those special-market vendors who are not as interested in the fundamentals of reach and cume (Naples 1979).

Finally, as might well be expected, advertisers are disinclined to offend potential customers, and so they shy away from controversial or potentially offensive programming. Thus, when the topic of abortion was addressed in a popular prime-time series, most advertisers shied away; there would be risk and no obvious advantage in placing ads there. In that particular case, for example, conservative citizens' groups that had heard about the program's content in advance vowed to publicize the issue and boycott the products of any advertiser associated with the program.

The economics of the new media

Thus far in this chapter, particular emphasis has been placed on the economics of the current media, in an attempt to understand the likely constraints that will be faced by the new media. What lessons can we draw from the current media economics to predict the levels of diversity and pluralism in the evolving public communications system?

Our fundamental conclusion is that the cultural and political environment for the average citizen will indeed be more pluralistic and diverse, but only modestly so. There are two caveats. First, such a prediction assumes that the nature of mass tastes and the low salience of complex political issues for the average citizen will remain the same. Second, it is assumed that the basic institutional structure of decision making and control over the public communications system in the United States will continue to be a predominantly commercial capitalist enterprise.

Both premises should seem reasonable. The general character of mass-audience media and mass tastes has demonstrated remarkable consistency from the development of the printing press through the sophisticated broadcast technologies. At each turning point, from the development of telegraphy to the inexpensive paperback book, those who predicted a cultural renaissance were disappointed. Furthermore, given the central political role and economic resources of the media conglomerates, coupled with a general public satisfaction with media performance, a major structural overhaul of public communications in the United States is rather unlikely (Comstock et al. 1978).

Nonetheless, there is room for gradual change. For those particularly disappointed with these pessimistic observations, the question might well be redefined in normative terms. The most effective strategy for reform of the system is to work at the margin with new technologies to try to nurture and broaden public tastes with innovative cultural formats and designs. Furthermore, if there is to be fundamental change in the diversity of content in the marketplace, structural rather than simply technological change will be required. A deregulated commercial system would not suddenly demonstrate a new enthusiasm for serving minority audiences. If serving such audiences is judged as a worthy goal, then new incentives from foundations, government institutions, or other sources will be necessary for the mix of the content and technology to be expanded.

Returning to the underlying properties of the new media, how might we expect each to contribute to a rich and responsive environment of public communications? The main points are summarized in Figure 5.10. In light of our study of the constraints of audience psychology and media economics, we can now group the nine elements of technological push in terms of four fundamental impacts.

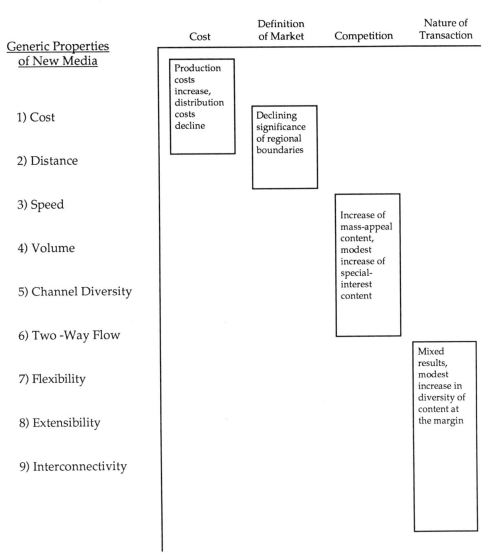

Figure 5.10. Impact of the new media on political and cultural diversity.

The cost of communication

What we have discovered in the area of cost is a double-edged sword. The costs of transmitting information from one point to another are indeed declining. That in itself is an important and laudable outcome. It encourages and enables those who may want to communicate with each other or with a social or cultural group or with a mass audience. The other edge of the sword is that the increased demand to communicate raises both production costs and competition for attention. In earlier days, the public hunger for information and ideas was relatively underserved by one-room schoolhouses, infrequent public debates on the commons, or even discussions around the cracker barrel at the general store. In such an environment, a crudely printed pamphlet such as Thomas Paine's *Common Sense* might well catch the public fancy and influence the direction of public debate.

In the new media age, the ante has been raised. A crudely printed pamphlet would be overmatched if pitted against a sophisticated television ad with a prominent spokesperson, background music, dramatic graphics, and imagery prepared at a cost of hundreds of thousands of dollars for, say, a major oil company. In the early days of the motion-picture industry and the recording industry, entrepreneurs with limited technical expertise produced major works literally in garages and backyards with a few colleagues and friends. Video production and editing have become rather sophisticated enterprises calling on the professional expertise of hundreds of specialists, the most talented of which are in great demand and thus charge appropriate rates for their services. Thomas Paine's pamphlet required an author, a printer, a printer's assistant, and several hundred dollars worth of equipment. An equivalent public-affairs program for television would require the contributions of several hundred highly trained professionals and between a half a million and several million dollars of capital.

Such prohibitive entry barriers are not necessarily characteristic of the print domain. One can imagine a young Thomas Paine at his computer terminal pouring his heart into an essay to be transmitted to all who might care to read it via an inexpensive digital communications network. In such a case, both production and access to transmission require capital measured in tens of dollars rather than millions of dollars. But here the problem of competition for public attention plays a constraining role. It is again a catch–22. Our young Mr. Paine is now competing not only with thousands of others at their terminals with equally urgent concerns to broadcast on the network but also with the vividly produced and promoted mass-audience media competing at an even more feverish pitch for the eye and ear of the average citizen.

The definition of the marketplace for communications

Regional boundaries will play a decreasing role in the definition of the communications marketplace. This is a clear-cut result of the declining costs of communications over long distances, and it may prove to be the technological push least constrained by factors of psychology and economics. In a frontier town in the American West, one can imagine that the publisher of the local paper played a particularly important role in providing information on what was happening back on the East Coast and in the world at large. The telegraph was a prohibitively expensive means of communications for general information. The mails were slow and unreliable. One might well read newspapers, books, and magazines from around the country or from Europe, but at a delay of weeks, months, and years. So the local editor did not have a complete monopoly in controlling the flow of public communications, but certainly much more control in the short run. Furthermore, the nature of economics and local government meant that much of what affected one's life took place nearby. Politics and culture were highly regionalized. The media system reinforced that.

Much has changed since the nineteenth century. In 1922, in an analysis of public awareness of events overseas, Lippmann marveled at the tensions between the complex events happening at a distance and the few fragments of information available to the average citizen who had to judge and evaluate them. That trend continues. National and international newspapers can be easily provided, electronically or otherwise, if there is a demand and a viable basis of direct-payment or advertising support. Satellites, optical fiber, and coaxial cable can bring to American audiences programming originally developed for Europe or Asia. As the production costs are covered by the country or region of origin, the marginal cost is only that required for transmission. Furthermore, transmission costs are low and continue to decrease.

If new local channels on cable television providing coverage of town meetings and the local high-school sports teams, suburban community weekly newspapers, and glossy metropolitan monthly magazines each find a niche in the media mix, that does not signal a dramatic rebirth of local concerns and neighborhood culture. It simply shows that distance is no longer a significant hurdle in communications and that the mix of media and coverage of neighborhood, regional, national, and international events will more closely reflect levels of interest rather than levels of availability.

Competition in public communications

As the technical constraints fall away, there will be more communications. The number of channels and the speed and capacity of each will continue to rise. The limiting factor is the attention span of the public at large. A clear conclusion, however, is that an increased diversity of channels will not lead inexorably to an increased diversity of available communications content. There will be an increase in the number of channels providing mass-appeal content – as before, primarily action and comedy entertainment, sports, and brief news headlines. So for those who have discriminating preferences for particular old Hollywood movies, soap operas, or mystery novels, the convenience of easy availability will be a distinct pleasure. With some irony, we conclude that the most prominent result of an expanded communications capacity will be intensified competition for mass-audience tastes.

At the margin, there will also be modest improvement in the availability of special-interest materials. Because of unchanging economic constraints, media supported primarily by advertising will not expand significantly into serving special-interest audiences. For small but highly motivated audiences, however, who care deeply about a particular set of political issues or a cultural form and who are willing to pay their proportionate share of the production costs directly, there will be channels of communication available. Video-cassettes, and later a greatly expanded public digital network, will be able to provide extremely inexpensive means of transmission. The limiting factors are audience interest and awareness in an increasingly competitive mass-audience marketplace.

The nature of the communications transaction

Technological developments, particularly the increasing interconnectivity and two-way properties of public communications, will have two effects on the way in which individuals access the communications marketplace. First, direct-payment transactions for communications between the audience and the producer will be facilitated. Most public communications in the United States currently are heavily subsidized by advertising. Thus, television is, by all appearances, a free good. Subscribers pay only 20% of the production and distribution costs for the newspapers they read. Because advertising support provides less income to the producer than will most forms of audience direct payment, producers will be motivated to explore and promote new ways of selling existing content directly and to develop new forms and formats that audiences are less accustomed to getting for free or for less than they cost to produce.

Second, information will be available in smaller units, less often bundled together as tends to be case for the production of magazines, newspapers, and television programs. Electronic filtering, storage, editing, and searching will allow those members of the audience who care to make the effort increased ability to edit their own packages of news and information. In the past, because of the historical constraints of printing and the spectrum constraints on broadcasting, and because of the premium in advertiser-supported media on maximally large mass audiences, the diversity of public interest, such as it is, was met by repackaging and reintegrating information and entertainment into recognizable publishing units, from magazines and encyclopedias to movie studios and television networks. Increasingly one will be able to order and pay for only the episode, the recipe, the news story, or the encyclopedia article one desires.

Although such technical potential sounds as though it should revolutionize public communications, it will not. People will continue to rely on the editorial judgment of established news media to relay what are deemed to be the significant headlines of world and national news. Packaging, formatting, filtering, and interpreting complex flows of information represent value-added components of public communications. In a more competitive, complex, and intense communications environment, that value-added component will be equally important to the individual citizen, if not more so.

6

The future of the mass audience

What are we to make of this technological juggernaut of the new media? On the one hand, we have been warned that these technologies pose an ominous threat to privacy and provide a tempting tool for the manipulation of a helpless mass public. On the other, we have heard of unprecedented opportunities for electronic participation, education, and communication. Lest the reader grow weary of this polarity or become suspicious that a pair of straw men lurk in the background of this concluding chapter, it may be appropriate to review how such a polarization of views arose in the first place and how we ought to respond to it.

First, such a polarity is a predictable outcome of the efforts of authors to attract attention to their views. In making the case that the structure and technology of communications are important to society, analysts tend to slide into pro or con views emphasizing threat or opportunity. Second, there is a natural tension between those who believe they stand to lose and those who expect to benefit from the developments in new, competing media. The most articulate champions of new media usually are investors and salesmen, who stand to profit directly. Their opposites, the Luddites, take their name from the frustrated workers of the early industrial revolution who calculated, quite correctly, that the new machines would threaten their traditional livelihood. Indeed, a number of forceful and sophisticated critiques of the new media have been written by those who continue to work for the old (Greenberger 1985; Noam 1985). Third, such contrapuntal worldviews frequently are tied to the prospect of disruptive and dramatic social change. The two sides in such debates concur that life will be very different. Change is more interesting that continuity. Tönnies predicted that the new technologies would lead to new forms of social organization, emphasizing market rather than personal relationships. Marx argued that history marches inevitably and irreversibly from capitalism to socialism. Weber characterized the modern age as moving toward rationalized bureaucratic social organization. It would be counter-intuitive to conclude that fundamental changes in the technology of com-

164

munications would not have equally fundamental effects on the flow of public information. But that, in large measure, is what the evidence indicates.

The shift to reliance on new means of communication will be evolutionary rather than revolutionary. The anticipated impacts of the new media are neither inevitable nor self-evident. It is not that our analysis leads to a prediction of no effects or no change. Far from it. Perhaps the appropriate analogy is a tug-of-war: On the two ends of a sturdy rope are powerful forces in tension. When new technologies conducive to increasingly diverse and smaller-scale mass communications emerge, commercial market forces and deeply ingrained media habits pull back hard in the other direction. If the rope moves only slowly in one direction or another, that should not be mistaken for evidence that the forces involved are not strong and significant.

But there is a further point. This process of change, although infused with conflicting vested political and economic interests, is still subject to our collective control. The key to controlling it is to understand the nature of these forces in tension. We stand at a historic threshold. A new electronic infrastructure is about to be built. How it is to be designed and used should be the subject of a self-conscious inquiry. Moving away from the mystique of historical inevitability and determinism can only be a step in the right direction.

Theories of technological effects

Some say that it is foolhardy to try to predict how the new technologies of communications will take shape, let alone to speculate on their social and political impacts. But the analysis here points to a clear-cut bottom line. The properties of digital electronics are convergent; they facilitate human calculations and communications. Getting a message to a large audience or to a select few will be cheaper and easier, in fact, dramatically so.

Given this conclusion about technological properties, how do we derive such a modest prediction about technological impacts? The answer is that although mediated political and cultural communications will change, the motivation to communicate will not. Communications are already remarkably inexpensive and convenient. It costs but a few dollars to make several telephone calls, write letters, or photocopy a newsletter. One can communicate with one's fellow citizens if moved to, but few are so moved. If there is an issue of great public concern, there are plentiful opportunities for the modern Thomas Paine to try to raise the consciousness of his fellow citizens. But such individuals are rare. Equally important, most citizens are not inclined to pay much attention (Neuman 1986).

Perhaps the lesson of Mancur Olson's analysis of the costs and benefits of direct participation in politics is most apt (Olson 1965): Who will participate in politics and how much effort they will put into it will depend on what they expect to get out of it. There is an informal but nonetheless rational set of ongoing calculations for individuals concerning whether or not political participation (like other forms of public activity) is worth the effort (Downs 1957). These insights have been reinforced by subsequent research, including that of Gamson (1975) and DeNardo (1985) on protest behavior and the work of Verba and his colleagues on political participation and voting (Verba and Nie 1972; Schlozman and Verba 1979). If many citizens are ill-informed, misinformed, or ambivalent about their civic duties, it is not because the price of a newspaper is too high or because television news is scheduled at an inconvenient time. Such public attitudes and behaviors are not the beginning of a new and ominous trend; they are political constants, the backdrop against which all new technologies are introduced.

Christopher Arterton (1987), in a study parallel to this, examined 20 demonstration projects in which new communications technologies were used to facilitate public participation in policy-making. The enthusiasm and energy, as well as the technical resources, invested in those diverse projects were impressive. Congressmen participated in computer conferences with their constituents; community groups were brought together by two-way cable; satellite technology connected remote villages; electronic town meetings included debates, polls, and plebiscites. The findings were the same in almost every case: The enthusiastic initiators of those projects embraced the new technological means to a idealistically democratic end. Sometimes, with great effort, they succeeded in attracting public attention and stimulating thought, debate, and participation. Sometimes, despite the considerable talents and resources of the organizers, the inertia of a semiattentive political process seemed unaffected. In every case but one, however, as soon as the demonstration project was completed, the initiative was dropped. Reports were written up, and people moved on to other projects. The technologies were dismantled or sat idle. The one activity that did continue under its own power involved a mayor and community groups that had a taste and a talent for using community cable television for public discussion. The mayor believed, probably correctly so, that there were political benefits from the activity, and she was pleased to continue it. Therein lies the key to the communications "revolution": It is less the push of the new media than the pull of the political cultures that may choose to use these technologies.

Pluralist versus mass society

A central question runs through this book and is reflected in its title: whether or not the proliferation of new communications channels will lead to fragmentation of the mass audience. Over the past 30 years, a number of mass-audience magazines have gone into decline and apparently been replaced by smaller, special-interest publications. Cable television channels have sprung up, providing specialized information for different interest and ethnic groups. The share of the viewing audience captured by the three national networks has declined dramatically. Economic pressures have raised the possibility that the networks may have to cut back on national news coverage. As a result, concern has arisen that the common cultural and political identity of Americans, traditionally reinforced by the mass media, may be eroding.

My approach to addressing this matter has been to identify it not as a new issue but rather as a continuing and central problematic of political communications. The key issue is that of balance: balance between the center and the periphery, between different interest factions, between competing elites, between an efficient and effective central authority and the conflicting demands of the broader electorate.

My strategy has been to draw on two theoretical traditions that emerged at the close of World War II – mass society theory and communications/development theory – and explore whether or not the questions they raise can provide a common framework for analysis. Mass society theory warned that an overly strong central authority in control of the communications media could debilitate local authority and participation. Communications/development theory pointed out the appropriately central role of the media in defining and maintaining a sense of national identity and collective interest.

The two traditions converge in their emphasis on two concepts: community and pluralism. A national identity is not the sum of a series of rational calculations of individual self-interest. A sense of community and belonging meets fundamental human needs that transcend self-interest calculations. It is, after all, somewhat difficult to imagine people engaging in wartime heroics or political mass movements, or even mass participation in elections, simply on the basis of hardheaded cost–benefit calculations.

Some national identities and political cultures emphasize obedience to authority and homogeneity. Others emphasize individual initiative and pluralism. The key to the future of the mass audience lies in the subtle interplay of cultural and political norms and the structures of the media that convey them. What might we expect from the interaction between the new media and the American political culture?

There are, as outlined earlier, three sets of factors: (1) the character of the technology, (2) the mass psychology of habitual audience behavior, and (3) the political economy of the communications industries. Some factors are more critical than others, and some are more amenable to change. Some mechanisms operate at the aggregate level, and others at the level of individual behavior; so it is difficult simply to add them together. But for the purposes of overview, it may be helpful to array the factors we have analyzed in terms of the general direction of the expected effects. In doing so, we are led to two predictions: a clear increase in communications volume, but not a corresponding increase in communications diversity.

These patterns are summarized in Figures 6.1 and 6.2. Figure 6.1 outlines the forces that tend to increase the volume of public communications. Virtually all of the technological factors have at least some component that is weighted toward greater communications volume. In the case of two-way interactive communications and the citizen's increased ability to electronically filter and scan the flow of information, it is not yet clear whether or not large segments of the public will exercise that control to decrease their exposure to news and public information. That is an important question for further research. The analysis of media psychology in Chapter 3 indicates, so far at least, a hearty appetite for the mass media, limited only by the simple constraint of available time. Exposure to broadcast media continues to climb, and the print media and even theatrical motion pictures appear to have held their own. The pattern of low-salience exposure means that people are not always highly attentive, but that leads to an increase rather than a decrease in overall communications volume. And finally, despite the constraints of market competition, the movement toward deregulation and the continuing profitability of the industry lead to an increased communications volume.

But increased volume, as we have noted, does not guarantee increased diversity. In fact, unless significant changes in the cultural norms or economics of mass communications evolve, the forces pushing in the direction of communications homogeneity appear to be as strong as ever. Figure 6.2 summarizes the technological effects. They would appear to be about evenly balanced in terms of homogeneity of content. Both media habits and media economics, however, continue to involve strong incentives toward common-denominator mass-audience content. These structures and incentives are subject to change, but the pressure for change is not necessarily evident in the character of digital electronics.

We might turn at this point to the equilibrium model introduced in Chapter 1. If mass society theory and communications/development theory settle on a common ideal of community and national identity, balanced against political and cultural pluralism, how is such an ideal to be achieved? Figure 6.3 reproduces the basic dimensions of the equilibrium model, but now from the point of view of the individual citizen, rather than the working of the political system as a whole. It emphasizes not just what is made available to the individual, but how individual choices in an open marketplace of information and media, in turn, can influence the direction of the market. Individuals do develop a sense of national identity and of civic duty. The mass media, as well as family and local institutions, are part of that process. Most individuals want to have a sense that they know what is going on in the world

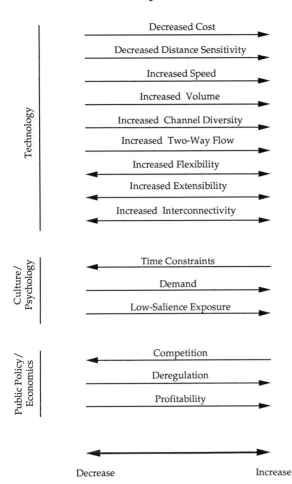

Figure 6.1. Pressures on communications volume.

around them. Few are so alienated as to seek isolation from this flow of public information. Given the electronic ability to cut themselves off from public life, to bury themselves in highly specialized hobbies or escapist entertainment, some will exercise it, but probably no more than those who have done so before perhaps by means of science-fiction novels or stamp collecting.

There is ample evidence that people are distrustful of overly centralized media. Studies of the domestic propaganda machine in Nazi Germany, as well as media behavior in modern totalitarian regimes, indicate that, on the whole, people seek out confirming information from other sources. When information ministries routinely exaggerate, people learn to discount the

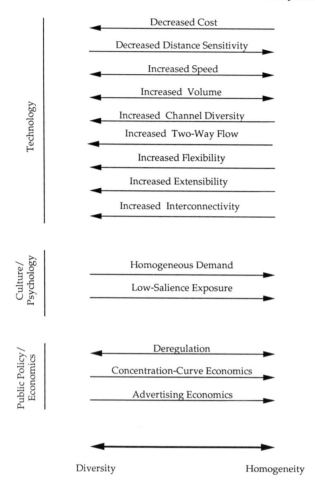

Figure 6.2. Pressures on communications homogeneity.

reports they are fed. Furthermore, when the hubbub of conflicting voices gets to be extreme, people retreat and seek solace in the common norms of national identity.

Thus, in terms of Figure 6.3, we might expect the center of gravity to move upward, toward higher levels of communications volume. But unless we have an emergence of political forces as yet unforeseen that are entirely independent of the technological developments, the horizontal equilibrium will remain in balance.

When Gutenberg developed his printing press in the 1450s, he began a

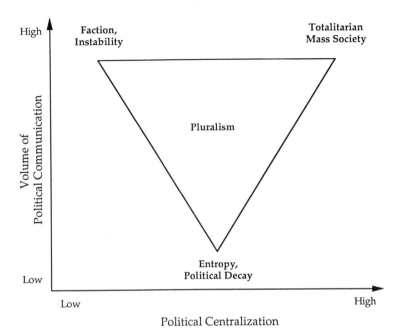

Figure 6.3. The equilibrium model revisited.

complex historical process that enhanced the ability of humans to communicate with each other across space and time. That process is still under way. Gutenberg, it can be presumed, had little trouble in deciding what book to print. It would be the Bible, of course. Much has changed as we stand on the threshold of the third millennium. The diversity of information available to us has increased manyfold. The satellite and optical fiber allow us to communicate text, voice, or moving images over thousands of miles almost effortlessly. One can imagine Gutenberg suddenly transported to our age and puzzling over the diversity of communications media at hand: People have so many books and other media available to them, he muses. What single book is most often found nowadays in the American home? It is the Bible, of course. Sometimes history moves at less than a revolutionary pace.

The critical epoch

Although we have seen that the pressures of the new communications technologies are unlikely to bring a revolution in national politics, we are not led by the foregoing analysis to conclude that these new developments will be without effects. In fact, they offer intriguing opportunities for experimentation.

The bulk of the data and research reported here draws on the recent American experience with publishing and cable and broadcast television. The two central themes are the nature of the media habit of the mass audience and the incentives of the commercial marketplace for the media elite. The two, in interaction, indicate a pattern of common-denominator and politically centrist mass communications. The new media will not change this, in the main. But what about changes at the margins?

The media habit is subject to gradual change. We have a habit of watching television passively that is, in part, a product of the television technology that evolved in the 1940s. As the number of channels grows and the ability to interact with them expands, new opportunities will arise. Most new experiments, as Arterton has demonstrated, will likely fail. But if the norms and expectations of public communications begin to change at the margin, we would be remiss not to follow these issues closely.

The odd fit, at this historical epoch, concerns the market economics of commercially supported mass communications. Our media have valuable qualities, but the fundamental conservatism of advertiser-supported media limits experimentation. If it takes a decade for the new, pluralistic, niche markets for cultural and political communications to evolve and define themselves, which is not an unreasonable expectation, we shall find few entrepreneurs willing to take the losses necessary to see the decade through. The commercial media need not be replaced or constrained, but they could be complemented by a diversity of administrative structures to match the diversity of new technological potentials.

The evolution of public broadcasting out of a virtually moribund system of educational broadcasting in 1967 represented an exciting step forward. Public broadcasting continues to counterprogram to complement the commercial broadcasting entities. At this point we need to assess where the new media are and where they are headed in the commercial sphere, in order to see if the time may have come again to add new structures and new voices as an experiment in testing the potential of the new media.

Narrowcast media

We have gotten used to the mass character of the mass media: newspapers with circulations in the tens of thousands, national magazines with hundreds of thousands of subscribers, and, of course, network television audiences in the tens of millions. New digital network technologies, however, will open up whole new domains of special-interest and special-purpose communications, narrowcasting rather than broadcasting. The outlook for a vibrant and dynamic cultural and political life in the United States is indeed positive.

Political theorists frequently remark on the importance of "issue publics," the virtual communities of like-minded individuals within a metropolitan area or around the country who will band together and speak out spontaneously in response to a public concern or event – an issue of religious or moral concern, or issues of self-interest among veterans, older citizens, or Hispanic-Americans. That was the essence of the vigorous citizen-based democracy that so impressed Alexis de Tocqueville when he toured the United States in the 1830s and wrote his classic *Democracy in America* (1856). What made that possible then was an extensive communications network within the small village. What may make it possible in the future for an urbanized, postindustrial society will be the rebirth of minimedia, the electronic soapbox, Thomas Paine on a computer network. We are seeing some evidence of that already.

Until recently, the natural separation between the telephone network and the broadcast networks led to a dichotomous choice between interpersonal communications or microcommunications and traditional mass communications. User-controlled, spontaneous, small-group communications, mixtures of a newsletter and a town meeting, create a new alternative: minicommunication. Figures I.1 and I.2 in the Introduction, for example, illustrate this exciting new potential of the advanced network. Minicommunication is not intended to replace interpersonal communications or put national news media out of business; it will supplement them both. Like interstate commerce and the postal system, it is a public good worth fostering.

Transactional services

There is another capacity of an advanced network that is just now being explored: transactional services. We are all familiar with the primitive forms of telephone transactions for the residential customer: We see a product advertised on late-night television and order it by telephone with a credit card, or perhaps order an item from a direct-mail catalog by touch-tone telephone. Sometimes that proves to be convenient and productive, and sometimes not. The irony of these primitive versions of transactional services is that they carry with them all of the limiting and negative features of the advertising-based mass media; that is, all the information at hand is supplied by the seller. One sees the advertising stimulus and has only the options to resist or respond. What intelligent, two-way systems will permit is instantaneous inquiry for other information resources by the consumer while the transaction is in process: Is the firm reliable? Is the product well designed? What are the ecological effects of using this product? Is it offered elsewhere at a lower price? These may seem like minor issues, and with respect to a single purchase they may well be. But blurring the distinction between a broadcast information network, with its ads and newscasts, and an electronic marketplace, where individuals can register their requests for a particular bundle of goods, may well have significant effects on how the market for things and the market for ideas operate. The integrated network will allow for more interconnection between the two markets, and that is likely to have beneficial effects.

In an earlier study (Neuman 1986), I described typical voters who had limited interest in and knowledge of politics, but who for reasons of good intentions and some social pressure found themselves in a voting booth: For whom should one vote? The names are vaguely familiar, but which one is which? I describe such voters as staring at their shoes in vain hope of some clue. Preceding any election there are debates, speeches, pamphlets, and numerous media reports and analyses of positions on the issues and candidate competencies, and from such a hubbub one may derive a vague sense of who the candidates are and who may best serve one's individual interests and those of the polity at large. But it is not easy. Well-paid media specialists in political campaigning continue to embellish the views and capacities of the candidate paying their bill, and to distort the views of the opponent.

Economists examining such a political marketplace might describe its operation as suboptimal. What would the economists and public-choice theorists suggest? Allow each consumer/voter to determine what criteria are of particular relevance to them. Allow them to gather information on those criteria from trusted independent sources. Allow them to gather this information at the time they need it, when a decision must be made.

The evolving integrated network will make it easier for information markets and product markets to approach such an ideal. It will take time, because cultural expectations and technical capacities interact in delicate chemistry. Some citizens will decline to take advantage of all the information resources offered to them, as do a great many people today. But even if only a few people do, imagine the consequences.

Notes

Introduction

1. One finds resurgent interest in these issues among the European left (Enzenberger 1974; Habermas 1989), as well as in mainstream American political theory (Mansbridge 1983; Barber 1984; Abramson, Arterton, and Orren 1988) and history (Czitrom 1982; Kielbowicz 1989).
2. Others, ranging from the academic to the popular treatments, have developed much longer and more comprehensive compendia of causes, effects, and thresholds. This list is drawn primarily from Bell (1973, 1979), Huntington (1974), Inglehart (1977), Piore and Sabel (1984), Beniger (1986), and Zuboff (1988).
3. The term "new media," as is customary in this literature, will be used more or less interchangeably with other terms for the evolving integrated network of digital communications technologies. In this context, the term may be a little misleading, because the plural may be taken to imply a multiplicity of separate and independent technologies. I shall argue shortly that what is truly unique about these digital systems is their capacity for integration and interconnection.
4. These potential effects will be addressed in turn in the sections ahead. For the record, a few of the key analyses of each in the literature are as follows: (1) information overload: Lipowski (1971), Blumler (1980). (2) decline of American political parties: Burnham (1982), Ranney (1983). (3) narrowcasting: Pool (1973), Abramson et al. (1988). (4) interactivity: Tydeman et al. (1982), Gagnon (1990). (5) privacy issues: Wicklein (1981), Yurow (1980). (6) small media: Pool (1973), Compaine (1988). (7) decline of advertising-based media: Vogel (1986), Collins, Garnham, and Locksley (1988). (8) globalization of communications: Dizard (1989), Tehranian (1990). (9) growth of executive-branch power: Grossman and Kumar (1984), Kernell (1986). (10) American cultural hegemony: Tunstall (1977), Fisher (1987). (11) pace of communications: Arterton (1987), Czitrom (1982). (12) pace of transactions: Keen (1988), Zuboff (1988). (13) information underclass: Mosco (1982), Barber (1984). (14) new class of communications technocrats: Huntington (1974), Bagdikian (1983). (15) teledemocracy: Meadow (1985), Arterton (1987).
5. An exception would be the community organizer and political activist frustrated by inability to get the attention of potential recruits because of competition from the glossy and dramatic commercial media (Schiller 1973).
6. Broadcast telephony is a most interesting outgrowth of digital telephone switching technology that makes it possible for an individual to set up a prearranged tele-

175

phone list, such as the members of a women's consciousness-raising group or a Little League baseball team, and call a special number that will record a message and then forward it on to all the members of the group automatically. If one of the numbers does not answer, the system will recall at a later time.

7. Technically speaking, "monism" refers to the philosophical school that posits that all matter is made of a single element. The term is used here in its more generic sense, as in Merton (1975).

8. "Balance theory" also has a more specific connotation in the study of social psychology and attitude change and is associated with the work of Heider and Festinger. It is used here, in contrast, in its generic sense. Recently, scholars in this tradition have been drawing on Long's concept (1958) of the ecology of games as a tool for the analysis of multilevel social phenomena. Long's work is especially enlightening because, in his vocabulary, one would understand a monist analysis as a focused study of one of many ongoing political or economic "games" under way at a particular historical period.

9. In Western circles, of course. Or, if one prefers, the appropriate parallel in the ethos of the left would be a "counterrevolutionary" or a "revisionist." It is not the stuff of casual conversation in either case.

10. The term is, as far as I know, a neologism. It is akin to the notion of meta-analysis developed by Glass and his colleagues (1981). But their approach to systematic assessment of empirical findings is much more quantitative and narrowly focused in its effort. Broadly focused meta-analytic studies are quite common in the social sciences, but for some reason the tradition lacks a methodological self-consciousness.

Chapter 1. Two theories of the communications revolution

1. Attentive readers may suspect a familiar tactic in such an approach. On examining the two extremes, we find that the truth of the matter appears to lie somewhere in between. But an examination of the normative polar views of evolving communications technology is hardly a scholarly diversion. As the argument unfolds, this polarization will prove to be central to the evolution of social theory in this field. When men and women invest significant energies in examining these issues, usually there is a strong driver of hope or of apprehension. That is probably as true in the academic literature as in the popular domain. It is endemic. As with the tradition of the ancient prophets who foresaw salvation or damnation, it is difficult to gather a crowd with a message of forces in tension and a search for equilibrium.

2. The technology of Orwell's Oceania plays a particularly important role in reinforcing its ideology. The telescreen, of course, carries only one channel, centrally controlled and totally political in its content. It is constant and pervasive. The telescreens are everywhere: every room, the halls, even the bathrooms. The novel's hero, Winston Smith, struggles to control his own thoughts against the tide of propaganda. The technological key, fittingly, comes from the preceding historical epoch. Smith finds a diary and a pen in an antique shop and takes to writing down his ideas on paper, an act punishable by death; ordinarily there are no pens and paper available to individuals. One is supposed to use a speak-write, a centrally controlled and monitored device that transcribes speech. When a document is to be thrown out, it is inserted into one of the many memory holes, slits in the wall leading to a central destruction chamber from which no

document can ever be retrieved. Smith is able to write in his diary only because of the unusual circumstance that his apartment has a small alcove out of view of the telescreen.

A special irony in *1984* was Orwell's choice of a bureaucratic career for his hero. Smith works at the Ministry of Truth, where he is assigned to edit old newspapers. His job is to correct prior statements and predictions of Big Brother so that all such statements will correspond with unfolding events. He uses the language Newspeak, as do all citizens. It is a controlled language that allows authorities to outlaw selected words and to change the meanings of others at will. Among the now-famous fundamental political slogans of Newspeak are "War is Peace," "Freedom is Slavery," and "Ignorance is Strength." Orwell had drawn on the insights of such linguistic scholars as Benjamin Whorf and Edward Sapir regarding the power of language to shape our understanding of the world around us (Pool and Grofman 1984). He was so convinced of the importance of control over language in the media that over the strong objections of his publisher he insisted on including an appendix to his novel on the principles of Newspeak and its subtle powers (Steinhoff 1975).

3. Unfortunately, such limited success has not discouraged other regimes from continuing to try to follow the theories of Lenin and Goebbels in turning every communications medium to the service of the central government. One perhaps thinks first of the spectacular attempt, and equally spectacular failure, of the Cultural Revolution in China to remake the consciousness of the citizenry. Similar efforts were undertaken by Pol Pot in Cambodia. Attempts quite different in direction, but of similar means, characterize the ayatollah Khomeini's regime in Iran and the ruling elite of South Africa.

4. For a development of the argument that mass communications theory is closely linked to sociological theory, see Alexander (1982), McQuail (1987), and De Fleur and Ball-Rokeach (1988).

5. It turns out, according to the ever-precise computer records, that *Captain Lust* did indeed attract a relatively large home viewing audience of paying customers, some 10,655 households. The jury found the movie exhibitors not guilty. After the trial was over, reporters found the words "contemporary community standards" written on the blackboard in the jury room (Burnham 1983, 247).

6. Huntington and Dominguez have a somewhat more jaded assessment of the enthusiasms of this generation of social scientists. As they put it, "after World War II, scholarship followed the flag into the Cold War" (1975, 1).

7. A similar model has been developed by Majid Tehranian in his *Technologies of Power* (1990).

Chapter 2. The logic of electronic integration

1. Some notable exceptions and excellent sources include the following: Abramson et al. (1988), Arterton (1987), Compaine (1988), Dertouzos and Moses (1979), Dizard (1989), Dutton, Blumler, and Krammer (1987), Nora and Minc (1980), Rice (1984), Nora and Minc (1980), Ferguson (1986, 1990), Pool (1983b), McQuail and Siune (1986), Robinson (1978), Smith (1980), Tehranian (1990), and Williams (1982). The two most widely read popular books that review these issues are by Naisbitt (1982) and Toffler (1980).

2. My notion of an underlying logic in digital electronic communications has evolved over a period of years, and I would like to acknowledge several scholarly sources and inspirations. Special acknowledgment is due to Professor Gary Orren and his

associate, Stephen Bates, of Harvard University, who developed the idea of generic properties of the new media and convinced me of the importance of that approach. Their list of six properties, especially the key concept (to me) of expanded user control (Abramson et al. 1988, 4–5), has clearly influenced my thinking. One particular difference between the Orren-Bates model and the approach taken here is that their concepts blur the properties of the technologies and their social effects, whereas I have attempted to keep them analytically separated. Somewhat more recently I have discovered that a similar effort to identify key properties that span the new media technologies had been undertaken by Professor Don Dillman (1985) of Washington State University. My focus on the phenomena of integration and networks has been greatly influenced by my colleagues at the Massachusetts Institute of Technology, particularly Charles Jonscher, Marvin Sirbu, and Richard Solomon.

3. The battle in computerized cryptography between those who code their messages and those who try to decode them makes an interesting story, but it lies outside the scope of this book; see Burnham (1983).

Chapter 5. The political economy of the mass media

1. Churchill was reported to have remarked that democracy was the worst form of government, except for all the others so far known to man.

2. These are useful tools because they allow the analyst to summarize the level of concentration in a single number, without constant recourse to the full Lorenz curve itself. Scherer (1980) summarizes the calculations and the logic underlying each.

References

Abel, Elie, ed. 1981. *What's News: The Media in American Society*. San Francisco: Institute for Contemporary Studies.

Abler, Ronald. 1977. "The Telephone and the Evolution of the American Metropolitan System," in Ithiel de Sola Pool, ed., *The Social Impact of the Telephone*, pp. 318–41. Cambridge, MA: MIT Press.

Abramson, Jeffrey B., F. Christopher Arterton, and Gary R. Orren. 1988. *The Electronic Commonwealth: The Impact of New Media Technologies on Democratic Politics*. New York: Basic Books.

Alexander, Jeffrey. 1982. "The Mass News Media in Systematic, Historical and Comparative Perspective," in Elihu Katz and Tamas Szecsko, eds., *Mass Media and Social Change*, pp. 17–52. Newbury Park, CA: Sage.

    ed. 1985. *Neofunctionalism*. Newbury Park, CA: Sage.

Alford, Robert R., and Roger Friedland. 1985. *Powers of Theory: Capitalism, the State and Democracy*. Cambridge University Press.

Almond, Gabriel A. 1990. "The Development of Political Development," in Gabriel A. Almond, ed., *A Discipline Divided: Schools and Sects in Political Science*, pp. 219–62. Newbury Park, CA: Sage.

Almond, Gabriel, and Sidney Verba. 1965. *Civic Culture*. Boston: Little, Brown.

Anania, Loretta. 1989. "The Politics of Integration: Telecommunications Planning in the Information Societies." Ph.D. dissertation, Massachusetts Institute of Technology.

Anderson, Daniel R., and E. P. Lorch. 1983. "Looking at Television," in James Bryant and Daniel R. Anderson, eds., *Children's Understanding of Television*, pp. 1–33. Orlando: Academic Press.

Arendt, Hannah. 1951. *The Origins of Totalitarianism*. New York: Harcourt Brace.

Arterton, F. Christopher. 1978. "Campaign Organizations Confront the Media-Political Environment," in James David Barber, ed., *Race for the Presidency*. Englewood Cliffs, NJ: Prentice-Hall.

    1987. *Teledemocracy: Can Technology Protect Democracy?* Newbury Park, CA: Sage.

Atkin, Charles K. 1973. "Instrumental Utilities and Information Seeking," in Peter Clarke, ed., *New Models for Mass Communications Research*, pp. 205–42. Beverly Hills: Sage.

Aumente, Jerome. 1987. *New Electronic Pathways: Videotex, Teletext, and Online Databases*. Newbury Park, CA: Sage.

Bach, Steven. 1985. *Final Cut*. New York: Morrow.

Backer, David. 1986. "Structures and Interactivity of Media." Ph.D. dissertation, Massachusetts Institute of Technology.

Baer, Walter. 1978. "Telecommunications Technology in the 1980's," in Glen O. Robinson, ed., *Communications Policy in Tomorrow*, pp. 61–123. New York: Praeger.

179

Bagdikian, Ben H. 1983. *The Media Monopoly*. Boston: Beacon Press.
Baldwin, Thomas F., and D. Stevens McVoy. 1983. *Cable Communication*. Englewood Cliffs, NJ: Prentice-Hall.
Barber, Benjamin J. 1984. *Strong Democracy: Participation Politics for a New Age*. Berkeley: University of California Press.
Barnouw, Erik. 1966. *A Tower in Babel*. Oxford University Press.
　1975. *Tube of Plenty*. Oxford University Press.
Bartlett, F. C. 1932. *Remembering: A Study in Experimental and Social Psychology*. Cambridge University Press.
Barwise, T. P., A. S. C. Ehrenberg, and G. J. Goodhardt. 1982. "Glued to the Box? Patterns of TV Repeat Viewing." *Journal of Communication* 32 (4):22–9.
Bechtel, Robert B., Clark Achenpohl, and Roger Akers. 1972. "Correlates Between Observed Behavior and Questionnaire Responses on Television Viewing," in Eli A. Rubinstein, George A. Comstock, and John P. Murray, eds., *Television and Social Behavior, Vol. IV*. Washington, DC: U.S. Department of Health, Education, and Welfare.
Becker, Lee B., and Klaus Shoenbach. 1989. *Audience Responses to Media Diversification: Coping with Plenty*. Hillsdale, NJ: Erlbaum.
Belair, Robert R. 1980. "Information Privacy," in Jane Yurow, ed., *Issues in Information Policy*, pp. 37–52. Washington, DC: National Telecommunication and Information Administration, U.S. Department of Commerce.
Bell, Daniel. 1962. *The End of Ideology*. New York: Free Press.
　1973. *The Coming of Post-Industrial Society: A Venture in Social Forecasting*. New York: Basic Books.
　1979. "The Social Framework of the Information Society," in Michael L. Dertouzos and Joel Moses, eds., *The Computer Age*, pp. 163–211. Cambridge, MA: MIT Press.
Bendix, Reinhard, and Seymour Martin Lipset, eds. 1966. *Class, Status and Power*. New York: Free Press.
Beniger, James R. 1986. *The Control Revolution: Technological and Economic Origins of the Information Society*. Cambridge, MA: Harvard University Press.
　1987. "Toward an Old New Paradigm: The Half-Century Flirtation with Mass Society." *Public Opinion Quarterly* 51 (Supplement):S46–S66.
Berelson, Bernard, Paul Lazarsfeld, and William McPhee. 1954. *Voting: A Study of Opinion Formation in a Presidential Campaign*. University of Chicago Press.
Berger, Suzanne, and Michael Piore. 1980. *Dualism and Discontinuity in Industrial Societies*. Cambridge University Press.
Blumenthal, Sidney. 1980. *The Permanent Campaign: Inside the World of Elite Political Operatives*. Boston: Beacon Press.
Blumler, Jay G. 1980. "Information Overload: Is there a Problem?" in Eberhard Witte, ed., *Human Aspects of Telecommunication*, pp. 229–63. New York: Springer-Verlag.
Blumler, Jay G., and Elihu Katz, eds. 1974. *The Uses of Mass Communications*. Newport Beach, CA: Sage.
Blumler, Jay G., and Denis McQuail. 1969. *Television in Politics*. University of Chicago Press.
Bolt, Richard A. 1984. *The Human Interface: Where People and Computers Meet*. Belmont, CA: Lifetime Learning Publications.
Boorstin, Daniel J. 1961. *The Image: A Guide to Pseudo-Events in America*. New York: Harper & Row.
Botein, Michael, and David M. Rice, eds. 1980. *Network Television and the Public Interest*. Lexington, MA: Lexington Books.
Bower, Robert T. 1973. *Television and the Public*. New York: Holt, Rinehart & Winston.
　1985. *The Changing Television Audience in America*. New York: Columbia University Press.
Bramson, Leon. 1961. *The Political Context of Sociology*. Princeton, NJ: Princeton University Press.

Brecht, Bertolt. 1932. "Theory of Radio," in Bertolt Brecht, ed., *Gesammelte Werke.*

Brock, Gerald W. 1981. *The Telecommunications Industry.* Cambridge, MA: Harvard University Press.

Burke Marketing Research. 1974. "Day-After-Recall Television Commercial Testing." Cincinnati, OH: Burke Marketing Research Inc.

Burnham, David. 1983. *The Rise of the Computer State.* New York: Random House.

Burnham, Walter Dean. 1970. *Critical Elections and the Mainsprings of American Politics.* New York: Norton.

1982. *The Current Crisis in American Politics.* Oxford University Press.

Bush, Vannevar. 1945. "As We May Think." *Atlantic Monthly* (July):101–8.

Campbell, Angus, Philip E. Converse, Warren E. Miller, and Donald E. Stokes. 1960. *The American Voter.* New York: Wiley.

Campbell, James A., and Hilary B. Thomas. 1981. "The Videotex Marketplace: A Theory of Evolution." *Telecommunications Policy* 5 (2):111–20.

Cannon, Don L., and Gerald Luecke. 1980. *Understanding Communications Systems.* Dallas: Texas Instruments Learning Center.

Cantril, Hadley. 1940. *The Invasion from Mars.* Princeton, NJ: Princeton University Press.

Channels of Communications. "Field Guide to the Electronic Environment" (yearly issue).

Chu, Godwin C., and Wilbur Schramm. 1967. *Learning from Television.* Stanford, CA: Stanford University Institute for Communications Research.

Cohen, Stephen S., and John Zysman. 1987. *Manufacturing Matters: The Myth of the Post-Industrial Economy.* New York: Basic Books.

Collins, Richard, Nicholas Garnham, and Gareth Locksley. 1988. *The Economics of Television.* London: Sage.

Compaine, Benjamin M., ed. 1982. *Who Owns the Media?* White Plains, NY: Knowledge Industries Press.

1988. *Issues in New Information Technology.* Norwood, NJ: Ablex.

Comstock, George, Steven Chaffee, Natan Katzman, Maxwell McCombs, and Donald Roberts. 1978. *Television and Human Behavior.* New York: Columbia University Press.

Comte, Auguste. [1851] 1875. *System of Positive Polity.* London: Longmans, Green & Co.

Cornish, Edward, ed. 1982. *Communications Tomorrow: The Coming of the Information Society.* Bethesda, MD: World Future Society.

Coser, Lewis A. 1956. *The Functions of Social Conflict.* New York: Free Press.

Cronbach, L. J., and R. E. Snow. 1977. *Aptitudes and Instructional Methods.* New York: Irvington.

Czitrom, Daniel J. 1982. *Media and the American Mind.* Chapel Hill: University of North Carolina Press.

Dahl, Robert A. 1989. *Democracy and Its Critics.* New Haven, CT: Yale University Press.

Dahrendorf, Ralf. 1959. *Class and Class Conflict in Industrial Society.* Stanford, CA: Stanford University Press.

Dalton, Russell J., Scott C. Flanagan, and Paul Allen Beck, eds. 1984. *Electoral Change in Advanced Industrial Democracies.* Princeton, NJ: Princeton University Press.

De Fleur, Melvin L., and Sandra Ball-Rokeach. 1988. *Theories of Mass Communication,* 5th ed. New York: Longman.

DeNardo, James. 1985. *Power in Numbers: The Political Strategy of Protest and Rebellion.* Princeton, NJ: Princeton University Press.

Dertouzos, Michael L., and Joel Moses. 1979. *The Computer Age: A Twenty-Year View.* Cambridge, MA: MIT Press.

de Tocqueville, Alexis. [1856] 1961. *Democracy in America.* New York: Schocken Books.

Deutsch, Karl. 1963. *The Nerves of Government.* New York: Free Press.

Diamond, Edwin, and Stephen Bates. 1984. *The Spot: The Rise of Political Advertising on Television.* Cambridge, MA: MIT Press.

Dillman, Don A. 1985. "The Social Impacts of Information Technologies in Rural North America." *Rural Sociology* 50 (1):1–26.

Dizard, Wilson P., Jr. 1989. *The Coming Information Age: An Overview of Technology, Economics, and Politics*, 3rd ed. New York: Longman.

Dominick, Joseph R., and Millard C. Pearce. 1976. "Trends in Network Prime-Time Programming: 1953–1974." *Journal of Communication* 26(1):70–80.

Dordick, Herbert S. 1986. *Understanding Telecommunications*. New York: McGraw-Hill.

Dorfman, Ariel. 1983. *The Empire's Old Clothes*. New York: Pantheon.

Downs, Anthony. 1957. *An Economic Theory of Democracy*. New York: Harper & Row.

Draper, Roger. 1986. "The Faithless Shepard." *New York Review of Books* (June 26):14–18.

Dubin, Robert, and R. Alan Hedley. 1969. *The Medium May Be Related to the Message*. Eugene, OR: Center for Advanced Study of Educational Administration.

Duch, Ray, and Peter Lemieux. 1986. "The Political Economy of Communications Development." Working Paper, Research Program on Communications Policy, Cambridge: Massachusetts Institute of Technology.

Durkheim, Emile. [1893] 1933. *The Division of Labor in Society*. New York: Macmillan.

Dutton, William H., Jay G. Blumler, and Kenneth L. Krammer, eds; 1987. *Wired Cities: Shaping the Future of Communications*, Boston: G. K. Hall.

Earnest, Olen J. 1985. "Star Wars: A Case Study of Motion Picture Marketing," in Bruce A. Austin, ed., *Current Research in Film, Vol. I*, pp. 1–18. Norwood, NJ: Ablex.

Egan, Bruce L. 1991. *Information Superhighways: The Economics of Advanced Public Communications Networks*. Boston: Artech House.

Eisenstein, Elizabeth L. 1979. *The Printing Press as an Agent of Change*. Cambridge University Press.

Elkington, Henry. 1988. "An Analysis of the Residential Demand for Broadband Telecommunications Services." Master's thesis, Massachusetts Institute of Technology.

Ellul, Jacques. 1964. *The Technological Society*. New York: Random House.

   1965. *Propaganda: The Formation of Men's Attitudes*. New York: Random House.

Elton, Martin C. J., ed. 1991. *Integrated Broadband Networks: The Public Policy Issues*. Amsterdam: North Holland.

Enelow, James M., and Melvin Hinich. 1984. *The Spatial Theory of Voting*. Cambridge University Press.

Enzenberger, Hans Magnus. 1974. *The Consciousness Industry*. New York: Seabury Press.

Epstein, Edward Jay. 1973. *News From Nowhere*. New York: Random House.

Ernst, Martin. 1981. "Report on the New Media." Cambridge, MA: Arthur D. Little Associates.

Fascell, Dante B., ed. 1979. *International News: Freedom Under Attack*. Beverly Hills: Sage.

Fedida, Sam, and Rex Malik. 1979. *The Viewdata Revolution*. New York: Wiley.

Feldman, Richard B. 1985. "MEDIACALC: The Development of a Forecasting Model for the Communications Industry." Master's thesis, Massachusetts Institute of Technology.

Ferguson, Marjorie, ed. 1986. *New Communications Technologies and the Public Interest: Comparative Perspectives on Policy and Research*. Newbury Park, CA: Sage.

   ed. 1990. *Public Communication: The New Imperatives*. Newbury Park, CA: Sage.

Festinger, Leon. 1957. *A Theory of Cognitive Dissonance*. Stanford, CA: Stanford University Press.

Fisher, Glen. 1987. *American Communications in a Global Society*. Norwood, NJ: Ablex.

Fiske, Susan T. 1986. "Schema-Based Versus Piecemeal Politics," in Richard R. Lau and David O. Sears, eds., *Political Cognition*, pp. 41–53. Hillsdale, NJ: Erlbaum.

Frank, Ronald E., and Marshall G. Greenberg. 1980. *The Public's Use of Television: Who Watches and Why*. Beverly Hills: Sage.

Frechter, Allen R. 1987. "TELECALC: A Telecommunications Demand Forecasting System with a Study of the Market for Residential Broadband ISDN." Master's thesis, Massachusetts Institute of Technology.

Freedman, Jonathan L., and David Sears. 1965. "Selective Exposure," in L. Berkowitz, ed., *Advances in Experimental Social Psychology, Vol. 2*, pp. 58–98. Orlando: Academic Press.

Frey, Frederick W. 1973. "Communication and Development," in Ithiel de Sola Pool and Wilbur Schramm, eds., *Handbook of Communication*, pp. 337–461. Chicago: Rand McNally.

Fromm, Erich. 1941. *Escape from Freedom*. New York: Farrar & Rinehart.

Gagnon, Diana. 1990. *Interactive Television: State of the Industry*. Bethesda, MD: Arlen Publications.

Gagnon, Diana, and Lee McKnight. 1983. "Arcade Video Games." Working paper, Research Program on Communications Policy, Massachusetts Institute of Technology.

Gagnon, Diana, W. Russell Neuman, and Gail Kosloff. 1988. "Interactive Shopping: A Trend for the Future?" Working paper, MIT Media Laboratory, Cambridge MA.

Gamson, William A. 1975. *The Strategy of Social Protest*. Chicago: Dorsey Press.

1988. "A Constructionist Approach to Mass Media and Public Opinion." *Symbolic Interaction* 11(2):161–74.

in press. *Talking Politics*.

Ganley, Gladys D., and Oswald H. Ganley. 1987. *Global Political Fallout: The First Decade of the VCR 1976–1985*. Cambridge, MA: Program on Information Resources Policy.

Ganley, Oswald H., and Gladys D. Ganley. 1982. *To Inform or to Control: The New Communications Networks*. New York: McGraw-Hill.

Gans, Herbert J. 1974. *Popular Culture and High Culture*. New York: Basic Books.

1979. *Deciding What's News*. New York: Pantheon Books.

Gantz, Walter. 1978. "How Uses and Gratifications Affect Recall of Television News." *Journalism Quarterly* 55:664–72.

Garcia, Linda, ed. 1990. *Critical Connections: Communication for the Future*. Washington, DC: U.S. Congress, Office of Technology Assessment.

Garramone, Gina M. 1983. "Issue versus Image Orientation and Effects of Political Advertising." *Communication Research* 10:59–76.

Gastil, Raymond D. 1986. *Freedom in the World*. New York: Freedom House.

Gerbner, George. 1972. "Violence in Television Drama," in G. A. Comstock and E. A. Rubinstein, eds., *Television and Social Behavior. Vol. 1: Media Content and Control*, pp. 28–187. Washington, DC: U.S. Government Printing Office.

Gerbner, George, Larry Gross, Michael Morgan, and Nancy Signorielli. 1980. "The 'Mainstreaming' of America: Violence Profile No. 11." *Journal of Communication* 30(3):10–29.

Giddens, Anthony. 1990. *Consequences of Modernity*. Stanford, CA: Stanford University Press.

Gilder, George. 1989. *Microcosm: The Quantum Revolution in Economics and Technology*. New York: Simon & Schuster.

Gilpin, Robert G. 1979. "The Computer in World Affairs," in Michael L. Dertouzos and Joel Moses, eds., *The Computer Age*, pp. 229–53. Cambridge, MA: MIT Press.

Giner, Salvador. 1976. *Mass Society*. San Diego: Academic Press.

Glass, G. V., B. McGaw, and M. L. Smith. 1981. *Meta-Analysis in Social Research*. Newbury Park, CA: Sage.

Goldsen, Rose K. 1978. *The Show and Tell Machine: How Television Works and Works You Over*. New York: Dell.

Goodhardt, G. J., A. S. C. Ehrenberg, and M. A. Collins. 1980. *The Television Audience: Patterns of Viewing*. Lexington, MA: Lexington Books.

Graber, Doris A. 1984. *Mass Media and American Politics*, 2nd ed. Washington, DC: Congressional Quarterly Press.

Grachev, A., and N. Yermoshkin. 1984. *A New Information Order or Psychological Warfare?* Moscow: Progress Publishers.

Greenberger, Martin, ed. 1985. *Electronic Publishing Plus: Media for a Technological Future.* White Plains, NY: Knowledge Industries Press.

Grossman, Michael Baruch, and Martha Joynt Kumar. 1984. *Portraying the President.* Baltimore: Johns Hopkins University Press.

Gunnell, John G. 1983. "Political Theory: The Evolution of a Sub-Field," in Ada W. Finiter, ed., *Political Science: The State of the Discipline*, pp. 3–46. Washington, DC: American Political Science Association.

Gunter, Barrie. 1981. "Forgetting the News." *Intermedia* 9(5):41–3.

Gupta, Anil K., and Amit Basu. 1989. "Information Technologies and Changing Patterns of Economic Coordination," in *Paradigms Revisited*, pp. 149–76. Queenstown, MD: Aspen Institute.

Habermas, Jürgen. 1981a. *The Theory of Communicative Action. Vol. 1: Reason and the Rationalization of Society.* Boston: Beacon Press.

1981b. *The Theory of Communicative Action. Vol. 2: Lifeworld and System.* Boston: Beacon Press.

[1962] 1989. *The Structural Transformation of the Public Sphere.* Cambridge, MA: MIT Press.

Hald, Alan P. 1982. "Toward an Information-Rich Society," in Edward Cornish, ed., *Communications Tomorrow*, pp. 9–12. Bethesda, MD: World Future Society.

Hamilton, Alexander, James Madison, and John Jay. [1787–8] 1961. *The Federalist Papers.* New York: New American Library.

Hamilton, Richard F. 1972. *Class and Politics in the United States.* New York: Wiley.

1982. *Who Voted for Hitler?* Princeton, NJ: Princeton University Press.

Hartz, Louis. 1955. *The Liberal Tradition in America.* New York: Harcourt Brace.

Heeter, Carrie, and Bradley S. Greenberg. 1988. *Cableviewing.* Norwood, NJ: Ablex.

Heider, F. 1958. *The Psychology of Interpersonal Relations.* New York: Wiley.

Herzog, Herta. 1944. "What Do We Really Know About Daytime Serial Listeners?" in Paul F. Lazarsfeld and Frank N. Stanton, eds., *Radio Research, 1942–43*, pp. 3–33. New York: Duell, Sloan & Pearce.

Hills, Jill. 1986. *Deregulating Telecoms: Competition and Control in the USA, Japan and Britain.* London: Pinter.

Hiltz, Starr Roxanne, and Murray Turoff. 1978. *The Network Nation: Human Communication via Computer.* Reading, MA: Addison-Wesley.

Hiniker, Paul J. 1966. "The Effects of Mass Communication in Communist China." Ph.D. dissertation, Massachusetts Institute of Technology.

Holmes, Urban Tigner. 1952. *Daily Living in the Twelfth Century.* University of Chicago Press.

Hornik, Jacob, and Mary Jane Schlenger. 1981. "Allocation of Time to the Mass Media." *Journal of Consumer Research* 7 (March):343–55.

Hotelling, Harold. 1929. "Stability in Competition." *Economic Journal* 34 (March):41–57.

Hovland, Carl, Irving Janis, and Harold H. Kelley. 1953. *Communication and Persuasion.* New Haven, CT: Yale University Press.

Huber, Peter. 1987. *The Geodesic Network.* Washington, DC: U.S. Department of Justice.

Huntington, Samuel P. 1968. *Political Order in Changing Societies.* New Haven, CT: Yale University Press.

1974. "Postindustrial Politics: How Benign Will It Be?" *Comparative Politics* 6:163–91.

1981. *American Politics: The Promise of Disharmony.* Cambridge, MA: Harvard University Press.

Huntington, Samuel P., and Jorge I. Dominguez. 1975. "Political Development," in Fred Greenstein and Nelson Polsby, eds., *Handbook of Political Science.* Reading, MA: Addison-Wesley.

Hyman, H., C. Wright, and J. Reed. 1975. *The Enduring Effects of Education.* University of Chicago Press.

Ide, Thomas Ranald. 1983. "The Technology," in Guenter Friedrichs and Adam Schaff, eds.,

Micro-Electronics and Society: A Report to the Club of Rome, pp. 36–86. New York: New American Library.

Inglehart, Ronald. 1977. *The Silent Revolution.* Princeton, NJ: Princeton University Press.

1990. *Culture Shift in Advanced Industrial Society.* Princeton, NJ: Princeton University Press.

Inkeles, Alex, and David H. Smith. 1974. *Becoming Modern.* Cambridge, MA: Harvard University Press.

Innis, Harold A. 1951. *The Bias of Communication.* University of Toronto Press.

Jacoby, Jacob, and Wayne D. Hoyer. 1982. "Viewer Miscomprehension of Televised Communication: Selected Findings." *Journal of Marketing* 46 (4):12–26.

Johnstone, John W. C. 1974. "Social Integration and Mass Media Use Among Adolescents," in Jay G. Blumler and Elihu Katz, eds., *The Uses of Mass Communications*, pp. 35–48. Beverly Hills: Sage.

Jonscher, Charles. 1983. "Information Resources and Economic Productivity." *Information Economics and Policy* 1 (1):13–35.

1986. "Information Technology and the United States Economy," in Gerald Faulhaber, Eli Noam, and Roberta Tasley, eds., *Services in Transition: The Impact of Information Technologies on Services.* Cambridge, MA: Ballinger.

Judice, C. N., E. J. Addeo, M. I. Eiger, and H. L. Lemberg. 1986. *Video on Demand: A Wideband Service or Myth?* Morristown, NJ: Bell Communications Research.

Kaplan, Gadi, and associates. 1985. "The High-Tech Home." *IEEE Spectrum* 22(5).

Kariel, Henry S. 1989. *The Desperate Politics of Postmodernism.* Amherst: University of Massachusetts Press.

Katz, Elihu, Hanna Adoni, and Pnina Parness. 1977. "Remember the News: What the Picture Adds to Recall." *Journalism Quarterly* 54 (Summer):231–9.

Katz, Elihu, Daniel Dayan, and Pierre Motyl. 1981. "In Defense of Media Events," in Robert W. Haigh, George Gerbner, and Richard B. Byrne, eds., *Communications in the Twenty-first Century*, pp. 43–59. New York: Wiley.

Katz, Elihu, and Paul F. Lazarsfeld. 1955. *Personal Influence: The Part Played by People in the Flow of Communications.* New York: Free Press.

Kecskemeti, Paul. 1973. "Propaganda," in Ithiel de Sola Pool and Wilbur Schramm, eds., *Handbook of Communication*, pp. 844–70. Chicago: Rand McNally.

Keen, Peter G. 1988. *Competing in Time: Using Telecommunications for Competitive Advantage.* Cambridge, MA: Ballinger.

Kernell, Samuel. 1986. *Going Public: New Strategies of Presidential Leadership.* Washington, DC: Congressional Quarterly Press.

Kerr, Clark, and Abraham Siegel. 1954. "The Interindustry Propensity to Strike – An International Comparison," in Arthur Kornhauser, R. Dubin, and A. Ross, eds., *Industrial Conflict.* New York: McGraw-Hill.

Kielbowicz, Richard B. 1989. *News in the Mail: The Press, Post Office and Public Information, 1770–1860s.* Westport, CT: Greenwood Press.

Klapp, Orrin E. 1978. *Opening and Closing: Strategies of Information Adaptation in Society.* Cambridge University Press.

Klapper, Joseph. 1960. *The Effects of Mass Communications.* New York: Free Press.

Klein, Paul. 1975. "The Television Audience and Program Mediocrity," in Alan Wells, ed., *Mass Media and Society*, pp. 74–7. Palo Alto, CA: Mayfield.

Kornhauser, William. 1959. *The Politics of Mass Society.* New York: Free Press.

1968. "Mass Society," in David Sills, ed., *The Encyclopedia of the Social Sciences.* New York: Free Press/Macmillan.

Krasnow, Erwin G., Lawrence D. Longley, and Herbert A. Terry. 1982. *The Politics of Broadcast Regulation.* New York: St. Martin's Press.

Kraus, Sidney, and Dennis Davis. 1976. *The Effects of Mass Communication on Political Behavior.* University Park: Pennsylvania State University Press.

Kris, Ernst, and Nathan Leites. 1950. "Trends in 20th Century Propaganda," in Bernard Berelson and Morris Janowitz, eds., *Reader in Public Opinion and Communication*, pp. 278–88. New York: Free Press.

Kuhn, Thomas. 1962. *The Structure of Scientific Revolutions*. University of Chicago Press.

Landis, Jack. 1979. "TV Factor Ratings." New York: Marketing Evaluations Inc.

Lau, Richard R. 1986. "Political Schemata, Candidate Evaluations and Voting Behavior," in Richard R. Lau and David O. Sears, eds., *Political Cognition*, pp. 95–126. Hillsdale, NJ: Erlbaum.

Lau, Richard, and David O. Sears, eds. 1986. *Political Cognition*. Hillsdale, NJ: Erlbaum.

Lazarus, William, and Lee McKnight. 1983. "Forecasting the New Media." Working paper, Research Program on Communications Policy, Massachusetts Institute of Technology.

Le Duc, Don R. 1987. *Beyond Broadcasting: Patterns in Policy and Law*. New York: Longman.

Lemieux, Peter. 1983. "The Multi-Channel Media Environment." Working paper, Future of the Mass Audience Project, Massachusetts Institute of Technology.

Lerner, Daniel. 1958. *The Passing of Traditional Society*. New York: Free Press.

Levin, Harvey J. 1971. *The Invisible Resource: Use and Regulation of the Radio Spectrum*. Baltimore: Johns Hopkins University Press.

1980. *Fact and Fancy in Television Regulation: An Economic Study of Policy Alternatives*. New York: Russell Sage.

Levy, Mark R. 1979. "Watching TV News as Para-Social Interaction." *Journal of Broadcasting* 23 (1):69–80.

ed. 1987. *The VCR Age, Special Issue of the American Behavioral Scientist*. Beverly Hills: Sage.

Levy, Mark R., and Sven Windahl. 1985. "The Concept of Audience Activity," in Karl Erik Rosengren, Lawrence A. Wenner, and Philip Palmgreen, eds., *Media Gratifications Research: Current Perspectives*, pp. 109–22. Newport Beach, CA: Sage.

Lewis, Oscar. 1959. *Five Families: Mexican Case Studies in the Culture of Poverty*. New York: Basic Books.

Lichtenberg, Judith, ed. 1990. *Democracy and Mass Media*. Cambridge University Press.

Liebow, Elliot. 1967. *Tally's Corner*. Boston: Little, Brown.

Linz, Juan, and Alfred Stepan, eds. 1978. *The Breakdown of Democratic Regimes*. Baltimore: Johns Hopkins University Press.

Lipowski, Z. J. 1971. "Surfeit of Attractive Information Inputs." *Behavioral Science* 16:467–71.

Lippman, Andrew. 1986. *Fifth Generation Television*. Cambridge, MA: MIT Media Laboratory.

Lippmann, Walter. [1922] 1965. *Public Opinion*. New York: Free Press.

Lipset, Seymour Martin. 1960. *Political Man*. New York: Doubleday.

1970. *Revolution and Counterrevolution: Change and Persistence in Social Structures*. Garden City, NY: Anchor Books.

1985. *Consensus and Conflict*. New Brunswick, NJ: Transaction Books.

Lipset, Seymour Martin, and Stein Rokkan. 1967. "Cleavage Structures, Party Systems, and Voter Alignments: An Introduction," in Seymour Martin Lipset and Stein Rokkan, eds., *Party Systems and Voter Alignments*, pp. 1–64. New York: Free Press.

Lodish, L. M. 1986. "The Use of Scanner Data." *Media and Marketing Decisions* (December).

Long, Norton E. 1958. "The Local Community as an Ecology of Games." *American Journal of Sociology* 64(November):251–61.

Lowery, Sharon, and Melvin L. De Fleur. 1983. *Milestones in Mass Communication*. New York: Longman.

MacBride, Sean. 1980. *Many Voices One World: Towards a New More Just and More Efficient World Information and Communication Order*. New York: Unipub.

McCrone, Donald J., and Charles F. Cnudde. 1967. "Toward a Communications Theory of Democratic Political Development." *American Political Science Review* 61 (March):72–9.

McGowan, J. J. 1967. "Competition, Regulation and Performance in Television Broadcasting." *Washington University Law Quarterly* (Fall).

McGuire, William J. 1969. "The Nature of Attitudes and Attitude Change," in Gardner Lindzey and Elliot Aronson, eds., *The Handbook of Social Psychology*, 2nd ed., pp. 136–314. Reading, MA: Addison-Wesley.

———. 1985. "Attitudes and Attitude Change," in Gardner Lindzey and Elliot Aronson, eds., *The Handbook of Social Psychology*, pp. 233–346. New York: Random House.

———. 1986. "The Myth of Massive Media Impact: Savagings and Salvagings," in George Comstock, ed., *Public Communication and Behavior*, pp. 173–257. Orlando: Academic Press.

Machlup, Fritz. 1962. *The Production and Distribution of Knowledge in the United States*. Princeton, NJ: Princeton University Press.

———. 1980–4. *Knowledge: Its Creation, Distribution and Economic Significance*, 3 vols. Princeton, NJ: Princeton University Press.

McHugh and Hoffman Inc. 1983. "Television Trends." Washington, DC: McHugh and Hoffman Inc.

McLeod, Jack M., and Byron Reeves. 1980. "On the Nature of Mass Media Effects," in Stephen B. Withey and Ronald P. Abeles, eds., *Television and Social Behavior*, pp. 17–54. Hillsdale, NJ: Erlbaum.

McLuhan, Marshall. 1964. *Understanding Media*. New York: American Library.

McQuail, Denis. 1986. "Is Media Theory Adequate to the Challenge of the New Communications Technologies?" in Marjorie Ferguson, ed., *New Communications Technologies and the Public Interest: Comparative Perspectives on Policy and Research*, pp. 1–17. Newbury Park, CA: Sage.

———. 1987. *Mass Communication Theory*, 2nd ed. Newbury Park, CA: Sage.

McQuail, Denis, and Karon Siune, eds. 1986. *New Media Politics: Comparative Perspectives in Western Europe*. Beverly Hills: Sage.

Maisel, Richard. 1973. "The Decline of the Mass Media." *Public Opinion Quarterly* 37:159–70.

Malik, Rex. 1986. "Beyond the Exponential Cascade." *Inter-Media* 14(2):14–31.

Malone, Thomas W., Joann Yates, and Richard I Benjamin. 1987. "Electronic Markets and Electronic Hierarchies: Effects of New Information Technologies on Market Structures and Corporate Strategies." *Communications of the ACM* 30 (June):484–97.

Mander, Jerry. 1978. *Four Arguments for the Elimination of Television*. New York: William Morrow.

Mankiewicz, Frank, and Joel Swerdlow. 1979. *Remote Control: Television and the Manipulation of American Life*. New York: Ballantine.

Mansbridge, Jane. 1983. *Beyond Adversary Democracy*. University of Chicago Press.

Marantz, S., and F. J. Dowaliby. 1973. "Individual Differences in Learning from Pictorial and Verbal Instruction." Unpublished paper, University of Massachusetts, Amherst.

Marcuse, Herbert. 1964. *One-Dimensional Man*. Boston: Beacon Press.

Markus, M. Lynn. 1987. "Toward a 'Critical Mass' Theory of Interactive Media: Universal Access, Interdependence and Diffusion." *Communication Research* 14 (5):491–511.

Martin, James. 1977. *Future Developments in Telecommunications*. Englewood Cliffs, NJ: Prentice-Hall.

Martin, L. John, and Anja Grover Chaudhary, eds. 1983. *Comparative Mass Media Systems*. New York: Longman.

Marx, Karl. [1852] 1963. *The Eighteenth Brumaire of Louis Bonaparte*. New York: International Publishers.

Marx, Karl. [1867] 1906. *Capital: A Critique of Political Economy*. New York: Modern Library.

Masuda, Yoneji. 1980. *The Information Society as Post-Industrial Society*. Bethesda, MD: World Future Society.

Mattelart, Armand. 1980. *Mass Media, Ideologies, and the Revolutionary Movement*. Sussex, England: Harvester Press.

Meadow, Robert G. 1985. *New Communication Technologies in Politics*. Washington, DC: The Washington Program of the Annenberg School of Communication.

Meier, R. L. 1962. *A Communication Theory of Urban Growth*. Cambridge, MA: MIT Press.

Merrill, John C. 1974. *The Imperative of Freedom*. New York: Hastings House.

Merrill, John C., and Ralph L. Lowenstein. 1971. *Media, Messages and Men: New Perspectives in Communication*. Columbia, MO: David McKay.

Merton, Robert K. 1975. "Structural Analysis in Sociology," in Peter M. Blau, ed., *Approaches to the Study of Social Structure*, pp. 21–52. New York: Free Press.

Mickiewicz, Ellen Propper. 1981. *Media and the Russian Public*. New York: Praeger.

Migdal, Joel S. 1983. "Studying the Politics of Development and Change: The State of the Art," in Ada W. Finifter, ed., *Political Science: The State of the Discipline*, pp. 309–38. Washington, DC: American Political Science Association.

Miles, Ian. 1985. "The New Post-Industrial State." *Futures* 17 (6):588–617.

Milgram, Stanley. 1965. "Some Conditions of Obedience and Disobedience to Authority." *Human Relations* 18:57–76.

———. 1970. "The Experience of Living in Cities." *Science* 167:1461–8.

Miller, George A. 1956. "The Magical Number Seven, Plus or Minus Two: Some Limits on Our Capacity for Processing Information." *Psychology Review* 63:81–97.

Miller, James G. 1960. "Information Input Overload and Psychopathology." *American Journal of Psychiatry* 116:695–704.

Millikan, Max F. 1967. "The Most Fundamental Technological Change," in Daniel Lerner and Wilbur Schramm, eds., *Communication and Change in the Developing Countries*, pp. 3–4. Honolulu: East-West Center Press.

Moore, Barrington. 1966. *Social Origins of Dictatorship and Democracy*. Boston: Beacon Press.

Mosco, Vincent. 1982. *Pushbutton Fantasies: Critical Information Technology*. Norwood, NJ: Ablex.

Mosco, Vincent. 1990. "The Mythology of Telecommunications Regulation." *Journal of Communication* 40(1):36–49.

Mueller, Claus. 1973. *The Politics of Communication*. Oxford University Press.

Naisbitt, John. 1982. *Megatrends*. New York: Warner Books.

Naples, Michael J. 1979. *Effective Frequency: The Relationship Between Frequency and Advertising Effectiveness*. New York: Association of National Advertisers.

Nelson, Theodore H. 1974. *Dream Machines and Computer Lib*. Chicago: Hugos.

Neuman, W. Russell. 1976. "Patterns of Recall Among Television News Viewers." *Public Opinion Quarterly* 40:115–23.

———. 1986. *The Paradox of Mass Politics*. Cambridge, MA: Harvard University Press.

———. 1989. "Parallel Content Analysis: Old Paradigms and New Proposals," in George Comstock, ed., *Public Communication and Behavior*, Vol. 2, pp. 205–89. Orlando: Academic Press.

———. 1991. "What Ever Happened to Mass Society Theory?" Paper presented at the American Association for Public Opinion Research annual conference, Phoenix.

———. in press. "Political Communication and Social Control," in George Comstock, ed., *Public Communication and Behavior*, Vol. 3. Orlando: Academic Press.

Neuman, W. Russell, and Teresa Cader. 1985. *Interactive Video: A Research Report*. Cambridge, MA: MIT Research Program on Communication Policy.

Neuman, W. Russell, Marion R. Just, and Ann N. Crigler. in press. *Common Knowledge: News and the Construction of Political Meaning*. University of Chicago Press.

Neuman, W. Russell, Lee McKnight, Shawn O'Donnell, Gail Kosloff, and Deborah Campbell. 1987. *Hard Copy Imaging in the Home of the 90s*. Cambridge, MA: MIT Media Laboratory.

Neuman, W. Russell, and Ithiel de Sola Pool. 1986. "The Flow of Communications into the Home," in Sandra J. Ball-Rokeach and Muriel Cantor, eds., *Media, Audience and Social Structure*, pp. 71–86. Beverly Hills: Sage.

Neustadt, Richard M. 1982. *The Birth of Electronic Publishing: Legal and Economic Issues in Telephone, Cable and Over-the-Air Teletext and Videotext.* White Plains, NY: Knowledge Industries Press.

Newberg, Paula, ed. 1989a. *New Directions in Telecommunications Policy. Vol. 1: Regulatory Policy: Telephony and Mass Media.* Durham, NC: Duke University Press.

ed. 1989b. *New Directions in Telecommunications Policy. Vol. 2: Information Policy and Economic Policy.* Durham, NC: Duke University Press.

Newspaper Advertising Bureau. 1983. "Newpaper Readership Project." New York: Newspaper Advertising Bureau.

Nicholas, Nicholas J., Jr., Gerald M. Levin, and Steven J. Ross. 1991. Press release, March 7, New York.

Nie, Norman, Sidney Verba, and John R. Petrocik. 1976. *The Changing American Voter.* Cambridge, MA: Harvard University Press.

Nielsen. 1986. "1986 Nielsen Report on Television." A. C. Nielsen Company, New York.

Nielsen Media Research News. 1990. New York: A. C. Nielsen Company.

Nisbett, Richard, and Lee Ross. 1980. *Human Inference Strategies and Shortcomings in Social Judgment.* Englewood Cliffs, NJ: Prentice-Hall.

Noam, Eli M., ed. 1985. *Video Media Competition: Regulation, Economics and Technology.* New York: Columbia University Press.

Noelle-Neumann, Elisabeth. 1984. *The Spiral of Silence.* University of Chicago Press.

Noll, R. G., M. J. Peck, and J. J. McGowan. 1973. *Economic Aspects of Television Regulation.* Washington, DC: Brookings Institution.

Nora, Simon, and Alain Minc. 1980. *The Computerization of Society.* Cambridge, MA: MIT Press.

Nordenstreng, Kaarle, and Herbert I. Schiller, eds. 1979. *National Sovereignty and International Communication.* Norwood, NJ: Ablex.

O'Donnell, Shawn. 1989. "Mortgaging the First Amendment: Strategic Use of the Regulatory Process in Electronic Media." Paper presented at the Seventeenth Annual Telecommunications Policy Research Conference, Airlie, VA.

Oettinger, Anthony G. 1969. *Run Computer, Run: The Mythology of Educational Innovation.* Cambridge, MA: Harvard University Press.

Ogan, Christine L. 1989. "The Effects of New Technologies on Communications Policy," in Jerry L. Salvaggio and Jennings Bryant, eds., *Media Use in the Information Age: Emerging Patterns of Adoption and Consumer Use*, pp. 43–60. Hillsdale, NJ: Erlbaum.

Ogburn, William Fielding. 1946. *The Social Effects of Aviation.* Boston: Houghton Mifflin.

Oliver, Pamela, Gerald Marwell, and Ruy Teixeira. 1985. "A Theory of Critical Mass I: Interdependence, Group Heterogeneity, and the Production of Collective Action." *American Journal of Sociology* 91 (3):522–56.

Olson, Mancur. 1965. *The Logic of Collective Action: Public Goods and the Theory of Groups.* Cambridge, MA: Harvard University Press.

Orwell, George. 1949. *1984.* New York: Signet Books.

Owen, Bruce M., Jack A. Beebe, Jr., and Willard G. Manning. 1975. *Television Economics.* Lexington, MA: Lexington Books.

Packard, Vance. 1957. *The Hidden Persuaders.* New York: McKay.

Papert, Seymour. 1980. *Mindstorms: Children, Computers and Powerful Ideas.* New York: Basic Books.

Parker, Edwin. 1970. "Information Utility and Mass Communications," in Harold Sackman and Norman Nie, eds., *Information Utility and Social Choice*, pp. 51–70. Montvale, NJ: AFIPS Press.

Petty, R. E., and J. T. Cacioppo. 1977. "Forewarning, Cognitive Responding and Resistance to Persuasion." *Journal of Personality and Social Psychology* 35:645–55.

Piaget, Jean. [1930] 1952. *The Origins of Intelligence in Children.* New York: International Universities Press.

Picard, Robert G. 1989. *Media Economics: Concepts and Issues*. Newbury Park, CA: Sage.

Picard, Robert G., Maxwell E. McCombs, James P. Winter, and Stephen Lacy, eds. 1988. *Press Concentration and Monopoly: New Perspectives on Newspaper Ownership and Operation*. Norwood, NJ: Ablex.

Pinard, Maurice. 1968. "Mass Society and Political Movements: A New Formulation." *American Journal of Sociology* 73 (May):682–90.

Piore, Michael J., and Charles F. Sabel. 1984. *The Second Industrial Divide*. New York: Basic Books.

Poltrack, David. 1983. *Television Marketing*. New York: McGraw-Hill.

Pool, Ithiel de Sola. 1963. "The Mass Media and Politics in the Modernization Process," in Lucian W. Pye, ed., *Communications and Political Development*, pp. 234–53. Princeton, NJ: Princeton University Press.

    1973. "Communication in Totalitarian Societies," in Ithiel de Sola Pool and Wilbur Schramm, eds., *Handbook of Communication*, pp. 462–511. Chicago: Rand McNally.

    ed. 1977. *The Social Impact of the Telephone*. Cambridge, MA: MIT Press.

    ed. 1977. *Talking Back: Citizen Feedback and Cable Technology*. Cambridge, MA: MIT Press.

    1978. "Future Perspectives on Communication." Paper presented at a Honda international symposium, Tokyo.

    1983a. *Forecasting the Telephone: A Retrospective Technology Assesment of the Telephone*. Norwood, NJ: Ablex.

    1983b. *Technologies of Freedom*. Cambridge, MA: Harvard University Press.

    1983c. "What Ferment? A Challenge for Empirical Research." *Journal of Communication* 33 (3):258–61.

    1990. *Technology Without Frontiers*. Cambridge, MA: Harvard University Press.

Pool, Ithiel de Sola, Hiroshi Inose, Nozomu Takasaki, and Roger Hurwitz. 1984. *Communications Flows: A Census in the United States and Japan*. Amsterdam: Elsevier/North Holland.

Pool, Jonathan, and Bernard Grofman. 1984. "Language as Political Control." Paper presented at the annual meeting of the American Political Science Association, Washington, DC.

Porter, Michael E. 1985. *Competitive Advantage*. New York: Free Press.

Postman, Neil. 1985. *Amusing Ourselves to Death*. New York: Viking.

Pred, Allan R. 1973. *Urban Growth and the Circulation of Information*. Cambridge, MA: Harvard University Press.

Price, Derek de Solla. 1963. *Little Science, Big Science*. New York: Columbia University Press.

Pye, Lucian W., and Sidney Verba, eds. 1965. *Communications and Political Development*. Princeton, NJ: Princeton University Press.

Ranney, Austin. 1983. *Channels of Power: The Impact of Television on American Politics*. New York: Basic Books.

Rawls, John. 1971. *A Theory of Justice*. Cambridge, MA: Harvard University Press.

Raymond, R. C. 1962. "Betting on the New Technologies," in J. R. Bright, ed., *Technological Planning at the Corporate Level*. Boston: Harvard Business School.

Read, Oliver, and Walter Welch. 1976. *From Tin Foil to Stereo*. Indianapolis: Sams.

Reeves, Byron, and Esther Thorson. 1986. "Watching Television: Experiments on the Viewing Process." *Communication Research* 13:343–61.

Rice, Ronald E. 1984. *The New Media*. Beverly Hills: Sage.

Rice, Ronald E., and Frederick Williams. 1984. "Theories Old and New: The Study of New Media," in Ronald E. Rice and Associates, eds., *The New Media*, pp. 55–80. Beverly Hills: Sage.

Riesman, David. 1953. *The Lonely Crowd*. Garden City, NY: Doubleday.

Robinson, Glen O., ed. 1978. *Communications for Tomorrow: Policy Perspectives for the 1980s*. New York: Praeger.

Robinson, John P. 1972. "Toward Defining the Functions of Television," in Eli Rubinstein, George Comstock, and John P. Murray, eds., *Television and Social Behavior, Vol. 4*, pp. 568–603. Washington, DC: U.S. Government Printing Office.

1977. *How Americans Use Time*. New York: Praeger.

Robinson, John, and Mark Levy. 1986. *The Main Source*. Beverly Hills: Sage.

Robinson, Michael J. 1976. "Public Affairs Television and the Growth of Political Malaise: The Case of "The Selling of the Pentagon." *American Political Science Review* 70.

Rogers, Everett. 1973. "Mass Media and Interpersonal Communications," in Ithiel de Sola Pool and Wilbur Schramm, eds., *Handbook of Communication*, pp. 290–310. Chicago: Rand McNally.

1976. "Communication and Development: The Passing of the Dominant Paradigm." *Communication Research* 3:121–33.

1983. *Diffusion of Innovations*. New York: Free Press.

Rosengren, Karl Erik, Lawrence A. Wenner, and Philip Palmgreen, eds. 1985. *Media Gratifications Research: Current Perspectives*. Beverly Hills: Sage.

Rosenthal, Robert. 1984. *Meta-Analytic Procedures for Social Research*. Newbury Park, CA: Sage.

Rostow, Walt W. 1967. *The Stages of Economic Growth: A Non-Communist Manifesto*. Cambridge University Press.

Rothenberg, J. 1962. "Consumer Sovereignty and the Economics of TV Programming." *Studies in Public Communication* 4 (Fall):45–54.

Rubin, Michael Rogers. 1983. *Information Economics and Policy in the United States*. Littleton, CO: Libraries Unlimited.

Russett, Bruce. 1964. "Inequality and Instability: The Relation of Land Tenure to Politics." *World Politics* 16 (April):442–54.

Rutkowski, Anthony. 1986. "Integrated Services Digital Network," in Anne W. Branscomb, ed., *Toward a Law of Global Communications Networks*, pp. 121–40. New York: Longman.

Sabato, Larry J. 1981. *The Rise of Political Consultants*. New York: Basic Books.

Salomon, Gavriel. 1979. *Interaction of Media Cognition and Learning*. San Francisco: Jossey-Bass.

Salomon, Gavriel, and Tamar Leigh. 1984. "Predispositions about Learning from Print and Television." *Journal of Communication* 34 (2):119–34.

Sapir, Edward. 1921. *Language: An Introduction to the Study of Speech*. New York: Harvest.

Scherer, F. M. 1979. "The Welfare Economics of Product Variety: An Application to the Ready-to-East Cereals Industry." *Journal of Industrial Economics* 28(2):113–34.

1980. *Industrial Market Structure and Economic Performance*. Chicago: Rand McNally.

Schiller, Dan. 1982. *Telematics and Government*. Norwood, NJ: Ablex.

Schiller, Herbert I. 1973. *The Mind Managers*. Boston: Beacon Press.

1989. *Culture, Inc.: The Corporate Takeover of Public Expression*. Oxford University Press.

Schlozman, Kay Lehman, and Sidney Verba. 1979. *Injury to Insult: Unemployment, Class and Political Participation*. Cambridge, MA: Harvard University Press.

Schmalensee, Richard. 1972. *The Economics of Advertising*. Amsterdam: North Holland.

Schneider, Steven M. 1988. "The Infancy of Telegraphy: Congressional Policy and Politics, 1837–1843." Master's thesis, University of Pennsylvania.

1990. "Managing the Information Tide: The Human Use of the New Media," in Institute for Information Studies, ed., *The Annual Review*, pp. 59–84. Queenstown, MD: Aspen Institute.

Schudson, Michael. 1984. *Advertising, the Uneasy Persuasion*. New York: Basic Books.

Schwartz, Tony. 1973. *The Responsive Chord*. Garden City, NY: Doubleday.

1983. *Media: The Second God*. Garden City, NY: Doubleday.

Sharkey, W. 1982. *The Theory of Natural Monopoly*. Cambridge University Press.

Sharon, Amiel T. 1972. *Reading Activities of American Adults*. Princeton, NJ: Educational Testing Service.

Sherif, M. 1935. "A Study of Some Factors in Perception." *Archives of Psychology* 187.

Shils, Edward. 1962. "The Theory of Mass Society." *Diogenes* 39 (Fall):45–66.

Shils, Edward A., and Morris Janowitz. 1948. "Cohesion and Disintegration in the Wehrmacht in World War II." *Public Opinion Quarterly* 12:289–315.

Shooshan, Harry M., III, ed. 1977. *Option Papers for the Subcommittee on Communications, Committee on Interstate and Foreign Commerce, House of Representatives, Ninety-Fifth Congress*. Washington, DC: U.S. Government Printing Office.

Siebert, Fred S., Theodore Peterson, and Wilbur Schramm. 1956. *Four Theories of the Press*. Urbana: University of Illinois Press.

Simon, Herbert A. 1976. *Administrative Behavior*. 3rd ed. New York: Free Press.

Singer, Jerome L., and Dorothy G. Singer. 1980. *Television, Imagination and Aggression: A Study of Preschoolers*. Hillsdale, NJ: Erlbaum.

Sirbu, Marvin, David Reed, and Frank Ferrante. 1989. "An Engineering and Policy Analysis of Fiber Introduction into the Residential Subscriber Loop." *Journal of Lightwave Technology* 7 (11):1876–86.

Slack, Jennifer Daryl. 1984. *Communication Technologies and Society*. Norwood, NJ: Ablex.

Smith, Adam. [1776] 1976. *The Wealth of Nations*. University of Chicago Press.

Smith, Anthony. 1973. *The Shadow in the Cave: The Broadcaster, His Audience, and the State*. Urbana: University of Illinois Press.

    1980. *Goodbye Gutenberg: The Newspaper Revolution of the 1980s*. Oxford University Press.

    1991. *The Age of Behemoths: The Globalization of Mass Media Firms*. New York: Priority Press.

Smith, Robert Ellis. 1979. *Privacy: How to Protect What's Left of It*. New York: Doubleday.

Smythe, Dallas W., and T. Van Dinh. 1983. "On Critical and Administrative Research: A New Critical Analysis." *Journal of Communication* (Summer):117–27.

Spengler, Oswald. 1939. *The Decline of the West*. New York: Knopf.

Steiner, P. O. 1952. "Program Patterns and Preferences and the Workability of Competition in Radio Broadcasting." *Quarterly Journal of Economics* (May).

Steinhoff, William. 1975. *George Orwell and the Origins of 1984*. Ann Arbor: University of Michigan Press.

Stinchcombe, Arthur L. 1968. *Constructing Social Theories*. New York: Harcourt Brace.

Strassman, Paul A. 1985. *Information Payoff*. New York: Free Press.

Strickell, David W. 1963. "A Critical Review of the Methodology and Results of Research Comparing Televised and Face-to-Face Instruction." Ph.D. dissertation, Pennsylvania State University.

Takeichi, Hideo. 1991. "The Meaning of Development Communication in Japan," in Fred L. Casmir, ed., *Communication in Development*, pp. 91–115. Norwood, NJ: Ablex.

Tanase, Masanao. 1985. *Behind the Telephone Debates*. Cambridge, MA: Harvard Program on Information Resources Policy.

Taylor, Shelley E., and Suzanne C. Thompson. 1982. "Stalking the Elusive 'Vividness' Effect." *Psychological Review* 89 (2):155–81.

Tebbel, John. 1974. *The Media in America*. New York: New American Libraries.

Techo, Robert. 1980. *Data Communications*. New York: Plenum.

Tehranian, Majid. 1990. *Technologies of Power: Information Machines and Democratic Prospects*. Norwood, NJ: Ablex.

Television Audience Assessment. 1984. *1984 Program Impact and Program Appeal: Qualitative Ratings and Commercial Effectiveness*. Cambridge, MA: Television Audience Assessment.

Toffler, Alvin. 1980. *The Third Wave*. New York: Morrow.

Tomita, Tetsuro. 1980. "The New Electronic Media and Their Place in the Information Market of the Future," in Anthony Smith, ed., *Newspapers and Democracy: Internatonal Essays on a Changing Medium*, pp. 49–62. Cambridge, MA: MIT Press.

Tönnies, Ferdinand. [1887] 1957. *Community and Society*. New York: Harper & Row.

Toynbee, Arnold J. 1934. *A Study of History*. Oxford University Press.

Tsuneki, Teruo. 1988. "An Experimental Study on the Measurement of the Amount of Information." *KEIO Communication Review* 9:33–51.

Tunstall, Jeremy. 1977. *The Media Are American*. New York: Columbia University Press.

1986. *Communications Deregulation: The Unleashing of America's Communications Industry*. New York: Basil Blackwell.

Tydeman, John, Hubert Lipinski, Richard P. Adler, Michael Nyhan, and Laurence Zwimpfer. 1982. *Teletext and Videotex in the United States: Market Potential, Technology and Public Policy Issues*. New York: McGraw-Hill.

United States Bureau of the Census. 1986. *Statistical Abstract of the United States*.

United States Department of Commerce. 1977. *The Information Economy*. Washington, DC: U.S. Government Printing Office.

Van Gigh, John P. 1976. "The Physical and Mental Load Components of Objective Complexity in Production Systems." *Behavioral Science* 21:497–8.

Verba, Sidney, and Norman H. Nie. 1972. *Participation in America: Political Democracy and Social Inequality*. New York: Harper & Row.

Vogel, Harold L. 1986. *Entertainment Industry Economics*. Cambridge University Press.

Wartella, Ellen, and Byron Reeves. 1985. "Historical Trends in Research on Children and the Media: 1900–1960." *Journal of Communication* 35 (2):118–33.

Weber, Max. [1905] 1958. *The Protestant Ethic*. New York: Scribner.

[1924] 1978. *Economy and Society*. Berkeley: University of California Press.

Weiss, W. 1968. "Effects of Mass Media Communication," in G. Lindzey and E. Aronson, eds., *Handbook of Social Psychology*, pp. 77–195. Reading, MA: Addison-Wesley.

Wenders, John T. 1987. *The Economics of Telecommunications*. Cambridge, MA: Ballinger.

Whorf, Benjamin L. 1956. *Language, Thought and Reality*. Cambridge, MA: MIT Press.

Wicklein, John. 1981. *Electronic Nightmare*. New York: Viking Press.

Wilensky, Harold L. 1964. "Mass Society and Mass Culture." *American Sociological Review* 29(2):173–97.

Wiles, P. 1963. "Pilkington and the Theory of Value." *Economic Journal* 73 (June).

Williams, Frederick. 1982. *The Communications Revolution*. Beverly Hills: Sage.

Williams, Martha E. 1985. "Electronic Databases." *Science* 228 (April 26):445–56.

Williams, Raymond. 1974. *Television: Technology and Cultural Form*. New York: Schocken Books.

Winn, Marie. 1977. *The Plug-In Drug*. New York: Viking.

Wolin, Sheldon S. 1960. *Politics and Vision*. Boston: Little, Brown.

Wright, P. L. 1974. "Analyzing Media Affects on Advertising Responses." *Public Opinion Quarterly* 38:192–205.

Yurow, Jane. 1980. "Issues in Information Policy." Special publication NTIA SP 80–9, National Telecommunication and Information Administration, U.S. Department of Commerce.

Zuboff, Shoshana. 1988. *In the Age of the Smart Machine*. New York: Basic Books.

Index